The Merry Baker

Of Riga

Boris(s) Zemtzov(s)

Stanford Oak Press

The Merry Baker of Riga
by Boris(s) Zemtzov(s)

The Merry Baker of Riga describes the author's experience of establishing a business in Latvia from 1992-1999 and reflects his opinions relating to the experience. Some names and descriptions of individuals mentioned in the book have changed to protect their privacy.

For further information, contact the author at:
Stanford Oak Press
2759 Woodley Place, N.W.
Washington, D.C. 20008
email: mbaker@stanfordoak.com
(202) 316-8515

Book design by:
The Floating Gallery
244 Madison Avenue, #254
New York, NY 10016-2819
(1-877) 822-2500

The Merry Baker of Riga
by Boris(s) Zemtzov(s)
1. Author 2. Title 3. Travel

Library of Congress Control Number 20031143223
ISBN 0-9747116-0-8 (Softcover)

Printed in Canada

To Inguna, Marcis, Liene, Tanya, Steve, Marcel and my mother Aline

(who still wonders when this stone will gather some moss).

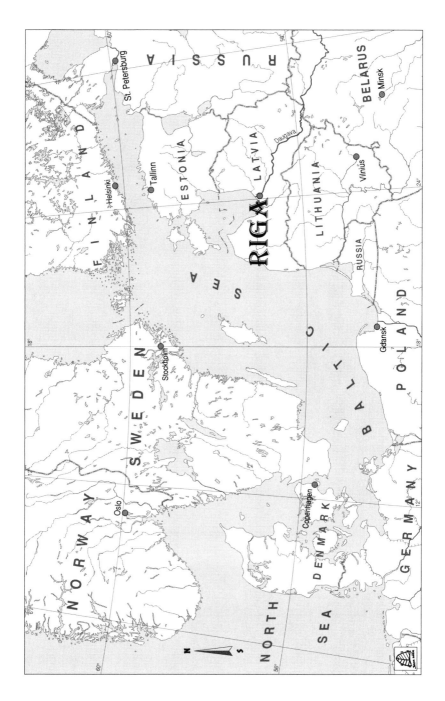

1

CAPITALIST

"Georgi Vladimirovich Petuhov could play master-level chess after having knocked back three hundred milliliters of 'Moskovskaya.'" The words rang in my ears as I boarded the train that would take me from the town of Ogre to Riga, to meet this persona. On this April day in 1992, the passenger cars were full of commuters. From the entry door of the one I entered, I spotted a free space on one of the benches towards the other end. I started down the aisle, careful to avoid the drunken men who were standing in the three-foot-wide space. On the way to the free spot, I passed a row that had been staked out by a group of *babushki*, each of whom was wearing a faded kerchief on her head. Four of these squatty women were sitting opposite five counterparts. All nine were huddled over a collection of netted-polyester or torn-plastic bags. They seemed convinced either that other passengers were dead-set on stealing these bags, or else that a play-action fake was the move required to leave the defensive back *babushka* reeling in confusion. They were grunting phrases in Russian to one another that, except for an occasional "*svoloch* 'bastard'" and "*Nu kak inache?!* 'How [could it be] otherwise?'" were incomprehensible to me.

While continuing my sot-avoiding waltz to the destination bench, I estimated that one quarter of the passengers were men and women who were commuting less between cities than between the state of consciousness and the "great vodka void." For some, like the thick-lipped man who was passed out and sprawling generously over what would otherwise be space for three people, the commute had lasted days before a clear destination emerged. The man's right eye was swollen — the surrounding tissue a deep burgundy hue. His left arm was marked by several rows of long thin scabs. At first glance, one would have thought, "heroin tracks." But they were too long and thick by far, as if he had been shooting up with a pastry syringe. No, he had probably initiated a wrestling match with some rosebush that had rudely obstructed his path to the great void.

Another four feet to go and I would be at my row. An extended family of gypsies occupied the row before mine. They were darker-complexioned than the other passengers, had manes of dense black hair and bantered in a language that was neither Latvian nor Russian. I recognized one older woman amongst them; I had seen her at the market a few days earlier — at least I thought so, and I wasn't too bad with faces. But although this proud matron also sported a hot-pink/grass-green-paisley-design-on-black kerchief over her hair and no fewer than seven gold crowns in her mouth, which flashed when she smiled at her children, her face was a model of serenity and calm. Her alter ego, the one that I had seen at the market, had been grimacing intensely while pleading, "Help...*PLEASE* h-e-l-p me" so emphatically, that I was sure her husband had just been crushed to a pulpy mass under a construction crane, while her children — the ones that hadn't already died of typhus or cholera or the plague — hadn't eaten in weeks. "Well," I thought to myself, "I trust that the money I put in her cup was enough to cover a few days' commute."

I finally edged my way between the knees of two men that I pigeon-holed to be low-rung government clerks, the variety that could get a brain aneurysm from the news that desks in their offices would be shifted a few inches. One was wearing a brown suit, dark beige shirt, a shimmering brown rayon tie and shoes the color of milk chocolate. The other wore a light gray suit, black shirt and gray patent leather shoes. In turn, they gaped at me as if I had just returned from Saturn. Nonplussed, I took my place on the wooden slat bench. As the train began its jerky acceleration over uneven tracks, I once again wished that I was twenty pounds heavier, with all of that fatty mass in my rear.

I wasn't the only man on the train with a briefcase, but I *was* the only one wearing a *Mano-a-Mano,* Italian-designed bone-white raincoat, and this random dress choice was beginning to attract sideways glances from the other commuters. I opened my newspaper, folded it into quarters and then eighths, the way I used to do — in observance of crowded-car etiquette — when I rode the subway in Manhattan two years earlier. I began reading an article about the imminent re-invasion of the country by *Spetsnazi.* However, within a few minutes of the doors' closing, my cognitive senses were occupied not by the counter-revolutionary plot I had started to read, but by the smell of half-digested garlic coming up for its last gasp before re-entering someone's stomach; by alcohol dehydrogenate that was not going to be processed by someone's liver but was instead offered up to fellow commuters with every breath; by socks that had probably not been washed since the re-declaration of Latvia's independence two years earlier; by underarm perspiration that had not only been preserved, but cultivated with some body odor fertilizer "*so znakom kachestvo* 'with a seal of quality'" over the span of several weeks. A solo waft of dried urine occasionally accompanied this quartet of scents. "This front-line civil defense is admirable for sure, but it won't be enough," I thought to myself. "Gas masks are standard issue for *Spetsnazi.*"

The train arrived in Riga Station fifty minutes later. I exited the train down the three narrow metal steps. Once on the platform, I stood still for a few seconds, re-adjusting to the new oxygen-filled environment. My head was feeling light. However, few of the other commuters bothered taking such a respite. I was reminded of my flagrant non-conformity when a *babushka* harpooned my lower back with her elbow. She carried on, pummeling a few more dawdlers. She followed each hit with a phrase; "Watch where you're going, *cretin!*" and "Don't know where you're headed? Should've stayed at home, *imbecile,*" were two I overheard. By virtue of her low center of gravity, her crow's sense of straight-line trajectory and her membership in the caste that no one is allowed to insult, she was unstoppable. Never was the "Tasmanian Devil" so well incarnated.

I reached the stairs to the terminal and descended, my back still smarting from the jab. I walked the forty yards down the corridor into the main terminal briskly, fearing that a slower pace would leave my midsection in welts. The mausoleum-like space of the terminal came into view. I reached the safety of the terminal and breathed a sigh of relief, only to be reminded, by the sight of a woman lying on her side with jars of fruits rolling in all directions from her bag, that it was too soon to relax. Although I would not be jabbed or pushed for sport any more this morning — this terminal was half the size of a football field, and thereby plenty large to absorb the flows of passengers to and fro — the floor was finished with the same slabs of gray, polished marble that covered the walls. Consequently, with the slightest moisture, the floor turned into a skating rink. And it always shocked me what decent-looking folk absolutely loved to launch Soyuz-sized spit missiles around here … without countdown.

People were already helping the lady up and gather her jars, so I walked on, past the newspaper stands, which were selling *Pravda* 'Truth,' *Neatkarīgā Rīta Avīze* 'Independent Morning Newspaper' and a few other newspapers with print-type that looked like it had been taped and pasted into place by four-year-olds with dyslexia. Alongside these newspapers was the traditional fare of Soviet news and sports journals, gardening and ladies' magazines. But there was also a *True Murder Mystery* tabloid, three or so *krimiḵi* 'criminal investigation' journals, and one *Ribald Anecdotes* paper, which would not have been seen here even six months earlier. The latter featured a panoply of impotent husband and lover-in-closet jokes, which sufficed to ensure that it was the first of the weekly journals to be sold out. To grasp what a bold step this publication was, one had to keep in mind that two years earlier, even gynecologists returning from obstetrics/gynecology conventions abroad had their bags examined and instructional manuals systematically confiscated, to make sure that nothing even instructionally lascivious entered the Soviet Union. Such repressed attitudes had even forced the railroad station prostitutes to be coy and take up poetry — *Tri rublya i ya tvoya* 'For rubles three, you'll have me' was a popular whore haiku.

The electronically manipulated Polish-manufactured electric train schedule board, listing train departure and arrival times and tracks, was broken once again, with every fourth route an unintelligible mixture of letters and numbers. One display line read "1T:R9 *Niz5ny Nov66rod — 3X*." As the new routes emerged, the malfunctioning slots would flutter uncontrollably, mimicking the sound of a stork's wings at takeoff. Ironically, in 1939, a Latvian company had been exporting the most advanced electric train schedule boards of the time, throughout Europe.

Upon exiting the terminal, I was greeted by the sight of a full line of taxis, and the smell of *Belyashi*. *Belyashi* were donuts that had been filled with nondescript meat and chopped onions, then deep-fried and left to linger — like flotsam — in the same dark yellow oil, until someone paid five Latvian rubles to buy one. The latter was done often, judging by the frequent dives of the *babushka*-vendor into her bin. As I passed by, the *babushka* reached down and, in one deft movement, lifted out a *belyash,* suspended on the end of the fork. She shook off some of the grease by knocking the fork against the side of the bin and then deposited the snack food onto one of the squares of beige paper that saw use as notepaper in post offices, napkins in cafes and toilet paper in the *prilichniye* 'proper' toilet stalls throughout the city. She handed the wrapped *belyash* to the customer. I hesitated a split-second. The smell emanating from the bin was hard to resist. But, upon seeing the dark yellow oil dripping through the paper onto the ground, I decided not to indulge so early in the day. This was probably the right decision; a fellow expat later recounted how he hadn't resisted, and had subsequently ended up chanting loudly over a bathtub for the better part of the night before regurgitating a holy hairball.

Thirty yards further, I got into a cab. The taxi took me the final mile up *Čhaka* Street, to my destination. In spite of the exotic name, there were neither

Babushka Bag-Seller

bright colors nor soul-stirring rhythms in this stretch of road. In fact, there were not even any pastel colors, or even loud chatter — just different shades of gray and varying pitches of bus motor. The taxi pulled up in front of the Little Rooster café and I got out. I walked to the door of the wooden building adjacent to the café.

Georgi Petuhov's office measured about seventeen by eleven feet, with an eleven-foot ceiling. It was covered from floor to ceiling in cherry wood-colored, plastic-laminated panels. The lamination on three of the panels was cracked and small pieces of it had since fallen off, revealing the light brown pressboard underneath. A seven-foot-long table abutted his desk. His desk, spotted with cigarette burns, supported three Soviet telephones. These were "VEF" phones. "VEF" stood for *Valsts Elektrotehniskā Fabrika*, State Electronics

Factory in Latvian. The year before, they had manufactured telephones for a quarter of the Soviet Union. This year, a quarter of the Soviet Union would get no new telephones — a result of some parliamentary decision to award "out-of-favor nation" status to the three Baltic States. By Soviet standards, a "three-phone" ranking was rather modest. Some of the mid-ranking officials I dealt with a few months earlier had upwards of six.

But when Georgi Vladimirovich Petuhov rose from his chair to accept my handshake, I forgot about his office. He stood at six feet three, had the physique of an Olympic wrestler, and the presence of Kublai Khan. His white hair was wavy and hadn't been cut or even combed in some time; he gave the impression of having just finished conducting one of Beethoven's symphonies.

Prior to this meeting, I learned that the sixty-three-year-old Georgi Petuhov (not his real name) had had, just a few years earlier, over six hundred employees. Now there were fewer than four hundred, and the number was dwindling weekly. They worked in more than thirty establishments in this district of the city. As I sat face-to-face with this white-haired legend, he adjusted his thick, grease-smeared glasses.

"Zemtzov — that's a Russian name there, isn't it?"

His voice boomed, coarsely.

"Yes, it is, Mr. Petuhov," I answered as matter-of-factly as possible, to impress upon him the fact that I wasn't particularly tied up with nationality questions.

"Call me Georgi Vladimirovich — you *do* use patronymics in America, do you not?"

"Yes we do—"

He smiled for no longer than two seconds after that response before stating "Now, let me just begin by saying that no parts of this *Trest* are for outright sale. You ... young capitalists, all seek to profit from the fall of the great Soviet Union. You know ... *we* beat the fascists for you. Then we built Riga. This was a small town of less than four hundred thousand in the nineteen forties. We [communists] made it into the million-person metropolis that it is today..."

To these heartfelt pronouncements I responded with nods or with feigned looks of gratitude or amazement, depending on what I had guessed the remark was meant to elicit. "Without us, there would be no *Pļavnieki* [district], no Purvciems, alone housing a hundred thousand people," he continued, with a defiant air.

"And not many other buildings which make Bronx housing projects look like Las Vegas hotels by comparison," I summarized to myself, but suppressed saying. To understand why, one had only to view a representative building complex in Purvciems. It consisted of the standard, reinforced concrete, fourteen-storied multiple apartment dwellings. In each stairwell were fifty-six apartments. Each building consisted of three stairwells and consequently was about forty yards long. The architects attached nine of these identical buildings to each other, but made sure that they followed the contour of the street, which curved gently one way and then the other. So one structure stood ten yards further back than the one on its left, while the one on its right was ten yards further back still. This undulating complex of buildings stood as long as the Empire State Building was high. By this time, large chunks of masonry were falling off, and the paint was missing in large patches. Latvians, ungrateful non-poets that they were, nicknamed these buildings *Ķīniešu Mūri* 'Chinese Walls.'

"Chinese Wall" housing complex, Purvciems

"*Vecmīlgrāvis* alone repairs more ships than all of Riga did in nineteen forty. And that entire *district* was built by the Soviets . . . ," Petuhov continued.

I rolled back in my seat, opening my eyes widely, pursed my lips, turned the sides of my mouth down and finally shook my head from side to side, emulating what I thought might be a passable "Wow, unbloody believable" expression.

"You'd have no *Trests*[1], which are *responsible* for feeding over *fifty* thousand people in this city, *every day*—," he bellowed.

"And no charming tooth-free smiles from serving personnel, happy to ladle tons of slop into the bowls of tens of thousands of gray frowning comrades," I quietly reflected.

He continued his list of Soviet accomplishments for another five or ten minutes, during which time I took the opportunity to exercise the full range of my facial muscles. Nonetheless, I did not interrupt him. Suddenly, perhaps because I had accidentally crinkled my nose, he posed a question, "So, do *you* think that you could manage over five hundred personnel?" I was caught unawares. I must have expressed surprise at that moment. The best response that I could muster was that I didn't know — I hadn't tried, and didn't think I'd have to for a long time, either.

"Right, right . . . well, come see me next week, when you've thought it through."

"Wait, wait, Georgi Vladimirovich — I have."

"Well, then, you'd like to be a partner?"

"Yes! That's what I'm here for."

"Well, listen then, I have been thinking about the fact that there is no baby formula plant here in Riga . . . anywhere."

"And?"

"That's something that we could do together."

"Excuse me, Georgi Vladimirovich, but . . . uh . . . I don't think so. I want to partner with you to set up a Western bakery."

"Well, what do you know? Are you saying that we don't know how to bake . . . *pecheniye* cookies?!"

"No, of course not. It's just that we'll make a larger assortment of different ones."

"Maybe, but you forget one thing — people here will have no money to buy those new cookies with."

"Not all, that's true, but there are already plenty of entrepreneurs here who are making more than enough to survive on, and soon they'll be followed by others."

"Maybe, someday . . . but listen, I don't have time to talk about this right now. I have another meeting to go to. My driver's waiting," he stated impatiently, while looking in the direction of the wall with the framed "Honorable Mention" of the Moscow Region of Riga's Public Food roster of companies plaque. "Call me later this week, and we'll meet again."

We met again — several times more. Each time, I felt like my brains had been run through a MIG-24's turbine and re-deposited in my head for later use on toast. A few times, for the purpose of trying to find an earnest reason to praise him, I visited his establishments. During one meeting, he had stated — with no little pride — that he had introduced the *Cheburek* to Riga. This Central Asian fast food is a puff pastry dough shell, the shape and size of half a Pita, filled with finely chopped beef, lamb, onion and fresh herbs, then sealed to have a frilly edge and deep-fried. So I decided one day to stop in his *Cheburechnaya*. I crossed the threshold into his establishment at the tail end of lunchtime — about two in the afternoon. The air inside was neither ventilated out nor filtered, and unfortunately, the *Cheburek* is deep-fried until the filling is thoroughly cooked, or, as in this case, until customers developed severe respiratory problems.

I waved my arm after taking a step in and once again, I could see the counter clearly. Three salads, deposited in the customary glass salad dish, were displayed behind the chipped glass. One was a beet salad, topped with sour cream or mayonnaise that had started to dry out and crack, looking like the Nevada salt flats in the process. The second was a "cube salad" — some cubes of fish, lard, apple, suet and egg white, thrown together and topped with a dollop of mayonnaise. The third was a tomato salad, about five ¼-inch-thick tomato slices, decorated with minced green onions and some dark gray object. I looked closer, and found not only that the tomatoes had already started shriveling, but that the dark object was a fly's wing. I straightened up. The clerk, having since emerged from the back room, was eyeing me as if I were another one of the neighborhood idiots.

"Well, do you want one, or did you just come by to visit?"

"Well, no, uh . . . actually, uh, one *Cheburek* please." I sat down, and five minutes later, a piping-hot *Cheburek* was served to me on a chipped, nondescript white plate. A crisscross of dark gray scratches emanated in all directions on the plate from underneath the *Cheburek*. I carefully picked up the golden brown object and bit the top of the half-moon. Through the bottom of the *Cheburek*, a wave of grease and meat juices splashed onto the plate. I looked up quickly at the counter, as if I were at a Red Lobster restaurant in the States, about to receive the attentions of a gracious waitress and, seconds thereafter, another bib. But my gaze was met only by the three salads that I had inspected earlier. My tie was now history. I glumly finished the *Cheburek*. It was quite good, almost good enough to offset the heartburn that came galloping up my trachea as soon as I stood up from the chair.

All told, I could sincerely compliment him on at least this one culinary tour-de-force. But the flattery didn't work either. I discovered that Petuhov was a shrewder strategist than his greasy-glasses image communicated. He kept his mind sharp through, amongst other things, a packed schedule of

chess matches. He did indeed prime himself for these by consuming vodka
— and his counterparts were known to have pleaded for him to stop, so that
they would have a chance of beating him. All this made for a situation wherein
I had to schedule my meetings for late morning, never on Mondays, and always
avoiding any of the Soviet holidays by two days. Although I didn't feel any
closer to having achieved my goal at the end of this series of meetings, I *did*
hear about how many hundreds of two-hundred-pound dough mixers Georgi
had brought to the city (whether he had done so by truck, or on the small of
his back was not clear to me); how many mouths there were to feed after the
war (a number which grew to engulf half the population of the Baltic countries
by the last of our meetings); how many factories (producing anti-American
ordnance and equipment) were built by the Soviets after the war. He
expounded on how these great big Soviet factories were able to produce great
big incredibly strategic equipment, thanks to their workers being fed beet
salads and *Solyanka*[2] created by his cooks.

Between these meetings, I tried every which way to find another site in
which to start up a bakery. I investigated a myriad of other buildings that had
been zoned for bakeries — I viewed spaces in factories, in restaurants, in hotels.
But the "public food sector," during Soviet times, had been the sacred ground
of the foxiest non-communist party members in the land. Now, the ex-
bartenders and ex-waiters — there were at least seven in parliament, cozily
sharing the reins of power with ex-doctors and lawyers — were damned if
they were going to let that strategically important sector, even its decrepit
stores and crumbling plants, fall into the hands of foreign *kapitālisti*.

Two weeks later, on the morning of the day that I figured would be the
one that I say, "*Dosvedanya tovarisch* 'you've wasted enough of my time,'" I
was standing on the platform in Ogre, awaiting my train. I couldn't help staring
at the windows of the Moscow-bound train as it pulled into the station.
Judging by the condensation on these windows, the air was starting to conduct
the intriguing aroma generated by the *babushka/gypsy/alcoholic* huddled
mass unit, throughout the car. In deference to my lungs, I walked to the taxi
stand fifty yards further. I negotiated a rate of five dollars, which was not much
for the twenty-five-mile ride. Depending on the time of the morning, the greed
of the driver and my choice of wardrobe on any particular day, the rate could
climb to three times as much. But today, luck was on my side. The driver of
this *Volga* had not only settled for a fiver, but he was fun as well. Most of the
taxi drivers made it a rule to avoid smiling, laughing or straying beyond some
canned monologue about the "new incompetent government" and "horrible,
chaotic times." Not this one. He was a musician, moonlighting as a taxi driver.
When he spoke, he sang; "I love the music of Waylon Jennings — play it all the

time…along with the *Šlāgeri* [Latvian country pub music] of course! But what I love…is that there's always work — a wedding here, a party there. The pay's not bad…and the women…," he said, breaking into deep laughter, "well… it is a beautiful life." I laughed in accompaniment, thinking how this place, in the end, is just like any other on earth; there's always going to be a core life rhythm that requires libidinous wedding singers. My mind then drifted to thoughts of how I would be approaching Petuhov on my final meeting, "He obviously needs some future income stream . . . he knows that his days as director of the *Trest* are numbered…on the other hand, he's so unpredictable …volatile…nitroglycerin. Last time, I told him that his pastries were inedible without the accompaniment of 'strong' coffee. I was being nice, 'plutonium-enriched' is more like it — and he threw me out." The taxi pulled up in front of the office. The driver jumped out, opened my door, shook my hand and wished me a good day — he meant it.

He was a perfect foil to Petuhov, who greeted me about thirty seconds later with his "oh, it's you again" scowl. After the usual exchange of greetings, accompanied by one of his statutory two-second smiles, he said, "So, let's get to the point…You want a partnership? I've decided that I'll give you the old bakery site that's no longer in use." My heart started pounding. A million-dollar smile was making its way from the deepest recesses of my cerebral cortex, when he added, "As long as you make a baby formula production site out of it —" I reset my lips to a pursed-and-incredulous mode. Petuhov continued, "You see, there is a complete shortage of baby formula in Latvia. The stores have none. Some Swiss came here and said that they wanted to do it, but they were slow…couldn't make up their minds. I have no patience for people like that." He then stopped talking, looking intensely through his 1950s-scientist glasses. The ball was squarely in my court.

"Look, Georgi Vladimirovich, with all due respect [a term that I am using *very* loosely now, because only a moron can ask for the same thing seven times in a row and not understand that the other party is *not i-n-t-e-r-e-s-t-e-d*], I repeat — I did not come here to start a baby formula plant [because *I* happen to *like* babies, and strongly doubt that vermin poop — a universal element of all your production sites — is an integral ingredient of formula]. If that's what *you* intend to do, then fine, go to it [especially if you assume that vodka is a baby formula, which I suspect you do]. But that's not what I came here to discuss."

I rose, looked at the door, and threw my coat, toreador-like, over my shoulders. Petuhov looked beyond me towards the window. After I corrected a sleeve and took a step towards the door, he said, "*Khorosho,* all right, let's talk about a bakery on this site." I looked at him as sternly as I could. He gestured for me to sit back down.

Once again, I removed my coat. A few minutes later, I wondered why I had done so. During the course of the ensuing negotiation, he made me promise not only to employ Zigrīda, his personnel director, but also Valdis Andersons and Dmitri Sholokhov. The former of the two was Petuhov's mechanical director, while the latter was, from what I could piece together, an electrician who had spent most of his adult life on nuclear submarines. I conceded that this was an optimal background to have for our project, when we need to go ballistic with sesame-seed-bun warheads.

"Furthermore, who's going to do your accounting?" He asked gruffly.

"I was —"

"Just as I thought, I recommend Natalia Nikitina . . . ," he continued, as if he had been talking to Bonzo on barbiturates all along.

The remaining terms were dictated to me over the next three minutes. I silently accepted the candidates and conditions that he proffered, there was little else for me to do at this point; I had to avoid insulting the pride of this paragon of [ex-] society and risk blowing the only real opportunity for a site that I had come across in over a month of searching. The roster of my start-up company would now read like the committee of honor of the Central District [Communist] Party Duma. "Oh boy," I thought to myself, "This much deadwood . . . it's insane — I'm going to be a one-man Social Security pension scheme." Nonetheless, I replied that although it seemed a bit heavy as a start-up structure, I would think it over. We then agreed to "do lunch" later that week to work out the *poslyedniye shtrikhi* 'final details' of the agreement. We both knew that this meant the agreement on his position in the new company and his percent of the business — his cut — a private topic that couldn't be discussed in the presence of the others currently sitting in the office.

The interior of the *Jever* restaurant was clean, the atmosphere calm, and the sofas and chairs plush — in short it could have been one of any number of pubs in Germany or Houlihan's restaurants. I hoped that this atmosphere, which differed so much from the one in his "if-I-swipe-the-air-with-my-twice-bent-and-thrice-straightened-aluminum-spoon-I'll-collect-enough-oil-to-moisten-my-shriveled-tomato-salad-with-fly-wing-garnish" establishments, would also give Petuhov an idea of the quality levels I was aiming for. Furthermore, this subdued atmosphere should keep him on his guard, perhaps even uncomfortable — if he was capable of feeling such a sentiment — with extorting more than his fair share in the new company. I waited for him at the door. When he arrived, he scarcely looked at me, instead fixing his stare on the ground. We then sat down at a table for two, set off from the other tables with diners. I had seen Petuhov before only in his natty office, so he seemed out of place in this environment of stylized bookshelves, potted plants, and soft, understated lighting. Rebuffing an offer of dishes ranging from goulash to grilled steak, he settled for four ounces of vodka and sliced salami. As soon as the waiter placed these items on the table, Petuhov proceeded to down half the vodka, and followed that with three slices of salami. He pushed his glasses further up the bridge of his massive nose, and leaned back on the sofa. Apparently, he now felt sufficiently primed to engage in *peregovory* negotiations.

"*Znayete chto, Boriss Viktorvich, menya voobshche ne interesuyet vashe predlozheniye* 'You know, Zemtzov, I'm not at all interested in your [bakery] offer,'" he said as if he had just been offered a job as the sifter of luminescent refuse at the Chernobyl station. "So I'll appreciate it if you make me another proposal on the spot."

I was at once relieved and nonplussed. In the previous negotiations, Petuhin had referred to the bakery almost as having been his first child, painstakingly raised and fed from his own breast. I had come expecting to negotiate 7 to 15 percent; instead, he was asking me to pay him *po chornomu* (literally 'in the black' [under-the-table]) and proceed without him.

"All right, I, I . . . what did you have in mind?"
    "Well, given that a space like that goes for five thousand dollars nowadays, I think that four thousand dollars would be appropriate."
    "Hunnh?! That's non-renovated space there. In fact, the basement leaks *and* is piled up with garbage two meters deep. To call it a 'bakery plant' is simply a wild exaggeration. I think that two thousand three hundred to two thousand five hundred dollars is more in line with that. And let's see, that's three years of your current salary —"
    "Without benefits," he interjected while leaning back and waving his beefy hand up and down.

He then coughed and loudly cleared his throat. He started squinting and then widening his eyes, as if he were trying to focus on me through his glasses — no mean feat if it could be done, it would have been like trying to focus on something through the bottoms of two emptied-but-unwashed jars of Vaseline. "My final offer is three thousand five hundred dollars. If you accept, then you have a bakery. If not . . . then you're not interested."

I took a deep breath.

"It's a deal ... on condition that we get to use the store on Spring Street to sell the products from."
He looked hard at his plate, then looked up again, passed his hand over his white hair, and leaned back; "*Khorosho* 'O.K.' ... But with these 'assurances' ..."

Within ten more minutes, it was settled. Petuhov would get a compensation of $3500 for letting the new company rent space over which he, Petuhov, had no title and no rights to sublet. He furthermore relieved his *Trest* of a store that was consistently incurring only monetary losses and rat droppings on a regular basis. In addition, he was to receive $1800 for a Finnish rack oven[3] which had been written off in 1983; $170 for inventory that included fifty liters of fermenting pickles and two barrels of year-old apple *povidla*[4], which was — he assured me — "the backbone of any *truly worthy* pastry production"; the satisfaction of knowing that at least for a certain time — his most faithful cronies or communist buddies would have job security. I admitted to myself after the encounter, that this "deal" had a surreal quality to it. The only item missing was a cow's eyeball. As to the flies, there were plenty of those ... they hovered in swarms above the barrel of *povidla*.

Footnotes

[1] All restaurants, cafes, and food service operations in the Soviet Union were subsumed under Trests [Trusts]. These Trests were divided along geographical lines, and the Directors were held responsible for attending to the sabiedriskais edinasana 'public eating' ("food service" would be the Western equivalent) operations in that section of the city.

[2] A dish that could be described as a bacon-onion-and tomato soup when prepared well, but most often resembled a lard, old sausage, rotten pickle and onion broth in Petuhov's establishments.

[3] A rack oven takes racks, filled with product, rather than individual trays. Formed breads and pastries are placed on trays, which are then placed in a rack, which holds from twelve to fifteen trays. The oven is therefore more vertical than a deck oven, the standard pre-war oven (resembling a pizza oven).

[4] "Povidla" was a substance that resembled apple butter in texture and color, but had the smell and taste of no fruit as yet found in nature.

2

DIVINE INSPIRATION

I HAD NEVER PLANNED FOR the apogee of my youth to include a bakery start-up in a forlorn corner of Europe. No, I had stumbled onto this business, and indeed Latvia, by accident. In the four years prior to my arrival here, I had had the fortune of experiencing two career-building jobs. But I was simply not convinced that either of them were where my future lay. The first involved marketing in a *Fortune* 500 pharmaceutical company in New York; the second job was as the Moscow-based director for a non-governmental organization that had, in the course of my fourteen months with them, delivered the largest amount of humanitarian assistance from America to the USSR since WWII.

Although each job had been fulfilling in its own right, neither had been both rewarding *and* challenging enough to keep me committed. The first one was rewarding, but left my passion for inventiveness unrequited. This was made clear to me when I once incorporated scenes from *Night of the Living Dead* into a sales manager training tape, in place of scenes from a patient's life when the patient aid videotape on rheumatoid arthritis hadn't been produced quite in time. I had assumed that the difference between a zombie smashing the windshield of the car with a rock and a well-groomed rheumatologist describing the symptoms of early-stage rheumatoid arthritis would have been stark enough to prevent anybody from associating the scenes from the 1950s film classic with a patient information tape. I felt that this unannounced substitution would provide some comic relief from otherwise brain-numbing sales training material. Alternatively, I would have had to show my own uninteresting mug and say that the patient aid videotape would be ready in three weeks. The sales managers were tickled by the swap. However, my initiative was met with enough frowns, raised eyebrows and thinly veiled threats from "upper management" that I most quickly realized the limits — decidedly lower than my own — of acceptable creativity in large companies, or else the inability of said upper managers to distinguish between rheumatologists and zombies. In either case, I knew that, for my own peace of mind, I had to go.

My second job was challenging enough for my spirit but left me anemic and dyspeptic. I acquired this condition as a result of having had to travel on a weekly basis to desolate towns within the Soviet Union and in said towns, within the span of a year, consume enough lamb's ears, vodka[1], frozen fish[2], raw horse meat, tainted water, and, at absolutely no additional charge, the parasites that accompanied the last three, to last several lifetimes.

So I decided, in early 1992, to cast my fortunes in a country, which was in its early stages of "emergence," as economists termed such states at the time, but bore the marks of having been a highly civilized one before the last world war [or revolution] had transformed it. I was searching for a place where — if I actually wanted to — I could eat a square worm-less meal. Latvia fit the bill. In 1992 it may have been gray, melancholy and impoverished, but its people aspired to more. Furthermore they had proven, forty-three years earlier, that they could become more than what Western Europeans expected any Eastern European country to be, which was terminally gray, melancholy and impoverished. I decided to bond — in what I hoped would be a mutually beneficial relationship — my ambitions with the *zeitgeist* of Riga, its capital. I decided that in this city of close to a million Latvians, Russians, Ukrainians, Poles, Livs and foreign humanitarian workers, I could engage successfully in a start-up business in any sphere that my personal interests led me. And I had another good reason to make a try here. It was a reason that anyone with my insatiably romantic character would find absolutely overpowering. Her name was Inge. I had met her when she was working in the Ministry of Health. On account of her and the city in which she had gone to college, my life was going to undergo a revolution which, little did I know at that point, would alter my existence by around 160 of the 180 degrees possible.

I have always been drawn to sweets and pastries. Since as long as I could remember, they have had a pacifying, almost sedative effect on me. For example, when I was twelve, my mother and stepfather took my older brother and me on a family trip to France. When in Paris, my parents wanted to go to the *Moulin Rouge*, but they were at a loss as to what to do with their [admittedly] bratty twelve-year-old son. My brother was old enough — by French law — to accompany them, and was hell-bent on seeing the dolphin take the top part of the bikini off the young maiden in the tank. So younger-brother-sitting was out of the question for him. A young-boy sitter was also not available for tourists of our socioeconomic class, on short notice, in Paris in 1972. So, after a twenty-minute brain-storming session behind closed doors, the parents hit on the idea of offering me — in exchange for staying quietly in the hotel for the evening, in front of a TV whose programs I couldn't begin to understand — a *big* box of French pastries. I agreed without hesitation. The offerings included a raspberry tart, a lemon tart, a strawberry tart, a cherry flan, a *rhum baba* (with a sugar-dusted violet on top) and three eclairs — coffee, of course, the chocolate ones being too pedestrian for my taste. After taking the better part of one hour to savor most of the above, I recall thinking something along the lines of, "I can't understand why my parents, being such intelligent people and all, hadn't hit upon this idea earlier. They should go watch these girlie shows more often … and not forget to take my psychotic brother with them *every* time."

Now, in the Spring of 1992, I was in this re-emerging Baltic metropolis, where people had all but forgotten that butter also had an application in store-bought pastries; where the only fruit-like substance that ever reached the inside of a torte or gateau was a syrupy "*džems* jam" or povidla; where, apparently for nutritional purposes — but more probably to keep the populace in constant preparedness for hand-to-hand combat against imperialist aggressors — air was squeezed out of the dough with such ferocity that bread could be used as a club just minutes after it emerged from the bakery oven. Although this texture was an integral characteristic of the dark brown *Senču Maize* for which Riga was famous[3], when white and whole-grain breads turned out like bricks, the visiting Germans, Italians, and Frenchmen cringed. The texture didn't go over too well for Northern Californians either; I felt that I had to take matters into my own hands. I began by exploring the possibility of importing baked goods. This turned out to be unfeasible; the prices were prohibitive, and freshness could not be maintained. I researched what was happening in the other two Baltic countries. The same dismal situation existed in Lithuania and Estonia, as concerned the stuff of life. I finally decided that my first business venture would, by necessity, involve establishing the first western-style bakery in Riga. After launching that, I could do something admittedly less primal — like establishing the first company providing Web-based software for managing pension benefits in Northeastern Europe.

Soviet-style bakery storefront

I started by searching for some local partners. Through Inge, I contacted some people from the Ministry of Finance, who had been assigned the responsibility of attracting foreign direct investments into the country. These people in turn referred me to someone from a state concern that was "falling apart" and whose current management was looking for partners. This manager's name was Zigrīda Auza — her summer *vasarnīca* dacha was across the street from the house of one of the Ministry officials. We met a few days later. She stood about five feet nine inches tall. She was not overweight but could be classified as a large-boned woman. I surmised from her wartime references that she was in her early fifties. She spoke Russian with no detectable accent but explained that she was Latvian, with one German grandparent. Her German-Latvian father had, furthermore, been sent to Siberia during the first series of deportations, when Germans and Soviets were still allies. This genealogical/historical rundown was, I later deduced, supposed to help me "place" Zigrīda in the alchemic table of nationalistic elements. It didn't. But I *was* encouraged by the fact that Zigrīda appeared sincerely content to have found a foreign investor. In turn, she told me that I would have to talk to Georgi Vladimirovich Petuhov, the General Director of the "*Avots* Public Eating *Trest.*"

The morning following the closure of the deal, I was sitting around a table in a café near Petuhov's office, with Zigrīda, Dmitri and Valdis. I briefly reflected, during my ride to the café, on the fact that it was probably unique for start-ups at this time that one manager was Latvian-German, another a devoutly Soviet Russian, and the last a Latvian-Russian with a Swedish family name — a consequence of the Swedish occupation of Riga three hundred years earlier. I also decided to tell Valdis and Dmitri that they should together attend to all the technical issues, while Zigrīda could expect to continue her role as a personnel director. Furthermore, no politics or history was to be discussed at work.

When I arrived, Dmitri and Zigrīda were seated, while Valdis was standing. Valdis Andersons was a man of moderate build, whose most salient feature was a pair of vigorously reddish-pink cheeks — a testimony to the fact that in his previous life he had been, like most Soviet factory managers, no teetotaler. But that his nose was not a deep crimson hue also testified to the fact that he had been relatively temperate, while his colleagues had been passing out on the toilet or crawling under the tables impersonating tanks at "the Front." In his previous life, he had been the "Mechanical Director" of Factory #65 — in its heyday a behemoth of more than five thousand employees. Its workers had manufactured ninety percent of all airport transport equipment, as well as the mechanical motorized stairways that drew up to the Tupolev-154 passenger aircraft, for the entire Soviet Union. And the whole production had been termed "*strategicheskaya*" by Moscow, so Valdis had had no room for error. Perhaps it was for this reason that most of his hair had fallen out, revealing a large bald spot between two tufts of brown hair. Valdis had come to work at the *Trest* on Georgi Petuhov's invitation less than one year earlier. At what I guessed to be 50 to 55 years of age, he was a veteran of the Soviet machines-with-moving-parts sphere — *that* sphere which was unknown and terrifying territory to me; even the screw sizes here differed from the standard U.S. or Western European ones.

Dmitri was older: I guessed about sixty-one. His hair was silver, with streaks of white. He wore a brown suit, with a light beige v-necked sweater underneath. Besides the fact that he had been Petuhin's technical man, and an officer on a nuclear sub, I knew nothing about him.

"So, guys, congratulations. We're in business!" I started, with bounding enthusiasm. I then told them what I would like to see as the ground rules of our management relationship. They had no questions, but smiled when I mentioned the "no politics and history" policy. I then started assigning tasks of contacting builders, organizing cleaning crews, re-wiring the plant, and finding bakery personnel — in short, all the things that one does when starting up a green-field bakery anywhere. I then launched into what I *thought* would be the fun part:

"Now, we need a name . . ." This phrase was meant to elicit a string of responses. Instead, it brought forth three perfectly blank stares.

"So, partners, what should we call it?" Stone silence. "Well, did you think about it since we last talked?" Stonier silence than before. I waited even longer, until the silence bordered on embarrassing. "How about something to do with this part of town?" From the silence that ensued, one could have deduced that this part of town was a black hole. "Hmm, I understand, I'm pulling teeth from a corpse . . . O.K., I understand that you haven't given this too much thought before. That's fine, we can think *now!*"

"How about the Latvian-American bakery?" asked Zigrīda, reservedly. This suggestion elicited no response from Valdis or Dmitri.

"*Not bad!* I mean, that *definitely* communicates that we'll be doing something *different,*" I replied enthusiastically, so as not to put an end to this show of initiative. "There's just one little problem . . ." Everyone looked at me inquisitively, probably wondering why I wouldn't just be bowled over by this idea. "I think that people would be expecting American baked goods, and, uh, to tell the truth, most American-style baked goods wouldn't be too popular here." All three looked stunned. "That's because, as I understand it, with the exception of cheesecake, they aren't popular in Germany, France, or Denmark. But that name's not bad — it's a good *start*. We'll keep it as a *rezervniy* variant. How about someone else, any suggestions?" My prompting was once again greeted by a deathly silence.

So as not to let spirits flag, I broke the silence by another name: "I've got an idea. The bar next to the *Avots Trest* office is closing down, isn't it?"

"Yes," they chimed in.

"Well, that's not a bad name . . . *Gailītis* 'Little Rooster' — doesn't that have the connotation of farms and freshness? We could just make it a big rooster, or a red one." Although no one uttered a word, I felt that I had touched a chord of some kind, as I saw some smiles. "We could have a rooster with a baker's cap as the logo. Whaddya think?" Valdis was looking at the ground, exposing his smooth scalp, which the receding hairline had left shiny and red, with just a hint of peachy fuzz, like on a baby's forearm. He lifted his head, and I could see that he was desperately trying to keep a straight face; he was on the verge of failing dismally. In the meantime, Zigrīda was looking out the window at this moment as if she were staring at a Seurat painting for the first time in her life and was trying to decipher which points comprised the people, which the boats. It was poignant, since out of *this* cracked and filthy window, one could at best see shadows of peoples' legs and bus tires.

"*Davai*⁴ Valdis, tell me what's so funny. Whazzit *mean*?!" I asked.

"Well, uh, 'rooster' has several meanings—," started Valdis, in his extra-deferential, studied way of answering difficult questions,

"Yeah, yeah, and?"

"You see 'rooster' could be just a bird...or it could be a man, let's say, that gets along with women...young ones...all of them."

"*Khvatit* 'enough'. I get it, stud bull...right?" Valdis nodded.

"O.K., 'Stud bull bakery' — hmm, probably not the image we want in this country. Who knows what kind of cakes people will be ordering...actually, I think I know what kind they'll be ordering...I just don't think that we'll find bakers to make those cakes. So that's two down. Any more suggestions, anyone?...Come on, I don't think that any could be worse than the one I just made."

"How about the 'Kliņģeris'?" asked Zigrīda.

"You mean a Latvian Sweet Golden Pretzel? *That's* a possibility," I said.

Dmitri then piped up, "But wouldn't others try to use it?"

"Yes, possibly," she replied.

I cautiously said, "That could cause problems, like calling a flower stand 'roses' or something, but we're not far off. Hey, what about something *else* that would give the notion of health and freshness and countryside...like, like...the 'Golden Eggs' bakery?" This suggestion was followed by an even more unnerving silence than my first one had triggered. "Well, what about it? ...If you don't like it, just say so — I won't be offended." Once again, Valdis and Dmitri started grinning widely and their faces turned red. Zigrīda now looked as though she would have gladly sacrificed all her family heirlooms to be on the moon, in a dump truck, on an overcrowded Indonesian fishing boat — *anywhere* outside the room now.

"O.K., what is it this time?" I asked, meekly.

"Well, Boriss, eggs have several meanings, you see, and uh...this could be misinterpreted...uh—"

"You want to say that 'eggs' mean something bad, right?"

"Not *bad*, just...anatomical."

"Valdis, stop taunting me, *what do 'eggs' mean?*"

"There are two of them between men's legs."

"Well...O.K....and 'golden' to boot," I murmured humbly.

I waited until everyone's cheeks resumed a paler shade of red, then gathered my nerve. I smiled and told myself that as I had succeeded reasonably well in conveying the image of being a sexual maniac, I had better shut up before some other perfectly normal (in my understanding of the language)

but in fact perfectly obscene (in everyone else's understanding of the language) phrase again were to escape my lips and remove all doubts.

I started boldly again, "O.K., that one probably wasn't so good — any other suggestions?... I can't believe that no one had given any thought to this earlier."

"The Spring Street Baker," Valdis proffered.

"Good... and simple, Valdis."

Zigrīda then said, "But Valdis, there's a 'Spring Street Café,' a 'Spring Street Hairdresser,' and I think that we'll sound just like another one of *our* establishments." Valdis and Dmitri nodded.

I waited another minute, and I was about to ask everyone to give it another week of thought, when, prodded by divine inspiration, I blurted out, "Hey, what about... 'The Merry Baker'?!"

For once, I saw expressions of positive surprise on people's faces. Valdis started nodding. Stone faces had been moved to human ones with the simple words — "The Merry Baker." Valdis chuckled a little, and said, "Yeah, yeah, it's *different*—"

"But still, to the point," added Dmitri.

"*Pravda* ... I think it could work," said Zigrīda, cautiously, "although... it's not really a *Latvian* expression."

Footnotes

[1] For purposes of brevity, "vodka" is mentioned only once in the sentence. Let it be noted, that in the Soviet Union, there was nothing brief, nor singular, in reference to vodka and foreign dignitaries. After one year of this routine, my liver was a few months away from doing a revolution of its own.

[2] A "fishsicle" of sorts. This is a specialty of northern Siberia.

[3] A twenty-year-old sample of the Soviet Union's most famous black bread can be viewed at the Air and Space Museum in Washington, D.C. It is a close copy of the bread that was provided to the cosmonauts on their first flight in space.

[4] "Come on" or "let's go," would be the two closest translations, depending on the context, of this expression, which today is used by both Russian speakers and Latvians in Latvia.

3

RESISTANCE

THE SMALL COUNTRY OF LATVIA is the success story of indigenous pagan tribes surviving close to one thousand years of attempted colonization and integration. Throughout its pre-colonial history, the territory of present-day Latvia was noted for two reasons: its prime location for trading, and its inhabitants' stubborn resistance to subjugation. The inhabitants of present-day Latvia had been mentioned in numerous Viking and Kievan Russian chronicles. Although the Vikings enjoyed skewering babies of defeated tribes on their spears for sport, they met their match in the *"Kurita"* (Cours), one of the three principal ethnic groups that comprise present-day Latvians. The Danish Vikings first tried in A.D. 854 with a sea invasion. [1] A year later the Swedish Vikings attempted to do the same, extending the attack over eight days. Although the losses on the Courish side were greater than those incurred during the previous year's campaign, the Swedes still had to depart with nothing to show for it. And for more than 300 years after that, through the use of innovative arms, such as the extended wooden sling[2], fierce fighting and even fiercer trading techniques, the Lats, Livs and Cours remained independent.

However, the Teutonic knights arrived in 1198, and proceeded, with Prussian efficiency, to seal the political fate of the trading village on the banks of the Daugava river. The Germans, through battle and artifice, subjugated the Livs and Lats in 1201. They christened the people and established a new administrative framework for governing them. A century later, they were also to put the city of Riga into a German-dominated economic framework called the Hanseatic Trading League, which was a medieval equivalent to COMECON, with the main beneficiary being Germany. Until the beginning of this century, Riga was a German trading post, colony, protectorate, enclave, and eventually provincial outpost. In fact, whenever a country engages in peaceful occupation of another for a period of even one century, significant assimilation takes place. Over the course of three centuries, this process is complete. After all, what self-respecting German would wish to marry a widow? She became a target for eligible Latvian men. For this reason, written accounts of German merchants of the sixteenth century bear hints that more than half of the inhabitants of the city, including the city elders were in fact — if not in name — Latvians. Nonetheless, as concerns the administrative, technical, political and economic framework, Riga was undeniably German for 714 years.

In the beginning of the First World War, Russia appropriated all major German-owned industries, subsequently dismantling and shipping key plant and equipment to western Siberia. The heretofore mighty German industrial class was reduced to naught. Furthermore, after achieving its first Independence in 1920, the Latvian government nationalized the great German estates and subsequently redistributed the lands among those soldiers who had fought for independence, and, eventually, to Latvian peasants. By 1922, a mere forty years after their heyday in the city, Germans remained prominent only as clergy in the Protestant church, professors, engineers, and small-scale landlords.

The inter-war period, from 1921 to 1940, marked the period of Latvia's economic boom. Within twenty years, Riga fully reacquired its pre-WWI status as the most dynamic port city on the Baltic Sea. There was a full economic resurgence of the agricultural sector, and a significant improvement in its industrial one. In 1937, Latvia was competing with Denmark for the burgeoning U.K. bacon and butter market, with Czechoslovakia for the opportunity to assemble BMWs and Fords, and with the rest of Northern Europe for dominance in "new technologies." One example of the latter was the *Minox* camera. A Latvian named Valters Caps (pronounced Tsaps) invented this camera while he was working in Tallinn. He offered to sell his invention to VEF (later the Soviet telephone manufacturer). The directors agreed to the offer, bought the license for the camera and hired him to lead the new department. The camera was a startling innovation for three reasons. Firstly, it presaged automatically advancing-film cameras of the 1980s because the user both shot a picture and advanced the film with just one movement. Secondly, the camera could precisely capture an image at a [then] remarkably close distance of fourteen inches from the object — an absolute must for nature and archeological photographers, to name a few. When these features were combined with the small size of the camera (17 x 28 x 80mm) — about the size of a cigarette lighter — one could well understand why it became the "spy camera" of choice in the war, and remained so for nearly twenty-five years afterwards. As such it appears prominently in all spy films produced in Hollywood and Europe in the '60s and early '70s.

Between 1937 and 1939, in an age prior to cheap and convenient air flight, Herbert Hoover and college junior John F. Kennedy were two of many Americans who made a point of visiting Latvia. After his trip, Hoover remarked that the standard of living in the Baltic States was "as high as any standard of living in Europe, possibly outside of Switzerland and Norway." In fact, statistics show that Latvia was one of three countries vying for eleventh place in the world, based on its per capita Gross National Product. Kennedy of course remarked that the girls were babes.

However, on June 17 1940, the Soviet Red Army troops pulled their tanks into town, and Riga was afflicted with "*Status Sovieticus,*" as Central Europeans refer to it. This condition was interrupted only by a brief interlude of vengeful Nazi German occupation. The occupation reduced the heretofore well-assimilated Jewish population to 10 percent of its pre-war size and decimated the ranks of eighteen- to thirty-year-old Latvians by forcing them to fight the SS's rearguard battles as they retreated. The Soviets, with their superior grasp of free market economics, subsequently reduced Latvia to beggarly status. Within five decades, the situation of the country was not close to comparable — not even in the same ballpark of international status — that it had enjoyed before the war. In a study of countries' wealth, conducted by the World Bank in 1998, Latvia ranked sixty-third in the world. Furthermore, this placement was in the process of being bypassed — by Romania. In the span of fifty years, Latvia had been soundly overtaken by more than ten other European countries, including Portugal, Spain, Greece, Italy and Finland. Latvia, the co-founder of Europe's basketball league, the country that gave filmmaking legend Serge Einstein his start, the nation that in 1939 boasted more university graduates per thousand inhabitants than France or Germany, was an economic wreck.

In the U.S., an appropriate comparison might be the case, almost one hundred years earlier, of Charleston. In 1848, Charleston was situated right behind New York City as a dynamic, fast-growing port city of the U.S.A. Among other accomplishments, its merchants had just financed the *longest* single railway stretch, at 136 miles long, in the United States. Private homes, such as the Aiken-Rhett residence, by their size, the novelty of their architecture, and the European art that hung on their walls put most all of the residences in Manhattan to shame. Charleston was grand. But by 1900 — one civil war and one industrial revolution later — the general populace of America was hard-pressed to remember that this city had ever mattered to anyone besides a few fat and greasy South Carolina plantation owners.

In the same way, by early 1993, Latvia was known — in select circles — for only two things. One was for the contract manufacture of certain pieces of *IKEA* furniture; the second was for harboring the largest modern production line of an illegal drug in the world[3]. The only college juniors who included Latvia in their itinerary were either Latvian-Americans who had had it drubbed into their heads by their grandparents and parents that it was their moral obligation to visit the *Tēvzeme* 'Fatherland' at least once, or those who wanted to get to a particularly clean stash of heroin — smuggled in from Afghanistan — on the cheap. The Latvians that I met consistently felt bitter about their situation, consistently referring to the urban legend of the Russian Officers' wives who got "all dressed up" to go to the Opera, in the slips, negligees and evening gowns of the previous occupants of the flat (who were probably in Siberia, feasting on rotten potatoes and fishbone *consomme*), thinking that this apparel was evening dress. I'm sure that this wasn't so terribly unwelcome in the Opera Hall; I suspect that for not a few other men in audience, these outfits prompted a standing ovation of sorts. The Latvians were bitter, however, at being occupied by what was, in short, a bunch of country hicks from Russia. But given that there had been so many of the hicks available to assure the occupation in 1940 — with about one hundred times more "hick" tanks — the results were unavoidable. Although some Latvians [still] feel that the Latvian army should have resisted, most historians agree that this action would have led to the Tatarstan-like elimination of Latvia from the map of Eastern Europe.

Since I had absolutely no Latvian roots, and a half-Russian heritage, I had no reason to be involved in any post-war "hate-ons". I did, however, have another reason for looking to settle here. Although her name was Scandinavian, Inge was distinctly non-Nordic in her appearance. A disinterested observer might even have said "Egyptian." She had dark brown hair, which reflected a tone of polished cherry wood when the sunlight hit it. She tanned wondrously. I had met her at the beginning of my humanitarian work in the Soviet Union and suspected, towards the end of my mission, that she might play a major role in my future, when I could concentrate on little else besides bouquets of wildflowers and Latvian folk melodies in her presence. In short, I had been swept away.

But swept away or not, I had to get this bakery up and running and profitable — my relationship with her depended on it ... it was part of the "Deal."

In late April I made an oblique marriage proposal to her. Inge hesitated. I was taken aback. After all, I was an American. Russian women were, already at this point, climbing over each other with stiletto-heeled crampons to get a "catch" like myself.

"So, Inge, you can't marry me until you're *sure?*"

"That's right."

"Well, what do you need to be 'sure' of?"

"Just a couple of things," she said as she smiled teasingly. She then said, very matter-of-factly. "Well, firstly, I've got two kids. They need a good father. I thought that theirs was, but ... but, I guess I was wrong."

I assured her as best I could that I would not, and that he must have been one of the dumbest men on earth to go running around with other women when he had a wife like her. I would be insane to do the same.

"We'll see," she quipped, while continuing to wipe the cabinets.

I detected a look of disillusionment. Apparently she was reflecting once again upon the fact that he had been cheating on her with what had turned out to be a Persian vizier's haremful of women, beginning some six years into an otherwise "normal" Soviet marriage — one result of which was two boisterous, intelligent kids.

"Secondly, we're speaking Russian—" she continued, like a lawyer making her closing remarks, "That's not a language that we can continue talking in. So either my English gets better ... or you must learn Latvian."

"Well, that makes sense. It shouldn't be too hard."

After all, I learned French after living for one year in France ... and that was among Parisians, whose blood-sport involved making mockery of foreigners who attempt to speak French. They always did so with looks that would normally be reserved for watching paralympic hopefuls; the phrase "*C'est drole, n'est ce pas, quand les petits Amerloques parle francais?*" still rings in my ear.

Inge looked away, and, while still smiling, said, "Finally, you're trying to set up a bakery in Latvia. Do you know what kind of people work in the *sabiedriskās ēdināšanas* 'public eating' sector?"

She asked it the way Livingstone's Mother probably asked her son if it was *absolutely* necessary for him to conquer the wilds of Africa.

"What … what do you mean?"

"Do you realize that these people were the richest, greasiest, most resented parasites that walked the territory of the Soviet Union?"

"Well, no, not really … I mean sure, some people everywhere in the food business steal, and restaurant owners always have to watch the wine in the kitchen, but it couldn't be *that* bad …"

"Boriss, these people had everyone begging at their feet — someone would approach them and say, 'We're having a family reunion next week, and I really needed three pounds of beef and one bottle of cognac — you wouldn't be able to arrange that for me, would you? Of course we'll pay you 15 rubles [three times the official price for it] and of course you can use the summer dacha anytime next June.' Their salaries were too small to live on. *Why?* Because it was taken for granted that they would *steal* the difference."

At this point Inge threw a glance that I believe I will remember for the rest of my life. The "look" involved eyes opened wide, lips pursed, and every muscle from the shoulders up, tensed. It sent shivers down to my Achilles tendon and communicated more clearly than any words could – "You might have business experience, and education, and some smarts, but you obviously have *no* idea what cunning, conniving, cutthroat beasts these people are." But the words came out softer.

"Well, let me just say, that you will be *challenged.* Just bear in mind that when all is said and done, we have two kids to support. I don't want them running around in their bare feet."

"Darling. I understand your concern. But, you see, how shall I say it — this isn't just going to be another Soviet bread bakery, making white bread-that-should-be-used-as-a-doorstop. This is going to be *Vyesyoliy Pekar* 'The Merry Baker'!"

Inadvertently, I continued in English and explained that it would be so good, that people will be coming from miles around to try the baked goods. And this wouldn't just be one store. No, that was *not* why I decided to go into business for myself *here*. We would set-up-a-chain-of-stores-like-Mrs. Field's Cookies-or-Noah's Bagel's-or-Winchell's Donuts.

I had to admit to myself that it was probably hard for her to imagine what I was talking about now — it was about as actual to her as Argentinean beef steak and tiger prawn salad would be for an Ethiopian. At the end, I assured her that she had nothing to worry about and that I hadn't dropped a job that paid what it did, and gone through the education that I did to set up some little corner bakery … I couldn't even bake.

"No, this'll be *big*—"

At this point Inge took my hand, which, after the wild gesticulation, I had placed back on the table with a clunk, squeezed it and said, "We'll just see." I caressed her hair until it was time to go, said goodnight to nine-year-old Markus and seven-year old Eliza, shut the door behind me, and set out for my apartment, two hundred yards down the street. We had a "deal."

Footnotes

[1] Rimbert, a chronicler of Viking exploits of the 9th century, writes that [in a.d. 854]; "The Danes gathered boats and outfitted them to attack the peoples on the lands of the [Kurs]. There were five [districts], and the warriors from those districts had quickly assembled. There were five thousand of them. The Danes, attacked and hoped to plunder the village and burn it to the ground. However, the warriors fought [fiercely] and at the end of the battle, half of the Danes lay on the battlefield. The [Cours] then went and plundered [their] boats, taking the gold and [previously] plundered stores."

[2] The extended wood sling consisted of a piece of wood that was approximately two feet long, at the end of which a receptacle pod was carved out. The rock would be placed into the pod and fastened with a thin strip of leather. The Lats discovered that the length gave more leverage than using a regular sling, and the rocks would travel up to fifty meters further than they would with ordinary slings. The Russians also discovered the effectiveness of this hand-held "catapult" as a result of being on the receiving end of stones hurled at them.

[3] Olainfarm was the largest of three pharmaceutical manufacturing companies in Latvia in 1992. Besides being the original producer of Rimantidine — the world's leading flu therapy — the factory manufactured several hundred other products, including amphetamines. The latter had been produced primarily for the Soviet army during the 1980s. Once the Afghan war had ended, and those trade ties were severed, the director of Olainfarm, Ilmars Penke, decided to re-orient sales of that product to Western customers, such as the drug users in Frankfurt. Through a series of Russian and Southeast Asian middlemen, he was able to sell several million dollars' worth of the product, until Interpol shut down the operation. When Penke was arrested, he stated that he was exporting it only for the sake of the workers, who would otherwise have lost their jobs. In his own defense, he stated that already, they hadn't "been paid for five months." Ironically, when the police raided his apartment, they found 700,000 deutschemarks (about $500,000) stuffed up his chimney — exactly enough to pay all the workers' back salaries.

4

A STATE OF THINGS

IT WAS NOW LATE MAY. I was standing outside the bakery. Dry gusts of wind hurled dust into the air. Three windows of the twelve on the street side of the stately turn-of-the-century apartment building across from the bakery were broken. Some windows on the first floor were shuttered. Others were not, but behind most of them hung sheets that substituted for drapes. Some of these appeared to have a floral design, which upon closer inspection turned out to be stylized initials of "MZ," or the Ministry of Health. The sheets had been the black market fare of Hospital Supply Warehouse directors or nurses desperate for a little hard cash to accompany the moral rewards of comforting untreated syphilitics and victims of hit-and-run accidents in their final moments.

Two wires ran the course of the street. Suspended on one of them were a handful of dark green bulb-less street lamps, swaying with each gust of wind. The other wire trolley buses sucked for power. A grime-covered pediment and peeling paint accented each of the buildings on the East side of the street. The paint was splintering off the six-storied Jugendstil stucco buildings, peeling off the wooden three-story houses — once the homes and stores of the Jewish merchants who had thrived on this street fifty-eight years earlier — in cusps. The paint was curling off the grocery store front and drugstore walls as if it had never been assigned the task of sticking to the surface on which it had been brushed. In patches it was suspended off the facade of the

Yeshiva, long since transformed into apartments for the proletarian masses arriving from the bowels of the Russian Federal Socialist Republic. Like tobacco leaves hung to dry, the paint hung off the walls of the "dairy products" store on the corner. I reflected on the state of these walls and concluded that the northernmost section of Avotu Iela resembled nothing remotely Western European, but may have drawn a respectable parallel to Puebla, Mexico, in December.

As they did on all workdays, the trolley buses were running along this street with frightening regularity. It was frightening primarily because they were the only vehicles allowed to use the eastbound lane on this otherwise one-way street, and they were surprisingly silent. The bus drivers operated these vehicles as if they were runaways on high-speed autobahns. I saw one bear down on a cat that was looking the wrong way. The cat was spared having to use up one of its lives by jumping back to the curb in the last possible millisecond before obliteration. People could be seen walking up or down the Avotu Street sidewalks in various stages of sobriety and undress. In spite of the heat, every second man was sporting a gray-brown or gray-blue woolen coat jacket, woolen pants, and a half-liter dark brown beer bottle bandaged with a gaudy paper label. These Rigans quaffed the beer at a rate that could sprain an Adam's apple, but judging by their hobble, they still couldn't get the liquid to relieve them of the heat fast enough. Then again, most of these very same guzzlers wore, below their wool jackets, three more layers of clothing. This dress code must have been, I surmised, a remnant of some bourgeois formality that had stubbornly resisted the forty-five-year reign of socialist sensibilities. Maybe it would have been unflattering to comrade Ivan or Pēteris, if someone "of position" were to see them wearing only a shirt. By sporting this nifty summer uniform the comrades could be confident that they were portraying the proper "noble-proletarian" image as they staggered from doorway ... to lamp-post ... to bus-sign, along their merry trek to oblivion. A few women, most of whom were wearing dresses with faded floral patterns, could be seen languidly walking between the stores and the apartment doorways. They frequently touched their coiffures, perhaps fearful that the heat and perspiration were wreaking havoc on their hair, which they were not. I guessed that it was around seventy-eight degrees Fahrenheit — late winter weather in most of California.

I stepped back into the bakery. It was three o'clock, one month and one day after we had sat down to name the company. The completion date of the bakery renovation had been pushed back twice already. I estimated that we were running one full month behind the originally scheduled date of June 10. Valdis was now telling the locksmith that the employee changing room

Avotu and Lienes Street intersections

would also require locks. Valdis had gathered together a seemingly qualified team of laborers, who were now helping push the project forward. I reflected frequently on my new partner. On the positive side, he appeared to know everything that was worth knowing about the psychology of the average Soviet laborer — knowledge that I was beginning to appreciate with each passing day. On the other hand, he had a major flaw.

"Valdis, mind if I give you a little word of advice?"

"Sure, I've always been the kind of person who's open to suggestions."

"Great. Well, there are some two weeks left before our new projected date of completion, right? And it seems that we are dangerously close to running behind *that* day, right?"

"Well, I don't know if you would use the word 'dangerously,' but yes, it appears that that date might also be slipping a tiny little bit," he replied with equanimity.

"Well, since our company has only nineteen people, and three of them are your [technical department] subordinates, that means that we pretty much need every pair of hands to be fully — how shall I say — *zadeystveniye* 'occupied'."

"Yes, and they are."

"Uh-hunh. Well, let me be blunt — experience in the West has shown that it's darned important for the troops to *occasionally* see that the officers are fighting too. It creates a sense of team."

This little pep talk was met with a blank stare. I wasn't communicating clearly.

"Let me put it another way — the uppermost managers at the top of the pyramid...," I continued, holding my right hand up, as if fingering the top of a triangle, "of a start-up company can *also* work with their own hands. Not only will the job get done more quickly, but it helps with morale."

I might as well have recommended a three-day spell in the felons' ward of the central prison to share the golden experience of incarceration. After a moment, his shocked expression faded, he nodded, smiled.

"Yes, I understand what you're saying, yes ... a bit like the work of students together with the workers during the summer work brigades . . . everyone, working for one goal, yes!"

He said it with the enthusiasm usually reserved for four-year-olds who have been promised a trip to the ice cream store.

I chuckled to myself and said, "O.K. let's try this. You choose something that you don't really want to do, as opposed to something that you *absolutely* don't want to do. Then treat it as a crisis, which by the way, we are *in* right now, and it will be resolved in no time at all."

He smiled widely and said, "No problem, really. No problem at all, I'll do, *s entuziazmom,* with enthusiasm whatever you tell me to."

"Valdis has, no doubt, been used to producing more than his fair share of unadulterated sycophancy at Communist Party cell meetings at the factory," I thought to myself.[1] He then walked off and proceeded to tell the plumber that the pipes should be lifted higher if possible (it wasn't), and for the refrigeration technician to fill up the refrigerator in the storage room with freon (which he had already done).

In spite of this management setback, on this particular day I could be pleased. About five hundred kilos of construction debris had been taken out of the basement, and the lift between the half-basement and the first floor turned out to be operable. This would be quite useful, explained Valdis, as heavy items could be brought upstairs this way. Little did either of us know that eight months later, twenty-two-pound cakes were the heaviest items that would be brought up on this lift that was constructed to take fifty times more — and sounded like it. "Creeagh, wakachaka, WHOOM," were some of the sounds that it generated during the thirty-second, seven-foot climb that the platform made between the half-basement and the first floor. The plumbing was now functional, and this left only the completion of the electrical system before the hired crew could begin the cosmetic finish of the bakery.

In the first week of July, one-and-one-half months later, the bakery's renovation was progressing at a pace between snails-on-hallucinogens or turtles-in-heat, with a leaning towards the former. This was so because between the last Pioneer camp and the next world war, work life had been marked by a series of "five-year plans" that would have been, in the West — under constant shareholder surveillance — compressed into six months or one year. Within this context, my "plan" for renovating the bakery by a certain date was not at all shared by the builders. But this fact did not prevent them from endlessly reassuring me, "*Nachal'nik – nye volnuysya – vsye budet kak skazish!* 'Boss — don't worry — everything will be as you say'." Shortly after saying so, they would go off to smoke for what appeared to be hours at a time.

I had to satisfy myself with the tempo of the rest of the preparations. In fact, there were three steps that I had to accomplish before I could breathe easily. I had to secure a retail location, I had to complete a plant, and to find a "master" who could train my bakers to make fine European pastries. Although cakes and bread also figured prominently in this business, I felt that the key to success was pastries. Pastries are how taste buds wake up in the morning. As a result, bakers are generally respected in Western European countries. In Latvia, I got the impression that they were viewed as societal degenerates. Even Zigrīda confided to me that "baking schools are the repositories of teenagers who had not only dropped out of high school, but had outworn their welcomes at home." I thought that France or Denmark or Austria could be rich sources of masters who fulfill the "calling" prerequisite. Out of convenience — there was a direct flight to that country — I started with Denmark.

A trip to the Culinary School of Copenhagen resulted in references to the baking schools of Denmark. Three major ones existed — but "Hillerod had a great baker who had worked abroad before, on a similar project in some backward country," the Director of the culinary school reflected aloud; "his name is Preben". So I called and arranged a meeting with Preben. Preben Rokamp was a man of medium height, with a prominent nose, a well-trimmed beard and a paunch that was part and parcel of his craft. Unlike myself — the inveterate ninety-pound weakling — Preben's midsection testified to the fact that he was not afraid to eat his own production.

Preben had also spent several years in Limerick, in the 1970s, where he had started a bakery. Although for various reasons, he had sold the bakery at a loss, he had very positive memories of establishing a Danish bakery in a foreign land. "Everything that I was baking was new to the people, and they loved it," he said with an Irish accent that made the intonation on the *o* in "love" rise to the stratosphere. "It was jolly fun for me, too, even though I had to import *everything*, from proper margarine to almond paste. Even the butter couldn't be used without the Danish fallin' apart." He had less pleasant things to say about his ex-wife, who had cheated on him, and about the financial situation that drove him back to Denmark. But he concluded optimistically. Several times, during the course of our conversation, students would come up to him and ask questions. Most of them laughed when he answered (I understood only the "*Hey, hey's*" uttered at the end of each exchange). He reminded me of the assistant coach on a high-school team that the players could confide their problems to first, before taking them to the Head Coach. I realized straightaway that he was the right man for the post, so I offered him the job on the spot. When he heard my proposal, he was amused, and said that it could be "jolly good fun" to train some Latvian bakers. It didn't take him long to reply, that it would be a pleasure for him to help me get this bakery started; he had no commitments at this time — "so who knows, maybe we can work on it together as partners later on — just don't ask me to make any Irish soda bread." We then agreed that he would come for two months to Riga, and take our bakers through the "basic training" course.

Finding the master baker had taken so little time that I found myself with two free days. Preben's mid-week day-off coincided with the last of these days, so he offered to introduce me to suppliers of tools and raw materials. These suppliers were quite impressed with the fact that someone was establishing something in "Lettland — so *far* away." In one case, this notion was uttered as if I were going to be the first client at the Sheraton Moon Hotel. In fact, Riga is only a one-hour, ten-minute flight from Copenhagen — Brussels is farther. At E.J. Frederickson's, we compiled our initial inventory of tools. Preben began by asking for twelve-inch-long cedar canes, about two inches thick, rounded at the ends. I thought it strange that simple hardwood sticks could play a role in the production of high-quality Danish — which the ones at Hillerod Technical School most definitely were.

"Preben, are these rounded sticks meant to beat the dough into submission?"

"No, Borisss, ya amateur," he said with a laugh, while shaking his bearded head from side to side, "they're for beatin' the bakers who don't listen."

"O.K., then why twelve?"

"Because sometimes, those skulls are harder than the wood, and my tech-n-i-i-que isn't what it used to be." When my laughter subsided, he explained that the small sticks of wood were used to flatten the dough.

"But Preben … uh … how shall I say this … Latvia does have rolling pins!"

"Oh, yes?! Then it's not a backward country a' tall, Boriss. But whatever the place is like, rolling pins are for housewives. Serious bakers use these." Once I gathered nerve to speak again, I asked which wood is acceptable. "Cedar, ash, work the best. Not pine, it's too soft." At the end of the visit, our cart was brimming with tools that I had never, ever associated with baking: at least none of the kind that I had seen done in my parents' kitchen. There were plastic scrapers, an item that looked like five pizza-cutters joined in the middle by a collapsible metal fence, thermometers in stainless steel casings and a myriad of instruments that looked to me like they belonged in a surgical ward, not a bakery. All of them Preben assured me were the most "basic" necessary for the production. I told him that I consent to all these purchases but that I wouldn't be bending over for any reason when I was in the bakery.

When I returned to Riga, Dmitri had also stumbled onto something hard — at least his teeth did — he had only one upper incisor, where six had previously hung. No clear explanation was forthcoming. Perhaps that was because he could no longer pronounce the letter ess. "*Malyenkaya Nepriatnoft,* "a little unpleafant-neff" was all that he offered in the way of explanation. He assured us, however, that all electrical wire-laying was proceeding at a "normal" pace, and that "there will be no delayf on *my* account."

At the same time, Zigrīda was screening the remaining bakers that would make up the production team. They were being selected on the basis of having as little bakery experience as possible. In Zigrīda's words, "enough to show commitment and aptitude, but not enough to show *experience.* Finally the apple *povidla* had been replaced with large jars of apricot marmalade and real Moldavian apples, peeled and canned for industrial use.

Two members of the local city council even came to visit the site. They asked me what I planned to do with the renovated bakery. I replied, "Well, it's pretty simple, I plan to train the bakers into world-class specialists, open some stores here, and once I change the quality of *konditereyas izstrādāyumi* 'pastries' in this city forever, then we open up superstores in London, Paris, Rome…" Their eyes opened so wide I thought that they would get strokes, so I quickly added, "O.K., no superstores, but we *will* be restoring the quality in pastries that has been lost since nineteen forty. Remember you had a pastry called Štopkūkas? We'll make them again." One of them nodded and said, "Yes, I remember — my grandmother used to tell me about them! It's a very good thing that you're doing — investing in renovating this building, in training this country's bakers, in being here. We are grateful for that, and if we can help in any way, just tell us. If only there were more foreigners like you!"

the council director told me, smiling from cheek to cheek while shaking my hand firmly. If I hadn't loosened my half of the grip after fifteen seconds, he would have offered his daughter's hand in marriage.

Footnotes

[1] Sessions of "self-criticism" were considered an important part of one's professional development in the Soviet Union, along with a heartfelt repetition of supervisors' plans and statements using one's own words. It was of paramount importance to include some virtue or another of long-dead supervisors and of course, Lenin, during the session.

5

RASPBERRIES

A MONTH LATER, I WAS staring at seven 30-liter plastic jars, arrayed neatly on the floor of the office, and filled to the neck with a bright magenta-colored mass. Next to me were Preben, Dmitri and Rolands, the driver. The perfume of wild raspberries filled the room.

"So Preben, you're saying that the aroma on these is very good, and that, at these prices, it will be better than importing the foreign product with too few raspberries, and high amounts of pectin added?"

"Yea, yea," the Dane replied enthusiastically.

"And Dmitri, you say that people won't be bothered by finding worms in the marmalade?" I asked in my oddly accented Russian.

"Yef, that'f right. We can minimife the quantity by fcrewing the topf on thefe jarf and depriving the wormf of air. They'll fcramble and float to the top, and we'll juft fkim them off."

"That's clever...do they all come up?"

"No, not all, but that'f not a problem though — people are ufed to a little worm meat with their rafpberry preserves — it juft provef that the ftuff is ecologically clean."

I chuckled to myself. Almost every time I heard that phrase it meant that someone in the ex-USSR was excusing himself or his establishment for a lack of the requisite sanitary standards that would remedy the situation. In one restaurant I overheard the waiter explain that the fact that the cockroaches are crawling over the food meant that they did not use pesticides, therefore the restaurant was doing a service to the environment.

"Oh Boriss, it'll just mean a little more pro-te-in fer the foulks here — besides the buggers are mighty small ... and cute, aren't they?" chimed in Preben. He followed that remark up with a guffaw.

"Well, I guess that ... when in Rome ... besides, you're right, Preben, the taste is divine."

After doing as Dmitri had suggested, we left to inspect the bakery plant. In half an hour we returned to the room and, sure enough, a 1/16-inch layer of light pink mass was squirming on the top of the raspberry puree, glistening with the juices that covered it. We skimmed the worms off and re-closed the jars and loaded them into the truck. Dmitri and Preben got into the car and drove, along with the raspberry-laden truck to the "Pūres Cehs" Company. Preben later recounted that upon arrival, they explained to the director of the jam factory that we needed an extremely thick marmalade, to withstand the high baking temperatures. "Otherwise," explained Dmitri, following instructions I had translated from Preben, "the jam will simply burst in the oven, and the oven sides will be sticky." From Preben's description The Director, Mrs. Kalniņa, a *tehnologs*[1], produced a vacant stare. According to Preben's description, it was apparently the first-stage neural coma triggered when new requirements were put forth, requirements unheard of in Soviet times, when all she had to do was produce a sugary syrup with a few fruit pieces that could be poured out of the jar onto the family's porridge. Preben's sentence "We also won't be able to sell them because the pastries will be empty in the middle and messy on the sides ..." received a "why in the world would anyone use our jam for anything besides topping porridge?! For *that* is *the* raison-d'être of *our* jam!" response. It apparently took another half hour of illustration to bring home the point that these seven plastic jars, holding thirty kilos of raspberry apiece, might be reduced to three, and that we were willing to pay the difference for the final product.

Preben's joviality helped me keep a normal perspective on the business. I wanted to set systems and controls and time the bakers as they made the products. Sometimes, Preben concurred that it was a good idea, but more often than not, he'd smile and shake his head, adding some phrase like, "Oh Boriss, ya gonna control how they pee, too?" When I expressed concern about the equipment arrangement in the newly refurbished bakery, he replied that if we didn't put it right the first time, we could move it around, and if there weren't enough people to move it, then we could just put plastic explosives underneath and *blow them into place.*

We had agreed with Petuhin that The Merry Baker could use the bakery plant behind the store to train our bakers until the time that our bakery plant up the street had been renovated. He agreed, albeit grudgingly, to let us use both the bakery plant and part of the store in which to sell the items that we baked. The hefty rent that we had settled on eventually left him amenable to this incursion on "his" space. The bakery plant area behind the store was being used, currently, to bake cookies that were sent all over this part of town. Ligita called the cookies "miracle cookies." This term she applied to all cookies that with virtually no sugar could stick together and, with only microscopic quantities of margarine, could still crumble. In the hands of less cunning bakers, they would have been straw-colored concrete biscuits. According to the agreement, we could use the bakery plant during the nine hours that the cookie bakers were not using it — from 10:00 A.M. to 7:00 P.M.

The bakery store itself was about six hundred square feet in size. Before the war, it had been a pin shop. But with a few cabinets, it was transformed, after the war, into a *konditer'skaya* — a term taken from the German *konditerei*. The store was located next to a bus stop, but Petuhin was not optimizing the location. This fact should have been no surprise to me; the merchandising techniques of this *Trest* matched the quality of the cookies and neither of the two was for the weak-spirited. For example, the pastries and cookies were displayed on white enamel trays. Such trays could be seen in photographs of American prisons in the 1950s, or WWII field hospitals. They were still used universally in Latvia and the ex-Soviet Union. Only their size and shape determined whether they were destined to display sugar cookies or to receive a freshly extracted appendix in the hospital operating room. Perhaps these trays were here and not in the operating ward of Hospital #4 up the street because the white enamel had chipped off the edges. In any event, the first thing that we made sure to do, even before replacing the cashier's abacus with an electric cash register, was to replace these trays with woven baskets. When the cashier from the "Avots" bakery saw this, she turned up her nose and walked out, saying, "So, our trays aren't *good* enough for them, eh? Soon, they'll be putting linen tablecloths under their baskets, *humph.*" We did.

The director of the bakery, both the store and the production, was a lady named Dzidra. Dzidra was in her late forties and displayed a weakness for the bottle — the one containing hair bleach. She would then take her miracle-white hair and arrange it into a beehive hairdo. When I first met her, I thought that she had stepped out of a Gary Larsen cartoon — any of the ones featuring the 1950s coffee-shop waitress. Dzidra's first words to me were, "So, you want to start a bakery business here, why in the world would you want to do *that*?! Oh well … you have a nice set of teeth." The latter she said as if having normal white teeth, along with a communist party card, were the two tickets to elite status in the Soviet Union. I later found out that she had been instructed by Petuhin to be accommodating to us. And throughout the first two weeks, she was. She patiently showed Preben the lay of the bakery, how to operate the oven and where the clean trays — as opposed to the ones caked with a quarter-inch-thick layer of cat hairs and rat droppings — were located. I translated for Preben as he clarified where the steaming controls on the oven were. Dzidra kept repeating, "*Nyet, nyet,*" while I pointed at the button marked with some symbol resembling a steaming showerhead. Finally, she said, "Yes, this *is* the button, but it doesn't work." Preben looked at her and smiled, answering, "no self-respecting baker would dare bake bread for sale to anyone but his mother-in-law, if it did not have a steam-started crust!" Dzidra laughed and shook her head wildly from side to side. Preben laughed as well, but his laughter had a very nervous edge. He then concluded that this flaw wouldn't affect most other items. We resumed our information exchange with Dzidra, but she was decidedly less patient from that moment on.

The following day, the bakers came at 10:00. Preben trained them to make cinnamon twists and three other items from sweet dough. He started by showing them how the dough should have the consistency of "goo" gel. The bakers stared intently, then whispered things among themselves — they seemed captivated. Preben measured the temperature of the dough with one of the thermometers — more whispers. He explained that the dough should be no more than twenty-seven degrees centigrade when it is taken for forming … that it was necessary to calculate the temperature of the water at the onset, to prevent over- or under-heating. The next day, he demonstrated how to make a walnut bread and a seven-grain bread. The bakers were amazed — nuts in a bread — "But it won't sell," I overheard one baker saying. In fact, it would not be long before the customers would soon be unable to buy this bread — it would sell out each day so quickly. Beginning some three days after the lessons started, store receipts demonstrated that the ex-Soviet citizens, who had been treated to three black breads and one white bread in their existence heretofore, were desperate to try something new. From the fifth day onwards, sales grew in geometric progression.

Within two weeks, Dzidra got wind of the fact that these "green" bakers, under the tutelage of Preben, were producing a product that was actually bringing *real* repeat customers into the store. Fine, upstanding family and business people were showing up, as opposed to alcoholics desperately trying to satisfy an attack of the munchies or harried mothers whose children wouldn't get on the bus without a "cookie" beforehand. One day Dzidra was at the bakery when I arrived. It was ten thirty in the morning, almost two hours after the time she would normally have left.

"So, Boriss, I understand that you have quite a few customers coming in for your . . . items," with a tone of voice implying that she would *never* have expected such a thing.

"I suppose so, yes they are."

"What's the secret?"

"The secret? — I couldn't begin to tell you. It's the Danish guy's fault," I said, smiling insipidly, "And, perhaps, because we include all the ingredients that are supposed to be in there."

"Ha-ha. But *that* won't last long, *dorogoy* dear, don't worry. With the crew that you've gathered, it'll soon be butter and margarine in their pockets, and flour and water'll be in the store."

I smiled again but said nothing.

"Another thing — the oven isn't working as well as it was before due to *all* the additional use that it's getting, and the bakery wasn't clean when we arrived last night."

I replied that I would have the oven checked and instruct the bakers to clean up better after themselves. That afternoon I arrived and told them what I had agreed to tell them. Preben chimed in afterwards, that they must clean up after themselves — it was a cardinal rule for any good baker. He followed that up with "Furthermore, don't let the rats run over the dough. Do it once, and the next thing you know, they'll be dancin' a jig on the cinnamon twists!" He looked at me and smiled, making sure that I understood that this bakery was a rat-infested sty. "But seriously, bakers, keeping the bakery clean is very important, *precisely* because otherwise it smells bad and attracts rodents."

Nonetheless, our attempts to leave a clean bakery — where none had existed before — fell short of Dzidra's expectations. Two days later, Dzidra was once again waiting for me and informed me that the bakers found two of our trays from the previous night to be unclean. She accompanied the statement with a cruel smile. I shared this impression with Zigrīda later.

"Boriss, don't pay her too much mind, she's *sawing*."

"*Sawing?*"

"Yes, when someone wants to change something here, or get somebody replaced, they complain about it — endlessly — to change the situation. It's called 'sawing'. She's no doubt doing this to Petuhin; she'll try to get something from you."

Sure enough, on the following day, Petuhin called me into his office. After uttering some preliminary niceties he said,

"We had an agreement, and *you* are going back on your part! Your people are working later in the evening than we had agreed. Furthermore, Dzidra says that we are receiving new orders from stores thirty-one and thirty-eight, and we can't fill them, because our bakers have to leave by ten."

I gathered myself, adjusted my tie and replied calmly,

"Georgi Vladimirovich, you are a man of honor, a man that others can rely on, or so I'm told. I have addressed the bakers with the problems that have been brought up by Dzidra. I am confident that they have righted the wrong conduct, and that the information that you're getting is wrong, or at the very least, greatly *priuvelitchenaya* 'exaggerated.' Now I know that you are a man of your word, a man, as I said, of honor. We had agreed that we could use the bakery kitchen until August 15. Today it is only the twentieth of July, three weeks after we had started," I paused, waiting for him to ponder the words.

He looked down at his desk and started shaking his head from side to side. Rather than listen to fresh accusations of being a young capitalist that I felt he was preparing to hurl at me (along, perhaps, with one of his cement and cinnamon cookies), I started with my back-up argument, which involved withholding his last installment. After all, we had a *"so-oglashenniye* agreement" and I had put my trust in him.

"Now, no reason to overreact — but we really *do* have to respect Dzidra's wishes — she is a *very* qualified bakery 'brigadir'[2]."

"Fine, I'll do everything in my power to make sure that we finish up on time, and the place is spotless when we leave."

"That's good, I trust you too," he answered, donning a sheepish smile.

As I walked out, I wondered what in the world our cleaning the bakery had to do with her qualities as a manager.

It was five o'clock in the afternoon when I re-entered the store. I counted seven people standing in line for our products. The pastries and cakes were flying off the shelves, bagfuls at a time. As I stood there, one man approached me and asked if I was the owner.

"Yes."

"You know, I work a lot with the Dutch — and I've been in Holland on several occasions, but I have never tasted anything as good as *this*," he said, pointing to the cinnamon stick, "When I was there ... this is just wonderful — I serve it to all our clients."

"Thanks, that's nice to hear, sir. By the way, have you tried this 'apple boat'? It's new. Here, have a couple of them on us," I replied, as I signaled to the salesclerk to put two in a bag for the man. He smiled in return and gave me a thumbs-up as he left.

Afterwards, the sales clerk approached me in wide-eyed terror and asked, "How ... how do I account for them? Zigrīda said that each one has been counted and if there is a shortage, it'll be taken out of my salary!" It took several minutes of explanation for me to calm her down.

On the following day, when I arrived, Dzidra was once again present. "Praying mantis" came to mind as she sprang out of her office and into my path. She was confronting me for the third time in five days.

"BorEESS, good *morning*," she uttered, as if she had just come from a five-day *Mind Spring* course. Besides the tone of her voice, I thought she looked a little different today, but I couldn't place why.

"You are looking dapper today — but that's usual," she continued. "Would you have time to talk about something?" she added, using a tone of voice that oozed conspiracy.

"Sure, for *you* . . . I *always* have time," I answered, oozing sticky sweet conspiracy in kind. It then dawned on me that Dzidra looked campy today because she was wearing cherry-red lipstick, and her "do" did not even have the odd strand out-of-place, which was usually the case after she had worked a shift. She had powdered her face whiter. Gary Larsen's diner waitress had gotten a Kabuki theatre makeover.

When I returned to her office a few minutes later, she began with the phrase, "Boriss, I appreciate your taking the time to talk with me. You are so *khorosho vospitanniy* 'well-bred.' I . . . I just wanted to tell you that I stayed yesterday, and listened to what this Danish baker was teaching ..." She paused and looked at me, apparently trying to determine if I would be shocked by her stab at spying. When she saw that I was taking it calmly (What?! You're actually observing what acts are being performed in *your* bakery by total strangers?!) she continued, "You know, there is nothing extraordinary in what he's teaching ... I know all of it ... in fact, I was a baking champion in nineteen seventy-eight —" I raised my eyebrows at that moment, feigning admiration.

"I could teach these things. We just stopped baking everything that way because nobody appreciated what we did."

I nodded, silently, but assumed a "please carry on" expression.

"And about the dirt . . . we can clean up too. Anyway, I was thinking, when this Dane leaves, who's going to manage your bakery?"

"We haven't decided yet."

"Well it certainly can't be Zigrīda — the lady has never set *foot* in a bakery plant before."

"No, it won't be Zigrīda."

"Well I think that you should take me — what do you need an office bureaucrat like Zigrīda for — I'll know what to do in the bakery."

"Well Dzidra, that's an interesting offer . . . but you see . . . we've set the number of employees that we can have, and we're at the limit. But tell you what, if an opportunity comes up — I'll make sure to consider your candidacy."

"Oh, all right . . . I hope it's positive," she said with a smile that bespoke of a wince.

"We'll see."

Later that day, I shared the gist of the discussion with Zigrīda. She laughed, albeit nervously, and then stated that if we want rat-eaten rolls made so hard that people break their teeth on them, then Dzidra'll guarantee that we get them. "But if you want to start something different from what you see all over this city today, then we're better off training Ligita." With difficulty, I assured her that I wasn't seriously considering the offer, but was just sharing information with her.

At the end of the training period — after the new bakery had opened — I apologized to Dzidra for the fact that we had no employment opportunities at the time. I also thanked her and said that we would keep her in mind. After all, she would be quite the find when we started a circa 1950s American-style donut shop.

One reason for Preben's easygoing attitude was that he had recently fallen head over heels in love with the secretary of the co-op board of the house where he was staying. All notions of partnership or serious involvement in the bakery that he might have entertained a few months earlier had, alas, gone with the wind. Instead, he kept in daily contact with Berit on a mobile telephone, in an era when they were a novelty and still the size of bricks. Setting up the telephone in his rental flat had been a half-hour endeavor; he had moved it from windowsill, to chest of drawers, to other flat surfaces, finally laying it on a chest of drawers that had been stolen from a large medieval castle. When he called, the radio waves disrupted all communication on the regular telephone line, made the radio inaudible, and probably paralyzed no small number of mosquitoes that were unlucky enough to have invaded the premises. When he talked, I could clearly understand only a series of *Hey, hey's, taks* 'hi, thanks,' interspersed with what must have been cooing remarks. Whether as a result of these, or of the separation, two weeks into the contract Preben asked if he couldn't shorten his stay by two-and-a-half weeks. Being in a hyper-romantic stage of my life at that point myself, I consented. In any event, the bakery renovation would *not* be completed by the originally agreed final day of his contract term.

Preben Rokamp, Danish Bakery Instructor, 1992

Footnotes

¹ Tehnologs 'technologist' was the combination of what in a western food manufacturing company would be a New Product Development Specialist and a Quality Control Director, and as such, in Soviet times, assured neither.

² Brigadir is taken from the military lexicon, and is the equivalent of a shift manager in America. Normally, these managers were responsible for weighing out the ingredients, and then mixing the dough. In larger operations, they merely oversaw those operations.

6

LITTLE TOWN BLUES

AT THIS POINT, THREE MONTHS later, I was still commuting from Ogre. This small industrial town was located some thirty-five kilometers from Riga, along the train route to Moscow. Concerning its transition history, there was nothing particularly unique about it. Throughout their empire, the Communist Party leaders had a habit of selecting a town with a particularly "bourgeois" pre-war profile (which meant that it was deriving most of its income from activity of a non-industrial nature such as silversmithing, horse-breeding, mineral-water baths, sailing or skiing) and blessing it with a factory employing ten thousand or more workers. The picturesque pre-war character of said towns was instantly relegated to "bourgeois history," and instead, these Ogres and Livanes began resembling any number of gray industrial towns in the Soviet Union. Each one boasted an off-the-shelf, monumentally sized yet nondescript concrete-and-glass factory building, which dominated the landscape. This eyesore was surrounded by dozens of four-, nine- and fourteen-storied apartment houses. These structures were also off-the-shelf designs, which were referred to by number — 105, 106, 109, and so on. In the process of building them, the Soviet planners made sure to raze several charming country homes or town houses, which had stood in their places. When all was said and done, only by comparing the surrounding landscape and climate could one differentiate these towns from one another.

This transformation from charming to industrial was accompanied by an equivalent change of the populace from predominantly local to "Soviet." The latter invariably meant largely ethnic Russian, with a smattering of people from other republics. In the best of cases, these "Soviet citizens" were experts in that particular industry. However, in most cases the population explosion consisted of simple Russian country folk who were searching for a better job. The latter was being trumpeted by local regional committees, on Moscow's orders, as the *raison d'être* (including bananas, sunshine and gorgeous single people) of the fringe republics.[1] Most of the immigrants were marginally educated, but harmless.

Valdis, Inge's father, was the administrative director of the department of housing of the Ogre Knitting Factory — the behemoth that Moscow had hoisted on Ogre. Valdis had chosen a job that granted him a significant degree of authority and respect, yet a good deal of flexibility in his schedule. Both were requisites for raising well-balanced children in the USSR, where both parents invariably had to work. As the administrative director, he oversaw both the management of currently existing buildings and the construction of new ones. The housing of fifteen thousand workers was no small matter, requiring a quadrupling of the housing stock that had existed prior to the war. To no small degree, I admired the man. Among other things, he preserved the use of the Latvian language in his immediate working environment. The central authorities had been — until the 1980s — bent on eradicating local languages, primarily by eliminating them from the workplace. All regional-level management, as well as the top management of all businesses, spoke only Russian. Nonetheless, by demonstrating that he had to employ local workers who "happened to have a poor command of Russian," Valdis maintained Latvian as the working language in his department.

Furthermore, Valdis had quietly played the role of chief conservationist of the town. In one case, in the 1970s, he had prevented the wanton cutting down of 155 twenty-year-old linden trees along the route to the newly constructed *Rembate* Soviet military airport. The *DorStroi* were widening the road. Rather than letting the trees be destroyed, Valdis petitioned his superiors to allow the trees to be uprooted, transported some fifteen kilometers away to Ogre and planted near the "high-rise" apartments that he was responsible for building. Although this achievement may be petty compared to the feats of the Sierra Club in the U.S. Pacific Northwest, it was a stupendous feat in the USSR, where to have declared oneself an ecologist or "green" in the 1970s was tantamount to treason against the Socialist State. *No one* could ever have, until the Chernobyl incident, publicly doubted that the Soviet Ministry of the Environment knew what was best for the environment and the people inhabiting it.

Valdis also kept up Christian traditions like Christmas and Easter, which his Polish Catholic grandmother had taught him to observe.

In other venues of his life and work, however, he was on a short leash — the only government-sanctioned architectural plans that he was allowed to "approve" resulted in high-rise apartments that looked exactly like the ones found everywhere else in the Soviet empire. He told me later, "There were only six plans to choose from. About three for nine-story buildings, and three for fourteen-story ones." They were drafty monoliths with inadequate infrastructures. The inconveniences ranged from a shortage of elevators to heating systems that defied regulation except through the opening and closing of windows; ceiling heights gave the newcomer an impression of being Alice in some new Wonderland after having drunk the "bigness" potion. But these were considered the *melochi zhizni* 'pocket change of life,' during the great progressive "Advanced Socialist"[2] era.

Furthermore, Valdis would be responsible for providing apartments to those relatives of the factory upper management or the city council, which clearly exceeded the norms permitted by the state, which was a grand total of nine meters — a hundred square feet, about one-fourth of a normal trailer home — per person. Occasionally, Valdis was able to help a relative obtain the same. In my case, he arranged a small studio apartment meant for short-term visitors to the factory. That was also one of his last work-related achievements, as he retired shortly thereafter, at the state-sanctioned age of sixty.

I was commuting to and from Riga because Inge lived in Ogre. During my commutes, I frequently reflected on my conversation with her about the "Deal." "O.K., so the tasks are clear to me. Now let me think about the game plan. Firstly about the kids … That's no problem, they're kids … I would have brought a monkey and a parrot along with the goat to that birthday party in 'Mrs. Doubtfire.' Second, I've got to start learning the language. I really should take courses. But I'll learn quickly enough through immersion, like I've done twice before. The business … a 'piece of cake …'"

In fact, up until this point, my conscious acquisition of the local language had not proceeded at all. Four months had passed since I had arrived in Latvia on the *Latvija* express train and three months had gone by since I had answered the first question posed to me, in coherent Latvian. The question "Do you find this language easy?" I had understood as "why did you go to the store?" and answered "after two bottles. This earned generous applause and boisterous laughter from those present, as they assumed that bottles would be filled with vodka. I found that between day-to-day survival in this country, starting up a new business, and trying to lead a family life, I had little energy to devote to learning this ancient language.[3] But I reasoned that *this* aspect of my life could wait a bit longer before remedying.

Foremost in my mind at this point, was that I was not pleased either with the general location or the living apart from Inge and the children. Small factory towns had never quite ignited my imagination, and I saw no reason to think differently now. Besides the plentitude of cultural activities, which in Ogre boasted a non-ventilated movie theater — which apparently banned entry to anyone who used antiperspirants) playing pirated Hollywood movies from the 1980s in which everyone spoke Russian with a whiny male voice, a disco for teenagers on Fridays, a small market three days a week and a fire-and-brimstone sermon from the newly arrived American preacher on Sundays, small towns moved at a pace which did not correspond at all to the ambitions of a thirty-two-year-old set to turn the ex-communist world upside down. More to the point, I felt that I would be missing out on the redevelopment that was taking place in Riga — the Swedish shoe store opening up on the corner of *Čaka* and *Dzirnavu* streets, or the new Italian restaurant that was to make its appearance, like a bright gondola on a gray Venice morning, in the Old Town. The city was now changing rapidly from the structured plans dictated by Moscow,[4] to the disorganized but socially responsive urban landscape that a free economy allowed.

Furthermore, I had to commute to town on the train. During the course of every commute to and from Riga, I ended up reflecting on the virtues of deodorants and how these virtues could be communicated to the train-riding, movie-watching populace. When nothing gelled, I started ruminating about some apartment in the center. One day, I just did the inevitable and agreed to meet a *maklyor* real estate agent that someone at the American Embassy had recommended to me.

The next day, I stepped off the train, ran down the stairs and sprinted past the newspaper and flower stands in the terminal and straight to the taxi line. I was running late, so I had to outmaneuver the freshly disembarked passengers from Nizhny Novgorod, to a taxi. I caught the eye of one taxi driver, at the end of the line of twenty-five taxis, and jogged to him. As I approached, I said; "Cēsu Iela 15 … take me there, and I'll make sure that you won't regret it." The taxi man took a long drag on his cigarette, looked in front at the clumsily forming line, exhaled, and said, "*Khorosho*, get in." I looked out the window as twenty people grouped at the first taxi, as if it were the last one leaving East Berlin before the border was sealed. "Thanks, cabbie; yes, looks like it'll be another fifteen minutes before they realize that the second, third, fourth and even tenth taxis are equipped with both accelerator pedals and steering wheels … although I realize that these may well be 'extras' by now in their hometown, I muttered, as the taxi entered the flow of traffic across town.

I arrived at the real estate office, opened the door and was greeted by the agent, who jumped to his feet. He was dressed in slacks, a shirt, tie and sweater.

He was also unshaven, and extremely nervous. He would have been an effective stand-in for any Brooklyn "bail-bond agent" auditioning in Hollywood.

"So, you are looking for an apartment of one hundred square meters, for a period of a year."

"Well, the amount of total space isn't so important, but the apartment must have three bedrooms and a living room, and must be located in the center of the city. However, it seems that, yes, these apartments tend to be in the range of one hundred square meters [1000 square feet]." The agent lit a cigarette and offered one to me.

"No, thanks. So, you mentioned over the phone that you have one?"

"M-hmm. Yes we do. In fact...," and he quickly glanced out the window, as if he were dealing in drugs and expecting a raid on his office at any moment, "we have three right now which fit your description. Only question is, can you share the space with anyone?"

I winced, using the entire range of muscles on the left side of my face, to make it painfully clear that he was being weirdly unreasonable, and responded curtly, "No, we cannot. We are not *desperate* for space."

"O.K., then that leaves two. How are you with your hands?"

"Whaddya mean?"

"I mean, can you fix a place up, if you move into one which isn't finished?"

"What do you mean by 'not finished'?"

"Well, some of the necessary pipes are in, but there's all the plumbing fixtures, the kitchen equipment... and most of the doors that still need to be done... along with the floor. But that's just in the back half of the house," he said, nodding as he calmly listed construction tasks sufficiently complex to keep the host of *This Old House* busy for two or three shows or to keep someone as lame at renovation work as myself tormented for decades.

So I put on my finest Brooklyn-sized sneer, arranged a piercing look on my face and said, "Look, don't be ridiculous, I have things to do — either you *have* a finished apartment, or you do *not!*"

"Whoa, whoa, just asking, it's all right, everything will be '*normal'no*,'" he said, as he threw out the cigarette and then jerked his head to the window.

"*Normal'no*" is one of the most popular expressions in the ex-Soviet Union, and means "O.K." However, the general understanding is that nothing that is "normal" is at a level equivalent to a U.S.-style "O.K.," because standards (and opportunities) are lower. The term *Zolīds* or "Solid" would be more equivalent to "O.K." of the West. However, no "*zolīds*" was forthcoming — I lowered my expectations accordingly — there would be rodents crawling on the floor, and holes in the wall... but they would be small. If he had used the term *Interyesno*, then I could have expected the place to be crawling with foot-long rats and an interior resembling a West Bank Hamas hideout after helicopters had strafed it.

"We have one, but it's expensive."

"How much?"

"He wants $500 per month."

"Well, it's more than I would have expected, but let's have a look. You know, that's pretty high, considering that the guy is probably paying about fifteen dollars a month for that space right now."

"Yeah, but you know how housing is around here — everyone is living in a tiny space and as soon as they can, they take up the big spaces, so don't expect a ... a New York apartment."

"Don't worry, the thought never even crossed my mind."

We sat in his car and drove ten minutes to the apartment. I was pleasantly surprised to see that the apartment building was located about six blocks from the bakery. That was not bad placement for a city that covered close to 120 square miles. The building was built in 1902. It was an Art Nouveau building, with balconies on each floor, overlooking the street. The apartment itself bore the hallmarks of a once-stylish residence, with a tiled central furnace, an art nouveau dresser and a piano, as well as intricate plaster relief on the ceilings, in the form of stylized irises. On the other hand, the post-Soviet features included a bathroom that seemed to collect and preserve the smells of every single toilet in the building; paneling in the kitchen that consisted of unplaned one-by-fours, guaranteeing a lifetime supply of splinters and destroyed sweaters; broken windows. Furthermore, the upright Art Nouveau piano was being used as a planter box. The real estate agent touted the spacious kitchen and central furnace, along with the Art Nouveau dresser, as being the highlights of the space. Even in my wildly imaginative opinion, they did not help terribly in offsetting the negatives of missing floorboards and deconstructed windowpanes. Nonetheless, I turned to the *maklyor* and said, "It's worth a try." I then proceeded to call Inge, who was also working in the city not far away. She agreed to inspect the premises with me two hours later.

When she arrived, her eyes opened to the size of half-dollars as she took in the vastness of the space. At first I thought that this look was simple awe — the country native-comes-to-Big-City amazement. Then she said, "*Ak Dievs* 'Oh my God'! ... The amount of cleaning and upkeep that *this* space will require on a *weekly* basis!"

After carrying out a closer inspection than the one I had done initially, we came to the brass-tacks synopsis of work required. Judging by the gaps between some of the floorboards in the children's rooms, and the manner in which they reverberated when stepped upon, we were sure that they had not been touched since before the war. The varnish had long since been rubbed off the boards, leaving bare wood in many places. Stout, square nails — the pre-war, Dracula-staking variety — protruded from the floor in other spots. One of the two panes in the window in the farthest room was broken. There was no insulation. Furthermore, the fit between window and frame could have accommodated a fourteen-dollar cigar. Nor were there any drapes, or curtain rods from which to hang them. "Inge, what do you think, why aren't there any curtain rods — not one in the entire house? I thought that most people have at least some sheets." "Yeah, well, Boriss, the sheets have other uses too — like straining the cabbage salad. I guess the children haven't reached puberty yet," she replied, while looking at the rows of windows of the adjacent house.

The door handles were sticks of wood run through the round cavity, which once held an ornate brass handle of one design or another. When the wooden handle was pressed, it drew the tongue back noisily. But, in fact, the entire mechanism was useless, insofar as each gust of wind that sailed through the window cracks provided sufficient force to keep the tongue of the lock slipping out of the crevice that had been carved in the side of the doorframe for it. Upon closer inspection, I saw that the crevice had been crudely carved out with a knife; I took this to be a positive sign — in most Soviet households the knife had been the *conscientious* handyman's tool for such cases. Most just used the axe/hammer tool — axe on one side, and hammer on the other. Although I myself am about as close to being a capable handyman as is Pee Wee Herman, I had trouble fathoming this degree of disrepair. After all, I had come from a world where ACE Hardware or Home Depot could provide the DIYer with every tool imaginable. As I later discovered, planers, drills, and chisels had, often enough, been available here. However the willingness to use them seldom surpassed the hypothetical. On the other hand, the combination axe/hammer was a gold standard relished by many ex-Soviet D-i-y'ers, possibly for the impressive visual effect that as little as one swing achieved. From observing most apartments, one could conclude that the goal of the "work" was to create an impressive volume of chips, splinters, dust and other fallout. Apparently, this secondary debris played an important role in cowing a demanding spouse into settling for a less-than-ideal finish of carpentry work in the home. In this particular apartment, the instrument had been used to hammer one windowpane into place, and to beat one stubborn nail into obedience — around the latter was a depression the size of a six-inch pie pan.

The plaster was also falling from above the window frame in the living room, leaving between crumb- and sugar-cookie-sized pieces of stucco on the wide pre-war windowsill. Finally, the bathroom boasted a circa- 1920s basin, nailed to the wall. To call it a "sink" would have been generous — "chipped ceramic on iron, with the latter component rusted where exposed" would have been fair. But besides these aesthetic snags, I reasoned, the place was A-O.K.

"I'm sure that within two or three weeks, we could make it comfortable," I muttered to Inge.

"I don't quite agree, but I'm sure that the place could be made 'livable,' with some hard work, within two or three months," replied Inge. "I'll ask my father and uncle to help out," she added, instinctively understanding that an inclination towards great adventure was not the only trait that I had in common with Mr. Herman.

"Fine, but it *is* an impressive apartment, isn't it? What with twelve-foot ceilings, and original turn-of-the-century plasterwork... *Nu*... do we take it?"

"O.K.... but only for three hundred dollars per month. The hundred-thirty-dollar difference between the sum he asks for and the monthly rental payment will be in the form of renovations for the apartment."

"Fine, then it's agreed." I turned to the real estate agent and said that we would probably take it, but not at the asked-for price, on account of the renovations that would be necessary to make. We then left, still in aftershock by the full 1400 square feet of the place. "By the way, I wonder who's living here now...?" Inge asked rhetorically.

On the next day, we met the leaseholder. He was a heavyset man, sporting a beard. He boasted a beer belly, full beard, beefy face, red nose, thinning, disheveled hair and grease-smeared glasses. In short, judging by my past experience with the profession, I thought he was an Orthodox priest. However, when he gruffly told his daughter, who was standing quietly nearby and looking at us, to "go play in the kitchen, or drink tea with Mother!" while lifting his beefy arm in a threatening position, he assumed the character of someone who was going to eat Englishmen after a good "fee-fi-fo-fum-ing." In short, preparing to follow the way of the cloth he was not, unless the "cloth" was a butcher's apron. He expressed a keen interest in our proposal and subsequently, in the details of the renovation that we were planning.

Fifteen minutes later, his wife left the kitchen and joined us. She was thin, stressed and suffering from the work of a third-circle-of-hell dentist. She was wearing oversize-framed, cherry-red sunglasses with mirror lenses, which she did not take off in our presence during the entire half hour that we were there.

She shifted nervously from side to side when we walked, as she commented on the grave sacrifice that they were making, letting this apartment out for twelve months. She ended her plaint with the question, *"Kto oni takiye? Ti uweren chto oni nye zdelayut sveniushnyu iz nashoi gnezdishkoi?"* Who are these people? Are you sure that they will not make a (pig sty) mess of our nest?'". During these seconds, I was startled by the sight of her incisors, all six of which had been struggling with one another, for most of her lifetime, to occupy the space directly under her nose. I also noticed a bluish-purple tint of skin just behind the upper left side of her glass frames. After hearing out his reply, she disappeared into the kitchen, where she quietly occupied herself with the children.

After ten minutes of negotiations, the leaseholder agreed to the decrease in rent, in exchange for the renovations, which we had made sure to describe in agonizing detail. Never in history had puttying a crevice been described as opulently as it was that afternoon. The procedures involved in restoring a damaged Rembrandt would have sounded like child's play compared to my rendition of sanding the plaster, applying putty, brushing off spare plaster, and other simple steps involved in concealing a crack.

I noticed that with every renovation I elaborated upon, no matter how minuscule, Inge's eyes flashed out warning messages like beacons on a moonless night. With time, I sensed less "warning" in the looks, than the collective hatred of several generations of Latvians towards all Russians, four of whom would now be reaping the benefits of a beautifully elaborated *remont* renovation. The negotiation was over. Hands were shaken all around. We paid the entire annual rental sum of $3,500 on the spot. In front of us, the real estate agent took his "procenti." When we finally walked out, carrying our lease and our list of committed-to repairs, Inge sighted me with a piercing stare.

"Why in the world did you promise to do so *much*?!"

"Oh, just a sense of fair play."

"*What*?!"

"Hey, just kidding. But if you think about it, we really aren't doing anything that we don't absolutely have to."

I then proceeded to calmly re-list the items we had earlier agreed would require repair. That if we didn't fix the floors in the children's rooms, the kids would fall through them. At the very least, on account of the exposed nails and splinters, Eliza would be able to walk around safely in her room only with the help of steel boots.

"As to the window in Marcus' room — maybe it's a bit of an indulgence, keeping the thrilling, chilling winds of November from racing through the house and chilling everyone's ... eggs. But I thought you told me that Markus was prone to colds. As to the bathroom — well, we can economize on back-brushes, just by lying down on the bathtub and moving around — provided that not too many ceramic chips lodge themselves between our shoulder blades..."

"O.K., O.K. You're right. But Boriss, we are not going to do *one more* thing than what you promised ... and whatever you do, make sure that it lasts for just *one* year. These Russians . . . or their parents — they kicked out good, honorable people from their homes, from *this* apartment — then they let it go to rot ... And *now*, we're fixing it for them ... Uggh."

Footnotes

[1] Russification of all the Baltics had been a goal of Stalin's, who cloaked it behind the following logic sequence: "Socialism is our goal; the state that has advanced furthest down the path of socialism is Russia. Ergo, by becoming Russian, one more rapidly progressed to Socialism." Coming from Uncle Joe, this line of reasoning stood second only to Einstein's theory of relativity in scientific soundness. As a consequence, an average of 14,000 new settlers per year came to Latvia between 1946 and 1976. Already by 1953, only 22 percent of the directors and chief engineers in major industrial enterprises were Latvian nationals and in all said enterprises, Russian had become the de facto official language of the working environment.

[2] Although no government official ever claimed that the mighty goal of "communism" had actually been reached, Stalin's heirs craftily redefined "socialism" to give the impression that great strides had been made along some well-defined path to the elusive "communism." The last defined milestone was "Developed Socialism," which was achieved sometime in the late 1970s, under Brezhnev's polemic tutelage.

[3] Latvian is very close to Lithuanian, the oldest form of Indo-European speech in existence today. Scholars of Sanskrit often learn Lithuanian prior to starting the study of Sanskrit.

[4] Moscow's Gorstroi, an Orwellian abbreviation for Gorodskoye Stroitel'stvennoye Organizatsia 'City Construction Organization' determined how many stores would be located in each of the high-rise buildings, and what their profile would be. A standard formula was used per 1,000 inhabitants. Other cities were relegated to inheriting this formula.

Z

SHTURMOVSHCHINA

Two incontrovertible elements of the Soviet working environment have always been the *shturmovshchina* 'storming,' and vodka consumption in large quantities.[1] However, the subtle methods and ways that they would affect the business were imponderable for me before this point. I was soon to learn firsthand.

It was now three weeks past our initial target date for opening, and now perilously close to target date number two. The bakery renovation was being completed in fits and starts. The tile work had initially been done at the rate of one square meter per day. The work had been punctuated by so many smoking breaks — with smokers in various reclining positions — that at times the bakery resembled an opium den. As I pressed and eventually threatened the contractor with non-payment, this limp turtle-with-trowel rate of tile-laying doubled to two square meters per day. However, the tile was now being laid on at angles that would have inspired a cubist. Finally, when I started holding back payments, the contractor began pressing the workers for both speed *and* quality. At that instant, some of the latter reached some kind of critical tolerance level of productivity. The quality of work that they began delivering at this point made the quality of work that they had delivered in the previous week appear divinely inspired. With one week to go, I took Valdis aside and told him that I couldn't believe what I was seeing here — smoking .

.. tea-drinking … "thinking" and work results as if the construction workers were abstract sculptors — and bad ones at that.

Valdis smiled, scratched his head, and blurted out,

"They should be controlled more strictly than they are now — they are beginning to drink … The peasant never crosses himself until after the lightning strikes."

"Fine, fine, whatever that means, Valdis, but I'd like to ask you to help get this renovation project back on track — as it is, I agreed to let Preben leave early, because we had *no* chance of finishing this place up before the end of his contract. But I can't extend the time in the old bakery either … Petuhin was already steaming mad when I asked to extend the second time … and not to mention Dzidra."

What I hadn't realized before, and that Valdis tried to explain to me now, was that the tile-layer was working beyond his "work-tolerance threshold," and had subsequently changed his diet. Valdis told me that the worker would begin adhering to a new diet, the cornerstone of which was not exactly a breakfast of oatmeal flakes and low-fat milk. It was four ounces of vodka. This amount, Valdis explained, was considered the maximum "permitted" by workers for daily consumption in their unwritten codex of acceptable self-government. It was apparently "common practice" in the factories for workers to consume one hundred milliliters — about four shots — for *tonizirovka* 'toning up' in the morning, and another one hundred milliliters at lunchtime [with or without food] for concentration. In the absence of the supervisor, twice this "tonic" was standard. Upon approaching the completion of a work quota or construction project, five hundred milliliters was the acknowledged daily norm. Finishing while in a sober state was not obligatory, nor expected, except in the strategically significant factories, such as the one that Valdis had worked in. "However, my policy on this issue, Boriss, was that my workers could — at the end of *that* day — put a bottle in their mouths, clench the neck of the bottle in their teeth, and gulp down the ingredients while they crawled out on all fours. Perfectly fine by me."

During the course of the week, I could only surmise that their strict adherence to this diet continued and, indeed, the consumption of the core ingredient had increased, because certain workers were disappearing. Valdis would inform me, throughout the course of the week, whenever the supervisor would find some worker stumbling up the stairs at the start of the day and send him off to "rest" — the Soviet man's favorite euphemism for getting drunk in some quiet out-of-the-way place. Occasionally, Valdis would tell me if a new worker showed up in the bakery to take the place of a sequestered one. Our bakery was no different, in this sense, from every other business that was doing renovations — and there were thousands. I had to accept the fact that Valdis and I were now powerless to change it.

But the hired crew was not the only team that was keeping my blood pressure high — my own technical "brigade" succeeded equally well in this task. Dmitri Sholokhov was rewiring the bakery. He couldn't tell me when it would be finished, but he never hesitated to launch into convoluted explanations of the work lying ahead: "And *thefe* wires *muft* be kept at leaft twenty centimeterf from the floor *without* croffing the *A's and B's* whereaf the outletf can *only* be fifty centimeterf, otherwife the infpectorf will be coming down on uf fafter-'en-a-Antonov-claff deftroyer on our H-47 fubmarine." Inevitably, the explanation would leave me running for the exit, while muttering to him not to confuse me with technical jargon — he was the electrician on a nuclear sub — not I.

But I also had reason for hope. One task, quite an insignificant one, involved the construction of a small platform, more of a wooden mat, in the shower stall. It was a simple task involving the sawing of some wooden slats and nailing them into a crisscross pattern. This would have been the equivalent of the second week's assignment in a junior high school woodshop class (which is fortunate, because after that week, I went into a [woodshop class selective] coma, from which I have only partially recovered). I volunteered to do it, seeing as one of Yuriy's people had come down ill the previous day. Valdis purchased the wooden sticks of 1" X 1" thickness, and left them for me in the basement in the afternoon. I arrived that evening in my jeans and a scruffy old shirt and started cutting the wooden sticks into slats of the necessary length. Some fifteen minutes into this work, Valdis showed up. He looked at me, and said, "So you meant that ... you would be doing this *yourself.*" He started rubbing his scalp. "Yep, sure . . . could you hand me one of those nails, please." He hesitated — he couldn't find the nails. When I looked up, he appeared agitated. "Be careful," he said as he finally handed them to me. He was pale. He hovered over me. Whenever I looked up, he would counter my gaze — usually with an expression of complete and utter astonishment — "Hey, he's still working." Did he fear that I would saw one or more of my limbs off, or else drive a nail through the family jewels in the course of a wild fit? Finally, when he was convinced that the sawing was being executed without significant bloodshed, he went off and did real work of some sort. Nonetheless, he returned periodically to view the progress of his little thirty-two-year-old. Valdis' face beamed when he viewed the shower floor, sawed, nailed and now fitting precisely in the space it had been meant to fit in. He had (perhaps with good reason) expected that the wooden slats, laid by the General-Director, would protrude into the locker room, and make the shower inaccessible, as tank traps did to Dieppe during the D-Day landing. But whatever the impressions made on him that day, during the last week prior to the finish date, Valdis came to work in some old slacks and worked alongside his *rebyata* boys.

Four days before the due date, the *shturmovka* began. Work went from the wee hours of the morning until late at night. Workers who had previously labored like zombies on Quaaludes now worked like Israeli commandos in the Entebbe raid. The cracks between the tiles were filled quickly and precisely, the paint was applied neatly to the window frames. All the while, the workers lived on three hours of sleep per night, and no sleep at all during the last twenty-four hours before "due date."

The equipment had been located, purchased, and was now in the process of being transported. When we arrived back at the bakery, we were pleased to see that the bed of the truck was empty. On this day, the male bakers were quietly sitting on the steps of the neighboring house. It dawned on me that I hadn't really seen them all together since the first day of training. With the exception of one, they were all in their mid- and early twenties. Most sported mustaches, which were *de rigeur* in Riga amongst the Latvian men — a compensation reflex to the inferiority complex preponderant amongst those raised in the LSSR during the period of high socialism.[2] This was a subtle revolt, along with the wearing of berets, to the unspoken no-facial hair policy of the Russians or to their habit of wearing Brezhnev-esque fur hats.

In any event, the bakers, now far removed from the political decisions made eighty and fifty-two years earlier, were smoking Latvian-produced cigarettes, the most popular one of which was "Elita." It would have been hard to imagine a more pointed insult to all bearers of that name, than this cigarette. Its tobacco had been grown in the Ukraine or Moldavia, harvested with roots, if not with dirt clods and manure, intact, sent on its way to Riga, and then processed — with virtually no loss of secondary or tertiary ingredient — into "Elita," the smoke of real men.

The bakery equipment arrived at just past two. With a hesitant but loud voice, Valdis said, "All right, the truck…is here, boys, let's start unloading." The bakers were visibly uninspired. With the exception of the oldest one, a thin man in his early thirties, who calmly flicked the cigarette on the dusty cobblestones, stood up and rubbed out the butt with his shoe, they kept sitting. Valdis ran to the truck and began talking to the truck driver, apparently describing to him where to back into the driveway. Gints, another baker, muttered, loudly enough for Valdis to hear, "All's you need now is a crane." He used a tone of voice, which suggested he had been invited to tell some sub-cretin of a building contractor to add water to the cement before mixing it. In fact these days, one couldn't find a basic taxi at the official taxi stand up the street 90 percent of the time; a crane-to-the-rescue was inconceivable. Besides, Valdis and I had concurred earlier in the week that in spite of a lack of equipment-moving experience on the part of the bakers — a situation that would very likely result in superficial damage to the equipment, some scraped walls, and even a few shins and forearms being bruised — the use of a crane on late Thursday afternoon would have been inviting disaster. To begin with, one had to assume that the driver would have "cooled off" with a few liters of 14-proof beer at lunch. Secondly, the Soviet cranes were generally as controllable as windsurf boards in a cyclone, so given the small space for maneuver, we would have been asking for a partial — or total — removal of the roof, wholesale destruction of two window frames and a decapitation of a baker to boot. Although we had acknowledged that the need for the latter might arise at some point in the future, it would probably be as a result of some wildly irresponsible behavior and *that* moment had not yet arrived.

The truck pulled up to the quay, and the driver pulled the piece of wood out of the crack in the flatbed of the truck, letting the side panel down. The bakers — by now realizing that no crane would be making its *deus ex machina* appearance to the site — let their cigarettes fly, and began helping the four stout workmen unload the equipment. The latter consisted of two standard four-foot-wide Soviet three-deck ovens, one Soviet rye-bread mixer, two Czech-made planetary mixers, five aluminum sinks, three stand-up Bulgarian refrigerators with Hitachi compressors, and one horizontal freezer. At this point, the equipment was similar to that which any American housewife could recognize when taking a stroll around the neighborhood shopping center, or through her own kitchen. The planetary mixers are like jumbo versions of the Kenwood "kitchen aid" mixers, with the same attachments, but ten times larger. The ovens were like three-deck pizza ovens, but with no windows. The refrigerators and freezers looked like the ones in the back sections of any supermarket.

Valdis had decided that a system of wooden rollers, reminiscent of that used by the ancient Egyptians to transport the sandstone blocks from the Nile to the site of the pyramids, was the best one to employ here. The bakers shuffled about with about the same enthusiasm as I imagine the slaves did, moving the objects from the vessel to the destinations. Satisfied that his minions were applying just the right quantity of bull's hide to his subjects, the Pharaoh departed to inspect the finished, protein-enriched raspberry marmalade that would soon be filling the pastries.

Late that afternoon, I walked into the new bakery plant. The two large yellow mixers dominated the mixing and forming room. I stepped past the wall that separated those rooms from the "baking" area. Three ovens, each measuring four and one half feet wide by five feet tall, stood side-by-side, aligning with the left wall. The walls throughout were covered with lemon yellow and olive green tiles. The floor was smoothly tiled with red clay tiles. The exposed sections of the walls were freshly painted. The three steps leading to the expediting room were neatly tiled, although in fitting with Soviet construction tradition, they were not of equal height. This was to lead to many trips and not a few falls at the beginning of the bakery's existence, until the spacing of *this* particular set of stairs was etched in the subconscious memory of the bakers. I went down the stairs to the basement section. I looked into the bathroom. My eyes reconciled, with difficulty, the post-modern melange of olive green tiles, light blue toilet bowl, and lemon yellow pastel paint above the metallic-gray hand dryer. According to Ray Kroc, the state of the bathroom was the way one could judge what kind of joint you're in. Using that measure, one could conclude that this one was the incoming patient toilet at the National Mental Institution. But *sanitary* it was — at least compared to all the hospitals in the country… not to mention those in the Ministry of Health. The basement space was also spotlessly clean, and significantly cooler than the upstairs. It would be perfect for the cakes. As I doubled-back past the bathroom, I noticed that one detail was missing. I turned to Valdis, "Good! Valdis, Dmitri, very, very good. I like this work. There just seems to be one small thing… you're not going to cheat these good folks of a toilet seat, now are you?" As Valdis was about to reply, Igors came down the stairs, and ran past me, gripping a bright orange object in a clear plastic bag. He ducked into the bathroom. Valdis gestured for me to follow him. My first thought, upon seeing the seat, was merely that it was large. As I saw it on the bowl, it was clear that someone could fall through it.

"It's *imported* — from P-O-L-A-N-D… very hard to come by," said Valdis, radiating with pride.

"Hmm," I replied, by now too tired to worry over the details of a bathroom that would have led any interior decorator with a smidgen of integrity to commit *hara-kiri* if ever his or her name would have been uttered in the same breath as "Bakery — Avotu Iela." But I was elated, for with the addition of this orange XX-large Polish toilet seat, the bakery plant was complete.

Some two hours later, all the upper management, directors, and shareholders — totaling six in number — filed in for the christening. Some were wearing their Sunday best, while others were dressed in everyday business outfits. Ligita sported a dark green medium-length dress; Valdis was in his black shirt, gray slacks, gray coat and a somber gray-black tie. Dmitri had not changed his brown jacket and vest uniform. These shareholders and upper managers pitched about nervously. They didn't know where to stand, as if they had been given numbered place tickets for a concert in a concert hall that had no numbered seats. I looked at them and smiled. Although I wouldn't openly admit it, I loved the formality, the occasional dressing-up, and the show of it all. Even though eight months had passed since my last press conference and eight years since I had been to a Viennese ball, I had never forgotten the electric feeling of a room when every person in it was on his best behavior. However, this sentiment did not coincide with that of the co-directors, who were growing more nervous with each passing second. I was later told, they associated public events and speeches with forced marches in sub-freezing weather — while holding up banners with embarrassingly stupid pronouncements.[3]

When the six partners and chief accountant took their makeshift places, finally forming a semi-circle, I began: "Today is a wonderful day. You may not know it, but it is a *momentous* occasion. You are the pioneers of something unique. Here on Avotu Iela, we will start a bakery business, which all the people of Riga, if not all the people of Latvia, will know about. It won't be built on the basis of a one-time trade, or a quick sell. This will be a *long-term* business, built on providing something wonderful to people. It will not be based solely on baking Latvian traditional baked goods, which are being produced now by a few Latvian bakers. Yet it won't be based on doing something 'Western' just for the sake of doing something different. No, this bakery will produce *unique foods*, which will have two things and two things alone in common . . . good taste and quality. Whether they are Latvian, American, Danish or *Chinese* recipes, they will be the best that they *can* be . . ." Everyone's eyes were riveted on me — the audience was awaiting the secret of good, effortless living. As I listed the various principles — including hard work, a little luck and devotion to the customer — upon which a successful business was founded, I saw another facial expression. It was a gaze that communicated either disdain, which would be a normal response to the ranting of "dreamers" such as Lenin and every high communist official who painted a utopian future, or else complete incomprehension, as if the words were being delivered in Church Slavonic.[4] Was it the "devotion to the customer" part that the audience doubted was one of the secrets to good living? Was it the international recipes? Undaunted, I continued, "and the champagne that we'll be drinking now . . . is an example of what one can do with quality . . ." I uncorked the bottle. The cork went flying into the ceiling and ricocheted off one of the tables before bouncing into the forty-liter bowl of the small mixer. I then signaled to Dmitri to pour into glasses and distribute them. "The champagne is called *Veuve Cliquot*. Does anyone know when it was first produced?" Zigrīda's head swayed nervously from side to side, as if pronouncing the wrong answer to the question would spell a very long trip to far eastern provinces of Russia. Most heads were still. "In seventeen seventy-two. Yes, this champagne factory has now been in existence for two hundred twenty years. And do you know how they could do it? . . . Only through an *unswerving* dedication to quality. Now, before we all take a gulp of it, I would like to say that I plan for The Merry Baker to be around for that long as well. Maybe not with the same recipes . . . probably not with the same people . . ." Two faces broke out in smiles. One even broke out in a snicker, which was instantly stifled. "But *yes*, with the same company name and the same company philosophy. *That* is my mission here, and I hope that if it isn't already, that it becomes yours as well. So, let's drink to a bakery that will be here for two hundred years." The glasses were lifted, I passed by each and clinked glasses. Among all the faces, I noted two in particular. Valdis and Ligita drank the champagne with vigor, as if they were consuming Dr. Jekyll's concoction. They put down the glasses and stood still, apparently waiting for the beverage to turn them into Frenchmen. When the suspense subsided, ten seconds later, and they realized that they were still Valdis and Ligita and not Charles Aznavour and Patricia Kass, they looked at one another with slightly puzzled expressions. Ligita mumbled, "I like *our* [Riga] champagne better."[5]

Footnotes

[1] Hedrick Smith, in The Russians wrote about these two things in great detail. Hedrick Smith, The Russians, pp. 222-227. New York Times Press. 1978.

[2] One could consult several texts on the political history of pre-independence and interwar Latvia. Two of them might be: John Hiden and Patrick Salmon, The Baltic Nations and Europe: Estonia, Latvia and Lithuania in the 20th Century (London, 1991) and Andrejs Plakans, Latvia; A Short History (Hoover Press, 1995).

[3] "'Yes' greets the Peoples' Soviet," "Lenin's word is truth!", "Communism is the power/fame of the people" were among the most popular banner lines of the 1980s.

[4] Old Church Slavonic. A language which formed the basis of biblical scholarship and writings from early Russia. It is the equivalent of Latin in the Roman Catholic Church, and plays the same obfuscatory role in the Orthodox Church as Latin did in the Catholic Church for lay parishioners in the eighteenth century. About half of the words are comprehensible to the fluent speaker of Russian.

[5] Riga Champagne. The name had been stolen from the French, but this method non-Champagnoise was developed locally. It involves fermenting the grape juice slightly in large stainless steel vats and adding additional alcohol and sugar at the last moment, before bottling. Consequently, unlike with the age-old French method, fermentation in the bottle is scant.

8

HANDS GROWING IN THE RIGHT PLACES

LATER THAT EVENING, I ASKED Inge to comment on the speech.

"Yes, you certainly have a polished delivery — but I'm not sure that it wasn't lost on them. They're used to very straight talk, ya know — *ar mietu pa pieri* 'board across the head' [simple].

"Sure, but this was the opening. What was I supposed to say, 'the bakery is now finished, let's start'? Inge, it's a mo-*men*-tous occasion."

"We'll see," said Inge as she looked away through the kitchen window towards the backyard, where two male alley cats were loudly clarifying their relations.

Shortly after our discussion about the "speech," Eliza came storming into the kitchen, seeking protection from an unseen foe. Eliza had some of her mother's character, but being a second child, her personality was smoother around the edges. She was fond of her stuffed animals, her knitting needles, and her collection of dolls. Most of the time, she was reclusive, quiet and deeply introspective. At other times, she was energetic and boisterous — for example when she was indulging in a good chase around the apartment. Her only physical shortcoming was the dishwater blond tone of her hair color, which evoked a reflexive hair-pulling response from her brother. Markus-the-hair-puller was quick-witted, and extroverted. To his mother and grandparents he was generous, big-hearted, and entertaining; to his friends, he was a fount of new ideas and entertaining games (which he played, like Bill Gates did in his youth, as long as he was winning them). His sister, however, he treated like a misplaced bean bag chair. Not a few times, we would be reviewing arithmetic, or the finger paintings that she did in her elementary school, when a pillow would come sailing into the room and lodge squarely in Eliza's face. "End of lesson!" we would hear, coming from the hallway.

Inge's response to these episodes was ambivalent. Usually they consisted of some comment about his suffering from the "new" situation, or that he had inherited some "traits" from his father, including the one demanding that he be the center of attention. The third time it happened, I couldn't resist responding that I didn't believe that that is the solution — I vividly recall being beaten across the backside with a thick leather belt whenever I tried such antics in the presence of my parents. I said that it instilled in me a greater attention to what I do to others, but quickly added that "I do though have a habit now of examining the thickness of the pants that I buy."

The comment elicited a little smile from Inge. However, it quickly turned into a stern frown: "Boriss, I've said this once before, but I'll say it again — if you lay your hands on Markus ... for any reason at all ... then I will immediately cancel the 'deal.' You just might not see — it's so brutish, showing helplessness in resolving a problem that can be solved in other ways. It's crude . . . it's *Russian!*"

"But what if he is causing physical pain to his sister? Don't you think that she should be protected in such cases?"

"Yes, but not by physical force. After all, they're brother and sister — didn't you ever fight with your brother?"

"Sure," I replied and related how he had been a constant pain in my side, until, at the ripe age of thirteen, I placed a left hook squarely across his jaw. I don't know how I had managed that, but he fell down on the bed. I thought that I had knocked him out cold, or worse. He got up, after half a minute, holding his jaw, and without looking at me, without saying a word, he left the room. From that moment on, he stopped physically tormenting me.

"Bravo, *Teofilo* ... but I'm not convinced that you should get involved in physically disciplining Markus."

"Fine, but I'm not convinced, Inge, that Eliza will ever be able to deliver such a knockout blow to her brother, when she's had absolutely enough. That's what fathers are for, don't you think?"

"No, I think that women have other tools at their disposal to keep themselves from being preyed on."

"You mean, like ... poisons?"

Inge laughed, but quickly added, "We can change him only by our example."

In the interest of leaving the small industrial town as quickly as possible, I now put all my spare energy into the renovation of the apartment in Riga. While living in an apartment undergoing renovation, I would head to the bakery every morning covered with a fine gray layer of construction dust, to see how the bakers were faring after the departure of Preben. I would come and inspect the production. Amongst other things, I saw how much was left unsold from the previous day, which helped me gauge buying patterns, and inspect production techniques. I was also getting to know my team of bakers better.

On this early September morning, Gints was the brigadier. He greeted me with his characteristically modest smile. I would never know, unless Gints broke out into an unconditional laugh, whether he was smiling or smirking. Gints had been a candidate member of the Special Forces of the Latvian Soviet Socialist Republic in 1990. In fact, these were the crack troops of the Soviet Army, and had heretofore been spirited around to all parts of the globe where socialism and communism were under threat from democracy. As such, they had been an elite within *the* elite (the Soviet military complex). But when Latvia's independence was recognized, worldwide, at the end of 1991, the corps not only lost its elite status, but in fact lost its very reason for being. So, as would be obvious to any straight-thinking opportunist, Gints understood that the logical career alternative was to become . . . a baker. Gints deserted the corps and enrolled in the State baking school. How much he had learned there Zigrīda feared to comment on, but he worked efficiently and reasonably well with his hands, especially when the work called for strength — Preben remarked that Gints was doing a particularly fine job of "punching down" the dough.

"*Sveiks* Gints. So, how goes it today?"

"Fine, fine, just fine. Everything is being produced on time, and getting out in precisely the right quantities."

I smiled, and held up my thumb. Then I saw the production results. Rolls were visibly soft-crusted and wrinkled, while at the same time 25 percent smaller than they should have been. I picked one up, broke it apart, and tasted a piece. More precisely, I *tried* to taste a piece of the roll, but since it was devoid of any, I just chewed it to oblivion.

"Yes, I see, Gints, but you do understand, that besides getting out in the right quantities, the items have to taste and look great. The recipes, including the salt, sugar, eggs that we have here are supposed to do that. That's why they are, how shall I say, not 'open to interpretation!'"

"But I followed the recipe precisely!"

I hesitated, and then continued, making clear that I did not believe him.

"Gints, our customers expect the best quality that can be provided them, and they expect it *every time*, not by shift. For this reason, we are different from the other bakeries."

Gints stared back with an expression that would have been appropriate had I been elucidating some aspect of Kant's "Foundations of the Metaphysics of Morals." He paused, looked at me with a vapid expression.

"And on time, right?"

"Yep, Gints, and on time of course."

Two full months had now passed since Preben's premature departure; the production resembled what he had taught the bakers to make less and less, with the exception, for some miraculous reason, of the Danish pastry. That product continued to have not only the golden brown look, but also the flaky texture, and indescribably pleasing, buttery taste, which made Denmark famous in the culinary world. Furthermore, customers could smell the items being made in the back of the store. So, in spite of some production inconsistencies that might have detracted from some of our products, the customers came in droves. One could understand perfectly well why Gints and Edvīns had been unmoved by the talk of "recipes to be followed," and "quality *every* time." I rationalized that it was a "cultural thing" and since the sales were increasing buoyantly, there was no need to establish steely quality control systems — yet.

More worrisome than the slight alteration of pastries was the fact that I had two technical directors who — now that the bakery was finished — had little to do but direct the same three workers, which they often did at cross-purposes. Both had a knack for prattle that would make a *tirgus vecene* 'market hag'[1] blush. But while they transformed themselves into mighty labor psychologists in my presence, expounding on work rhythms and workplace rituals of a time and place well before the present, they seemed to fret over nails that wouldn't remove themselves from a beam by their own force. Since the bakery renovation was now finished, they were doubling in their maintenance responsibilities, and subtly blaming each other for non-performance. I decided that one of the two would have to go. Since by local standards, both were receiving exceptional salaries, I wasn't sure that either would go voluntarily. Furthermore, I wasn't sure which one provided the set of skills most fitting the company's needs.

Valdis was more energetic and enthusiastic, appearing to possess a more professional attitude towards work and personnel management, with less smoking and complaining. On the other hand, Sholokhov was monitoring all the electrical circuiting, and seemed to know a great deal more about the functioning and maintenance of the equipment, having worked in this industry for far longer than Valdis. At the same time, the quality of some of his work was coming under doubt; I specifically heard, through Valdis, that a few bakers had complained of getting a shock from some of the equipment. I decided to get to the crux of the issue and asked Dmitri to come and see me. I started, as usual, with an upbeat, enthusiastic tone of voice.

"So, Dmitri, you have finished the electrical wiring for the third oven, is that correct?"

"Yes, sure *if,* you're good to go."

"Excellent, now would you mind doing something else right away?"

"Why no, not at all. You know me — I'm alway*f*ready… why, there'*f*nothing I hate more than people who*fe* hand*f juft* grow out of their *rear endf.*"

"Pretty strong words there, Dmitri. Now, here's the problem — I've heard from one of the brigadiers that somebody received a little jolt when they used the proving cabinet. Maybe you could fix that… but right away, please."

"*Fure, fure, reft affured,* you'll have no more problem*f* with that… If there even *if* a problem … you know how it *if* with the*fe* baker*f*… they hammer *f*omething with their knive*f* and tray*f* until it break*f,* and then *f*ay that it never worked right in the fir*ft* pla*fe.*"

We agreed that I would follow up in three days.

Certain other problems in company growth were emerging. The transition from small to mid-size was not easy to make. I knew, however, that this transition would have to be made as quickly as possible, to assure a continual flow of funds sufficient to pay the bakers' wages, the salaries of five partners who were active in managing the enterprise and the ongoing training that Preben would assure. This small company would definitely require a secretary. Since I was finding it harder and harder to express my thoughts on developing the business in Russian, she would have to at least know rudimentary English. Amongst others, the terms "team," "control systems," and "quotas" sounded either threadbare or downright socialist.[2] In the future, I would have to convey my thoughts in English or Latvian only. Furthermore, handwritten letters were no longer portraying an acceptable image of the company. We subsequently agreed that Zigrīda would scout around for a full-time secretary.

The following week, I interviewed several secretaries. Professionally, they were all weak. On the other hand, they were nothing short of drop-dead gorgeous. Any one of them, I reasoned, could have been a *Cosmopolitan* cover girl. However, since *Soviet Women* magazine tended to look for other traits in their cover ladies, such as "goat-milking mastery" and "potato-digging dominance," none of these would ever have appeared on the cover of that journal. One of the candidates had been a secretary in the Ministry of Health. She wanted to get into a sector where she could earn a little more money — perhaps one which would allow her to receive a salary sufficient to support herself and her child, she explained to us. The secretarial position at the Ministry no longer afforded that luxury. The state salaries were notoriously low … so payment was often received "in kind." She explained that this was pretty good if you work at the Ministry of Health and had a health problem requiring western pharmaceuticals — which could be "arranged" from the Ministry — but not so useful for someone in full health. I thought that she was the best, from a professional point of view, but could sense a tension between her and my partners during the interview. Zigrīda later said, "Boriss, she can obviously type well, but I think that when a baker comes here with questions of some sort, she will treat him like the lowest cur in the street. Oh, and I don't see her walking to the stationery store for pencils." I concurred, and left it at that. Another candidate had been a waitress in a German-Latvian joint-venture restaurant. She was hoping to change employment locations because of the establishment's steamy environment — not so much in the kitchens during restaurant hours, as in the private apartments above the dining room afterwards. Her typing was not nearly up to the forty words per minute that I would have been satisfied with, and unlike 99 percent of my peers, I actually considered this a fundamental shortcoming for this job. Other *General'niy Direktor'i* would have given me kudos for my catch of a secretary; in the unspoken competition of company prestige, a beautiful secretary ranked high. The assumption, I later learned, was that her most demanding work would be judged from a horizontal position.

When the list of candidates was exhausted, my disappointment must have shown, because Zigrīda approached me at the end of the day.

"I understand that you don't think any of these are appropriate … you know there was one who had stopped by on Friday—"

"And—"

"I didn't think to tell you about that one …"

"What do you exactly mean by 'didn't think to tell you?!'"

Zigrīda froze. She stood silently, with an expression like a six-year-old's — that of the child who had just been called to the front of the class because she had forgotten to return a book to the library for two weeks.

"Hmm. Zigrīda, I had completely forgotten to go over the new sanitation requirements of the workers' dressing room. Let's go to the *bakery*."

Once we were outside the office, I asked what happened.

"Boriss, I don't know how I should say this, but there was a *sluchiye* 'incident' that took place last Friday. A good candidate had stopped by and rang the doorbell. She apparently waited a long time outside. When she heard some sounds coming from inside, she decided to try the door. It was unlocked and she walked in. Boriss, she, uh, saw a man sprawled out on the desk. According to her, he lifted his head towards her as high as he could, which wasn't very, and said something about prostitutes making office calls — then he passed out . . ."

"*CHTO?!What?!*"

I began mulling over the question, *who* could have been in the office on Friday, and concluded that it could only be the new sales manager or the technical guys.

"O.K., was he young or old, the guy . . . on the desk."

"Older, according to her, and with a face flushed red."

After prying, I received more details of the incident; it was either Valdis or Dmitri. Zigrīda then stated that yes, during that time, Valdis had been in the store, repairing the display cabinet. Zigrīda then asked if we should ask the candidate to come back.

"Yes, Zigrīda, please do, with appropriate apologies of course . . . this isn't the image that we would like to portray of The Merry Baker, is it?"

I wondered where Dmitri would say his hands were "growing from." It couldn't be his rear end — according to the account, his rear end was not in contact with anything. It was floundering aimlessly, pointed upwards towards the ceiling. Perhaps out of his liver, insofar as it was this organ that was doing the most amount of work at the point that the young student had walked into the office. "Furthermore, the liver was most closely pressed to the desk, while in fact, only one measly ankle was in contact with the chair," I surmised. Perhaps for Dmitri, the hands grew out of one location on Mondays through Thursdays, and another on Fridays through Sundays. In any event, the intellectual thrill that analyzing this incident provided did not prevent me from dismissing Sholokhov the next day. He was to gather his tools and receive compensation for his shares in the company on Friday at three o'clock.

In the meantime, I decided to investigate the situation with the equipment, more closely. I walked into the bakery that evening, shortly after the shift began working. I saw the brigadier holding the mixer with a mitt on his hands.

"Hey, Edvins, why are you using a mitt while mixing the dough? Isn't that awkward?"

"Hello. Well, Borees Viktorvitch, I'm just preventing my hand from touching the metal."

"Good, you're doing it out of concern for cleanliness, right?"

"Well, no, you see, I get a little shock from the mixer when I turn it on."

"Oh, is it like a little rush, or something more?" I asked as I smiled nonchalantly.

Edvins stared at me, obviously trying very hard to decipher the underlying purpose of the question. As he smiled and continued searching for a reply, I asked him if I could see for myself.

"Well, go ahead, but are you sure you don't want to use the mitt?"

"No, go ahead . . . turn it on."

As I touched the machine, I received a jolt that knocked me off my feet, or at least, that is where I ended up. My ears were ringing, and I had the strange sensation of having been beaten all over my body; my heart was racing madly. I rose up off the floor and staggered off, shaking my head, like a cat that's been pummelled across its face.

As it turned out, the toothless electrician had had the last word; the mixer turned out to be the only part of what turned out to be something closer to a mad scientist's dungeon more than a bakery. Apparently my co-directors, for reasons that I could not surmise, had downplayed the degree of shock that the bakers underwent in the course of making each day's production. Besides turning on the lights or opening the oven doors, every other contact with equipment resulted in a hair-raising jolt for the bakers. Dmitri had crossed enough wires, and left enough machinery ungrounded, that the plant would have been a more appropriate site for the study of environment-mediated stress responses in large yaks, than a production site for pastries. The wiring would have to be redone from scratch. Even the diagram for the wiring, which was posted on the door of the electric cabinet — for use in case of emergency — had no basis in reality.

Whatever the technical explanation of cause, the motivation was found in the fact that Sholokhov had never taken the enterprise seriously. He had decided, sometime in July, to retire. As luck would have it, his *dacha* stood on territory not far from St. Petersburg and the plot had turned out to be an ideal location for a camping trailer park that some Finnish travel agency intended to establish. Overnight, Sholokhov's personal transition problems had been solved; as he aptly stated during his exit interview, "I don't need to work anymore . . . don't need the *ftreff*. Why should I, when I can collect four thou*f*and dollar*f* a year ju*ft* for . . . living." And he gave a final, one-toothed grin, as he signed away his shares.

"Dmitri, but what you did was both unethical and downright . . . *dangerous.*"

He shrugged his shoulders, turned to Zigrīda and Valdis, and said, "*You foolf* can kill your*f*elve*f*, working to make thi*f capitalift* rich — I won't."

After he left, Zigrīda said, "So, looks like he can finally let his hands grow out of the 'right place.'" After a few laughs, we agreed that fried bakers were not a commodity of particularly high value at that time; we disbanded and

Valdis went to tell the bakers to work with dry hands and clean up spills right away.

By the end of that summer, the apartment was also nearly completed, although to what quality parameters was another question. When I had asked the construction people who were finishing the bakery if they could fix the stucco on the wall of my apartment at their earliest opportunity, I forgot to mention that this would be for separate pay. So when I returned from my supply-purchasing trip in Germany, I found that the plaster had been fixed definitively . . . with cement. When I had come back to the apartment, and saw the faded yellow wallpaper highlighted by patches and veins of hard, gray concrete for a length of six feet, at times flush with the wall, at times protruding up to an inch out, I was in a state of shock. I hadn't remembered seeing this treatment when the bakery walls were done, but then, I hadn't remembered there being any plasterwork either. I decided to broach the subject on the following Tuesday, during a scheduled meeting with the builders.

After dispensing with details of final payment for the bakery renovation, I took the director aside: "By the way, Misha, about the apartment work that I had asked for . . . you know, I didn't expect concrete on the wall." The dark-complexioned man looked to the side, with what was the equivalent of a roll of the eyeballs, and said, "These do-the-private-apartment-for-the-director jobs are all the same. You guys always want us to do it for free. Well, I tell you, the only material that we had left over . . . was cement." I glared. Misha continued, "It'll hold, that's for damn sure, in case you're wondering. That plaster was coming off in chunks, 'cause there was a leak underneath. We sealed that off."

"Yeah, O.K., *now* I understand. But Misha, can you fix it right? . . . I intend to *pay* you for it."

"Oh, that's a different story. Whaddya want us to do?"

I told him that since it was no longer possible to take it off, could he at least sand it down so that he *could* cover it with plaster or putty.

"And it should be completely smooth, instead of looking like we had commissioned one of those nineteen seventies Soviet Socialist abstract bas-relief sculptures, you know, the ones with the little kids and their mommies and the guys in the lab-coats looking at the space ship." [3]

"Yes, yes, I understand . . . It's O.K. All will be 'normal.'"

Footnotes

[1] Renowned for gossiping idly, particularly in the presence of a line of customers.

[2] 'Team' — Most appropriately translated as Kommanda. In unofficial socialist lexicon — 'sportsmen trained to beat the Amerikantsy to a pulp in a team sport during the Olympics and guaranteed a lifetime of luxury living if successful, or coaching little Mongol soccer players in Ulan Bator as exchange trainers if choke during a key moment.' 'Control systems' — Kontrol'nije sistemi — Systems whereby some really nice person who is working alongside you is also in the employ of the boss or Regional Party Committee as an informant (stukatch) and will turn you in after you have confided your deepest, darkest secrets. In all cases, control systems were regarded solely as manipulative tools of management to get workers to do the managers' bidding. 'Quotas' —Norma — Either unachievable or pathetically low production targets that had to be striven at monthly, yearly, and quinquennial intervals by the kommanda. Since the targets were seldom linked to real demand, as a result one would see glaring market imbalances, such as an overabundance of Lenin's Complete Writings, under whose weight bookstore shelves would regularly be warping. At the same time, finding mouthwash or good toothpaste would be a cause for celebration, as these items so seldom appeared in stores. Apparently, the Central Planners envisioned an ideal society as being one comprising a lot of socialist intellectuals coercing sceptics — with their halitosis — into embracing socialism.

[3] Standard sculptures commissioned for new Soviet-built schools. The scene depicted little Soviet children in pioneer uniforms (short-sleeved shirts and scarves) waiting to go into the rocket-ship-which-will-fly-them-to-some-over-sized-planet, while doctors-in-starched-lab-coats-and-thick-lens-glasses look on. Besides the different characters and rocket ship, one indelible characteristic of these socialist-realism dream scenes was the massive, immovable volume of brass, copper and other colored metals of which these bas-reliefs were composed. I once asked a Soviet artist acquaintance if the Ministry of Culture paid sculptors by the kilo of art produced. He was taken aback and replied "No, of course not! The commissioning institution paid per square meter!"

2

MARKET

DURING THE FIRST WORLD WAR the Germans had built Zeppelin hangars in the small Latvian-Lithuanian border town of Vaiņode, for use in constructing the aircraft that was really useful in bombing the daylights out of enemy forces. When the Zeppelins failed to bomb the requisite daylights out of the enemy forces and the Kaiser's dreams of conquest failed him, the Germans left these massive iron structures, each the size of a football field and 150 feet high, to blot the landscape near the otherwise charming town. In 1924, the buildings were close to collapsing. A clerk at the Ministry of Agriculture heard of these structures and came up with the idea of using them to replace the decrepit, red brick buildings — at the time teeming with rats — used as markets along the riverbank. He passed this thought by two engineers, Isayevs and Žagars, who embraced the idea. Together with an architect named Paulis Dreimanis, they drew up the plans to have five of the Zeppelin hangars taken down and reconstructed on the site of the present-day market. Furthermore, they added an underground tunnel linking the pavilions to a canal, forty yards away. Each pavilion was also fitted with a basement, in some cases a refrigerated one, and a series of elevators. Produce could be supplied to the stalls at any time during the day without disturbing trade. To compare, it was a far cleaner act than *Les Halles* in Paris in 1938, where all goods had to be delivered by merchants in the wee hours of the morning. Although the single delivery prompted the establishment of restaurants, which for almost a century served up the best onion soup and pig's knuckles on the face of the earth, to cater to this early-morning clientele, the single delivery system in pre-war *Les Halles* did not have much else going for it. Whatever meat was not sold in the course of the morning gradually rotted at, or next to, the seller's stand. On average, that morning would be fifteen degrees Fahrenheit warmer than the one in Riga, but the E.coli and salmonella bacteria the same. So this Latvian "swords-into-ploughshares" feat had created the most modern, hygienic market in 1930s Europe.

Although, by 1992, the market had fallen far behind its Western counterparts in its sanitary conditions, it surpassed them in exotic flair. About that time, Inge and I went on our first big new-apartment-stocking trip. On this particular Saturday in September, we approached it from the side facing the Ministry of Transport. A throng of old and middle-aged ladies each greeted us by holding up a particular item of clothing as we passed. It was a strange feeling, like advancing through a dance line, except nobody was clapping to the music.

'Temple of Meat' — Riga Central Market

Instead, the women — mostly *babushki* — were bellowing, "*pants,*" "*stockings,*" "*brassieres,*" "*fine cloths*" at all passersby. Inge started inspecting some materials that a lady was holding, while I started wondering where a lady would go to try a brassiere on, should the need for trying this foreign-made bra arise.

"How much do you have?" asked Inge.

"Twenty-five meters." I looked hard, and even with my pitiful knowledge of sewing, could tell that she was holding no more than five meters worth of cloth. "Come this way," she continued. She led us to a flatbed truck some thirty yards away, where the materials were piled five high in thick rolls, each one four meters long. We inspected the cloths, whose patterns ranged from oriental gaudy to funereal, and whose texture ran from silky-finished rayon to coarse wool. Inge started eyeing some gray-black material with a coffin lid relief too closely for my comfort, before finally settling on an understated olive and beige wool material for our curtains. We then returned to the "line" and finished another thirty-yard-long shuffle, serenaded by a chorus of "it's cheap" and "today's a special deal'." We emerged in the open-air fruit section of the market.

The fruits were stacked in large piles under the open sky, or else lay in the soiled wooden crates in which they had been transported. The crates were invariably smeared a blackish brown and one or more of the slats were broken. Next to each of the crates were some fallen produce — peaches, or tomatoes, or apples. There was nothing orderly or polished about this section — this was not the Saturday morning market of Blois, France. Instead, the seemingly ad hoc arrangements, the grime, all suggested that the vendors had stepped off the caravan just a few moments earlier, paid someone for the use of the table (or just as often propped up the full box of fruit on top of two that had been placed upside down), spread out a tablecloth, laid out their scales, and started selling. We saw Uzbekhis, adorning their square *tubiteika*[1] hats, selling melons from their native country. Some Azerbaijanis were selling pomegranates, whose juice was staining the table with bright pink puddles. The *babushki* that had taken the local train in were now selling their usual assortment of mealy potatoes, soiled carrots, unfiltered gooseberry jam and pickled garlic, which they had successfully protected from the philistine commuting hordes.

At no time in my previous life had I ever witnessed such diverse selling methods as the ones the sellers employed here. The simplest one was sampling. As we passed the apple tables, a seventy-year-old vendor uttered, "Try a piece of this apple — you'll see how good it is . . ." with infectious enthusiasm. He promptly whipped out a pocketknife. It had residue from the previously cut fruit hanging on the rust-speckled edge. He looked at us and smiled, as if he were our favorite uncle, sharing the last truffle from the table with us. We froze in our places. After all, how could we just walk away and leave this sweet old man. He deftly cut away at the apple. Before we could utter a word, the old man was holding a slice under Inge's nose. Too late to refuse — what was he going to do now with a slice of apple? I had seen that most buyers were too accustomed to the unwashed hands and rusty knife-blade to make a fuss.

We each tried a piece. The vendor asked, "Sweet and juicy, *won't you agree? 'Kogda li biy proboli takoye yabloko?* 'Have you ever tasted an apple like this one before?'" At that moment, my mental database of lifetime apple tastings failed to boot up. I couldn't recall whether the red apples from Grandma's yard, or the neighbors' *Macintoshes* were in the same league as what we were trying — I felt obliged to agree that this apple was quite good. There was nothing left to do but buy a kilo (2.2 pounds).

Two stalls further, we were inspecting various imported fruits, and the seller said to Inge, "My, *you* look nice in that outfit today." This of course lowered resistance to the "Would you care to buy some very nice bananas?" that followed. The sale of at least one kilogram was thereby assured. The compliments were not limited to the ladies either. I was completely disarmed by the "You speak with an accent, 'Pan'²" approach. This technique served the vendor well in unloading one kilo of gamy cucumbers.

As we were eyeing blood oranges piled high on one table, the vendor from the adjacent table blurted out, "What are you doing looking at *those* oranges?! Trust me —" he said while putting his right hand to his chest, the Central Asian gesture connoting "I am *your humble servant*," "*Oni vo obshche ne godyatsa.* 'Those are absolutely no good.'" The seller at the first stand, whose oranges we were now examining, looked angrily at the other one, and said, "*Ne vmeshivaysya v chyuzhikh delakh.* 'Mind your *own* business!'" Not paying attention to this reproach, the initiator continued, "*On vas obmanivayet. Obyazatel'no deshevlye . . . oni upali s gruzovika.* 'You're getting ripped off. Sure, they're cheaper … they fell off the truck …'" The first one then turned to us, and said, "*Nye slushayete yevo, on boltuun nastoyashchi.* 'Don't listen to him, he's a real liar.'" The heckler piped back, "*Nu posmotriite na etich . . . poprobuyete odno, vidite cok kak tyechot.* 'Now look at these … try one, see the juice?!'" He cut one with his standard-issue rusted-blade knife. The first seller was caught off guard. He glanced backwards quickly. He had apparently given his knife to his wife; she was standing about twenty meters away, using it to cut some cords. For all intents, he was now dead in the water. We floated to the second [honest] vendor, mesmerized by his enthusiasm. Within a minute, we ended up with two kilos of oranges. Half of these, we discovered later, had not only fallen off a truck, but must have been used for a cricket test match earlier in the day.

While buying some peaches, I overheard a mustachioed young vendor from the next table saying, "*Krasi-vaja zhenschina, vy bi ne hoteli poprobats krassniy perets, ili dinya, ona takoye svezhoye. Sladki kak myed, no nye takoye sladkoye kak moi potseluy!* 'Beautiful woman, would you like to try some red pepper? Or how about a melon, it is so fresh. Sweeter than honey … but not as sweet as my kiss!'" He spoke this with an intriguing southern accent. In any of the countries that I had lived in for the previous twenty years, this phrase would have met with a slap — at least a vicious look. But in this case, he not only avoided getting slapped in the face, but he actually made a sale. Judging by her smile, he probably scored a date on top of that.

Further on, Turkic-featured women with bright scarves on their heads were selling nuts, seeds, and spices. And all of these were piled up in one-foot-high mounds. The paprika looked like a miniature Ayers Rock at sunset, while the poppy seeds were a small hill of coal. Next to the mounds stood the same twelve-faceted glass that is used for vodka consumption. A customer paid the agreed-upon sum and the vendor, a wizened woman of fifty, took a sheet of newspaper and rolled it up into a cone. Into this receptacle, she poured a vodka-glass full of spices. From that point on, it was the task of the buyer to make sure that the purchase didn't spill all over the bottom of their bag or onto the kitchen floor. Of course (as I later found out myself) a newspaper rolled up into a cone does not maintain its shape when one isn't holding it. Another fact is that paprika finds the smallest nooks in a canvas bag to bury itself in — for months afterwards, random cheeses, vegetables and fruits carried in this bag were three-alarm hot.

Furthermore, these women were radically different from the men that were selling fruit. They each wore the same pained expression on their faces, the kind that they thought said, "You need these more than I, and who knows if I'll be here tomorrow — so you're a fool not to buy *now*." Instead it communicated something more along the lines of, "YES, I've got an attitude and I don't know how I got stuck here, but now that I AM here, I'm going to make sure *you* suffer." I approached one, hoping to find out what the gray-green mound of dust was. "Poppyseed, cinnamon, spices," the plump lady said. I pointed to something yellow and she replied, "Ginger. How about a glassful?" When I refused it, she asked, "Then what about some paprika?" She asked it though with an undertone that meant, "Are you congenitally stupid, or are you purposely getting on my nerves?" The enthusiasm that positively glowed from the men was absent here. The women probably hadn't consumed enough of their own poppy seeds before starting work.

Behind several other tables, one could see members of the extended family, from young children to very old men, performing various weighing and stacking tasks. As I looked into the distance, I saw tables extending at least one hundred meters further, buckling under the weight of locally produced fruits and vegetables that one would expect to find in the markets in any Northern European country — apples, pears, cabbage, carrots; to herbs from the Caucasus; motor oil from Volgograd; *kinza* spices from Georgia; melons from Uzbekhistan; screwdrivers from the Ukraine; *Vyatka* washing machines from Northern Russia. These were just a handful of the thousands of items available at the Central Market at the time. The sellers hawking these items appeared to have arrived from those destinations as well. The vendor of the Vyatka washing machines, named after the city a few hundred kilometers due east of St. Petersburg, boasted a thin face, a thick red beard and pale skin. This reminded one of the fact that the Mongol hordes had failed to penetrate the bog-filled regions of Russia's North and left the gene pool there untainted.

In my Western understanding of retailing, it would have been more effective to find an importer/agent to distribute these items in a country a thousand miles from home. However, this framework was *not* the standard practice in the spring of 1993. Asking the vendors only earned me glares and some gruff "what's it to you's", so I could only surmise at the possible reasons driving this "hands-on" approach — Perhaps no one could be trusted to sell these strategic goods the right way. The second reason why I supposed that local agents were not used was that most often, these were single, dark-complexioned men from Muslim regions — or Christian ones that did not tolerate sex out of wedlock — in a city boasting more fair-haired beauties per hundred inhabitants than downtown Stockholm. The combination of selling charms on one hand and looks on the other made for a combustible combination. The third reason was probably inertia. It was the way selling had always been done. In Soviet times, people from Georgia and southern states would travel to markets of all major cities, with their panoply of goods in tow. In those times, gasoline cost twelve cents a liter (forty-five cents a gallon), and besides one's personal car, other means could always be found to get one's *defitsitniye* goods to the market of choice.[3] That by 1995, only three years later, spices would be readily available from every country in Asia, poppyseeds would be shipped in from Australia and washing machines delivered from Germany, could not have been foreseen by any of these vendors at the time.

Our final stop for the day was the meat pavilion. It was the size of a football field, sidelines and stands included. This was a meat-eater's temple, and today, the temple was full. The *myasnoy pavilyon* was no "meat department" of some grocery store, where one had to strain one's imagination to recall that the rib roast or T-bone steak sitting on a white Styrofoam under-container, neatly overwrapped with a plastic film, was once a little part of a minor muscle group of a thousand-pound beast, whose head alone weighed forty pounds. No, in *this* market, one could almost feel the last gasps of the beasts as they fell. Skinned oxtails were hanging every ten yards, like blood-red whips, from the edge of the metal bars that supported the lamps above the booths. A half of a pig's head, sawn precisely between its eyes, was displayed on a few stands, either to communicate "pork sold here," or else to remind people that even the animals' extremities could be chopped or sawn to specification. Apparently unable to suppress some deeply surrealist sensibilities, one of the butchers skinned a cow's head to the nose, but left its eyes in their sockets. The blood had congealed and the whole head was now a burgundy color, except for the brown horns, black nose, white eyes, and black eyelashes.

For nearsighted customers, who might have had trouble differentiating the pigs' heads from the *liellopu*[4] heads, cardboard signs were placed above the meats. "Lamb," "Liver" or "Veal," was singled out most frequently — and always in red letters. Sides of beef hung in the back of every third stand, and men with arms as thick as softballs were constantly unloading the carts — each one about five feet long and three feet wide — loaded with sides, quarters and shanks. These men would then cut the pieces into smaller sections, using two-foot-long hacksaws. The sawing was done on blocks hewn from the transsection of oak trees a yard in diameter. Others were wielding what looked like battle-axes. With no more than two swings these men were cutting through bones three inches thick. One needed little imagination to envision these butchers' forefathers swinging such an axe a few hundred years earlier to split the skulls of marauding enemies. Red was the color of the place, in shades ranging from the crimson of fresh pig's blood, to the magenta of lamb's blood, to the sienna — like a bordeaux wine about to go off — of blood dried half a day earlier. Even the gray-white-black countertops, now worn down by the decades of butchering, scraping, polishing with bleach and drying at the end of the day, had a pink sheen to them. The only colors to break the monotony of red were the black iron frames of each booth and the yellowish-blue fluorescent lamps, around which the flies hovered, when they weren't sucking on the carne below.

As to customers, they were standing three-in-line at each booth, haggling for better prices on a bit of lamb, or "reserving" the beef loin, or leaving an order for pork chops. We needed to buy some good pieces — it was the weekend. I pointed to some cuts, laid out on the previously mentioned white ceramic-on-metal trays. Inge said, "I don't think so . . . we'd be chewing that for a long, long time. Better take this one," she said as she pointed to a piece that did not look noticeably different to me from the ones that I had suggested taking. I shrugged my shoulders. "Yes, it looks a little marbley, but it's filet, Boriss. Trust me, it's the best cut of meat available." I deferred to her judgment on it. After all, the last time that I had purchased what I thought was a "roast" happened to be so far down on the shank as to be the kind of stewing meat that requires about 137 hours in a pressure cooker with a meat tenderizer before you could break it down with less than forty-three chews. We were made keenly aware of the absence of steak knives in Latvia as we attempted to saw through the fried meat with our Soviet standard-issue "stage-prop" knives. Eliza, who had a real hankering for any meat that wasn't moving (and perhaps for some that did), was the only one who didn't complain about it. She just went about it in her finest Neanderthalic style.

We crossed from the middle aisle to one of the two side ones. As Inge purchased some veal shanks and filets, I couldn't help noticing that some dogs had entered the fray. Some were begging humbly — a paw at a time, while others were jumping and getting what they could. One particularly spunky black mongrel, some cross between a chihuahua, a fox terrier and a con artist, zeroed in on people that were buying something. Its signal was the buyer's outstretched hand, holding money. At that point, it approached, bumping the customer's leg. While the customer turned around, the dog sat down. While making eye contact with its target, it lifted one paw up, and cocked his head, as if to say, "You haven't forgotten about me now, have you?" Its eyes, which then opened to take up one tenth of his body volume, apparently made it difficult for people not to pay a few santimes more for some bones. As soon as it saw some additional movement the dog stood up on its rear legs and put its small paws on the counter. It then lifted its snout to the counter, as if someone had promised it dinner. This mutt did the same at two stands. And it wasn't the only one that didn't go away hungry. Another brown mongrel, close in appearance to a hyena, actually stole a small rack of ribs while the customer was fishing around for change in her pocketbook. The butcher, after bumping his way out of the booth, started running after it. The hyena-dog escaped nonetheless, because as the butcher started closing the gap, one of the meat pavilion carts was pushed into the intersection, blocking the butcher's path. The cart was loaded with at least two hundred kilos (440 lbs) of various parts. Not only was jumping over it out of the question, but he stopped just in time to prevent getting gored by the horns protruding from a bull's head girded for battle and backed up by the full weight of a two-hundred-pound pig carcass.

On that particular day, we, along with at least two mongrels, were satisfied. Inge had all the material that she needed for the drapes. I had a honeydew melon from Uzbekhistan and the kids had a filet of beef, which like all the "filets" here, was actually a composite of five filet mignons . . . for a laughable $2.60. As I reflected on the relative success of our expedition, I was suddenly overwhelmed with a sense of awe for Kolya, our *snabzhenits* 'purchaser.' For Kolya, this market was not just an amusing Saturday outing — finding high-quality raw materials for the bakery, ranging from cinnamon to apples, to ham — was part of his daily work.

Footnotes

[1] Tubiteikas are a square-shaped skullcap, often embroidered with intricate designs, which are the traditional headgear of peoples from the 'Stan Republics.

[2] Polish for "Sir," with a noble connotation.

[3] In Soviet times, the government controlled supplies of all major foodstuffs and beverages. However, to augment the vitamin intake of those inhabitants who could afford it, and to assure a constant supply of flowers — not to mention the bribes to government officials that would accompany these items — private traders were allowed to bring and sell their grown products in the "co-operative" markets. Basically, this applied to all the markets in cities of around half a million inhabitants or more. The most profitable business was flowers. Although the modest fortunes of several Latvians, including that of the Prime Minister of the country in the beginning of 2000, were built this way, the recognized magnates in this field were Georgians and Armenians. That the latter had amassed sizeable capital this way was demonstrated in a scandal that became semipublic information in the late 1970s. Some entrepreneurial Georgians had combined forces, and, using every loophole and corrupt official in the Ministry of Aviation, created a business matching only the Dutch one in scale. They began by building houses on their private plots, which were up to 25 percent larger than that allowed by law, with permission bought from local authorities. They then built flat roofs on the houses. By law, everything grown on the private plots (including rooftop gardens) could be sold on the market. On one such roof it was possible to grow ten thousand forget-me-nots. Each year, four plantings could be made [the weather in Georgia is not dissimilar to that of Sonoma County]. Each forget-me-not could be sold in the market of St. Petersburg for no less than 75 kopecks (0,75 rubles). This translated to between 7,500 and 10,000 rubles that could be generated four times per year, or gross revenues of approximately 32,000 rubles. Even with the bribes that were necessary for local officials, there was plenty left over for shipping costs. Of course, the government had assumed that the sales would be limited to what the Georgians could bring to the markets in their private cars. They believed that at least two people would have to go, and that the flowers could not be placed on top of one another, the net income to the

family would have been marginal. But what Soviet Marxist economists hadn't expected was that these Georgians would pool their resources and bribe a whole string of Aeroflot officials — both in Georgia and Moscow — to be allowed to "charter" an Aeroflot flight to Leningrad or Moscow. On the airplane would be their family [the sales team]… and fifty thousand flowers. That two hundred regular passengers suddenly and inexplicably found themselves stranded and waiting for another flight was of little concern to either the byeeznessmyen or the Aeroflot officials, who had been generously bribed into cooperation. The net income on such a deal was still 5,000 rubles for each family, or about twenty times the monthly income of the average Soviet family. Done four times a year, this resulted in a net income exceeding 20,000 rubles. Compared to a 2400-ruble salary earned in a conventional way, selling one's own produce was about the most worthwhile venture one could have in the USSR.

[4] Beef cattle. In Latvian, literally 'large stock.'

10

THE GREAT REFORMER

AUTUMN MARKED THE RETURN TO school. Inge was happy to have gotten the children into one of the top five schools in the city. This one had a liberal arts bent. To get the children into this school, I had to attend several meetings with the director. The first involved assessing the capabilities of the children, with a review of their grades in Ogre, and so on. The second meeting involved scrutinizing the parents, or so I felt, when the questions focused on our positions and the organizations for which we worked. After the second meeting, it was not clear to me at all whether the four of us had passed our respective scrutiny.

In my case, the crucial meeting was the third one, which I was to hold alone with the director — a tête-à-tête of sorts. At the beginning, I could sense that the director of the school was having trouble sizing me up. I didn't realize, until much later, that he was probably waiting for me to start off by offering a bottle of cognac, or at least a fortified wine along with two glasses. Furthermore, I didn't speak either of the two languages with a local accent. Finally, I wasn't reacting emotionally to, let alone *using* the Soviet catchwords *'Plan'*, *'achievements,' and 'Soviet exceeder'* that he was reeling off poetically, in *my* conversation. But I caught his drift when he started retracting his previous intentions to let the kids come to the school, on account of the children's "rural" upbringing.

"The environment here at this school, tied to its urban setting, could prove to be an [he grimaced] . . . insurmountable challenge for your children. They may need, among other things, to be tutored by the teachers after class . . . for separate pay." He then added, "But the teachers are sometimes not available, being as they have their own lives to live, you understand . . ."

"Of course that's understandable. I believe that it is the parents' duty to help the children assimilate."

The comment elicited no visible reaction. In fact, in the silence that ensued, I noticed his expression getting more and more sallow. I wasn't connecting — let alone bonding — with him, and started fidgeting, until the answer hit me; "I also think that perhaps you need some gifts from those parents who can donate something, to 'modernize' the school in some ways . . ."

"Yes, you understand correctly. The needs of the school are . . . great," he replied, as he nodded. "One parent, for example — the director of a large company — had our large hall refurbished, with new seats and lighting. . ."

"Oh, well that's certainly a large company that he must be directing."

"Yes, certainly . . . well a company of your size might be more amenable to sponsoring one of the teachers' trips abroad . . . You know continuing education is so important for our pedagogues these days. And yet, on their meager salaries, they can ill afford to go, even by bus, to England. And what, may I ask, is an English teacher good for, if she hasn't been to England, not to mention the U.S., the cradle of the 'new language.' By the way, the teachers have invitations to go—"

"And what possible good could come from a physics teacher, if he hasn't been to NASA and . . . the EPCOTT Center, or even seen the Leaning Tower of *Pisa*," I wanted to answer, but didn't, for the kids' sake. Instead, I replied, "Mr. Director, I'm sure that you and the teachers can best decide how to use the donations. I believe that our company can donate three hundred fifty dollars towards the 'augmentation of professional qualifications' of one or more of the teachers, as you see fit."

"Thank you. I will certainly inform you to what end this donation will have been used — and I think, finally, that children as bright as *yours*, should be able to acclimate themselves to the rigorous academic environment of this school. I'll see to it personally, that they get the supplemental attention that's needed."

"Thank you. Your sincere concern is greatly appreciated."

I decided to start the year off on an academic foot as well, and signed up for Latvian classes. During the summer, I had assumed that any language wherein the accent fell squarely on the first syllable, without exception, couldn't be so difficult to learn. And had it not been for the hundreds of nuances, almost undetectable to the foreign ear, in the vowels and grammatical constructions, then I would have been right. To accelerate the learning curve, I signed up for private courses with a professor of English at the University. The overnight devaluation of the ruble, combined with the paucity of government coffers, resulted in many low-ranking state employees (amongst whom were found all University professors) scrambling to make a living through moonlighting. I offered to pay the handsome rate of $5.00 per hour for my Latvian-language course. The tutor was a Latvian professor of English language, so she could explain the errors that I was making, in a language that I understood.

By late October, the temperatures, with wind chill, were reaching the mid-20s Fahrenheit. I occasionally wondered whether this perpetu-gray climate wouldn't lead me to a deeply depressive state; after all, the fact that the Swedes, Finns and Russians were regularly competing with each other for the top spot on the suicide charts wasn't lost on me. However, suffice it for me to walk out of the cold gray air at three o'clock in the afternoon, into a cozy cafe, sit down to a cup of strong tea from fine Ceylon leaves, topped off with milk so fresh that the cream floated cloud-like on top of the liquid, accompanied by a slice of a freshly baked German chocolate cake, and my doubts vanished with the first bite. It was doubly satisfying for me when I realized that my bakers had baked this cake, and it was now being sold in several more cafes throughout the city.

Within a week of our conversation, Valdis had found a highly qualified and motivated electrician without any well-located *dachas* to redo everything correctly. The environment soon returned to a safe, user-friendly status. It was "safe," that is, except for the "one-armed" rye bread dough mixer. This model of mixer had been the mainstay of most all of the Soviet bakeries. Its most prominent feature was a solid steel arm about thirty inches in length and two inches in diameter, which was bent in the middle. This elbow bend permitted the end of the arm to descend vertically onto the dough, that was kept moving constantly by the bowl, which rotated independently of and in the opposite direction to, the arching arm. On the end of the arm was nothing other than a propeller — a demonstration of the effective incorporation of military-industrial innovation into the production site of the common worker. In fact, I am quite sure that if it had been technologically possible to knead bread by detonating hand grenades, then this methodology would have been incorporated as standard protocol in every bakery in the USSR. The propeller, true to its function, first ripped and tugged at the hapless dough, until finally, after twenty minutes, the dough was propelled into submission. In spite of its slow functioning, and its ability to maim the user, this machine remained a favorite of the intermediate and master-level *mitzitays* 'doughmixer' — a specialist subcategory of the general 'baker.' The latter apparently reveled in the challenge that it presented, not unlike the matador who is thrilled by the challenge of a *toro* bull facing him. "Oh, it mixes better than the Western models. Sure, it might take a little longer, but it's the finest machine around," said Alberts, the most experienced konditor of those present, as he timed his pushing down of the dough to take place in precisely the three seconds that the arm gyrated to the other side. When I commented once that it looked dangerous, Alberts merely smiled. In spite of Preben's long explanations about workers' safety and my repeated offers to replace it, they wouldn't part with this "dive bomber" for even the most advanced, not to mention safest of Western equivalents. The best that Preben and I were able to do was to persuade them to limit its use to the occasional large batch of Riga-style just-wouldn't-taste-the-same-if-it-were-mixed-differently rye bread or Christmas gingerbread cookies.

Preben and I also objected to the presence of the cats, which we felt had no place on the production floor of a modern bakery. Although Preben had long left for Denmark, I broached the subject at an ad hoc meeting that we had at the bakery, "Ligita, why do we still have the cat here?" Ligita shrugged her shoulders and gave a look which I would never be able to decipher, but I supposed to be a combination of futility, earnest ignorance as to the answer, mingled with a reflexive resistance to ideas proffered from above. "Please understand me correctly, I personally love cats. But I believe you'll recall that Preben said that the cat has no business being in a bakery," I said as I watched the pregnant feline negotiate, like a little oil tanker, between the legs of the bakers as we stood. "Well, what's the danger? She catches mice," replied Ligita, just at the moment that the cat, sensing that she was — finally — the center of attention, dropped on her side. "The danger?! The *danger?!* How do I know that you're not going to chop her up, put her in the *maltās gaļas pīrādziņi* when I'm not looking, and make 'Cat *belyashi*'?" I said. Ligita smiled only when I started chuckling.

"But seriously, there are rat extermination services. They are paid to do it, and we don't have to risk cat smells getting into our custard, or cat hairs getting into our production."

"All right, we'll see. In the meantime . . . I'll take the cat home."

During that meeting, I also addressed the bakers about the necessity of cutting the cinnamon swirls as uniformly as possible, and with as small a width of braids as possible. This item was our best seller when cut neatly, as Inese did. The finished product was a pleasure to look at, resembling eight golden brown bow-ties laid out and overlapping each other slightly. When cut sloppily, it looked like seven or eight flattened bananas, pushed together in the middle to prevent disintegration. "Now, I know that it is not easy — it takes practice and concentration. I wouldn't be talking about this now, except that you see, the customer is not *obligated* to buy any of them. And Zigrīda has told me that the Latvian customer is very picky. If he or she sees one like this...," I said while pointing to a neatly cut one, "then the salespersons have no problem selling them. If, however, they look like this one...," I said while pointing to a lopsided specimen, "they will probably not be able to sell them. And as we know, the more we sell, the better off the company will be, and subsequently *you* will be."

I had noticed, during the talk, that on the wall without the shelves [for the trays to rest on], the bakers had put up a poster of Aerosmith. To end the talk on a positive note after delivering the criticism, I said that "the little apple boats are delicious — and *popular* ... like Aerosmith. I like that group too — good music."

Losing no time, Valdis arranged for the rat exterminator to come the following day. In his previous life, the exterminator had been a researcher at the Institute of Applied Biochemistry. His intense gaze and glasses with lenses the thickness of Oreo cookies, gave him away as the scientist that he was, although his soiled, shredded shirt made me wonder a little at first. "Hello sir, a pleasure to make your acquaintance, what can we do to make your task easier," I started. He then replied, in a very polished, academic Russian, "Although the rats should find the poison more appealing than the bread products, it is possible that some *outliers* might prefer *your* products. For this reason, you would do well to hide all of the breads and pastries during the times that the bakers are not baking."

"Fine, then we will dye the dough clay-red, and mask the production as bricks-in-process.'" The exterminator started pondering this offer, until I broke in, "Just kidding. O.K. I understand. Valdis, please ask the bakers to do as the gentleman says."

Over the course of the next hour, the exterminator proceeded to place turquoise blue pieces of some material that closely resembled driftwood chunks, along the walls of the bakery. "This poison is taken from the Vitamin D group. It is experimental, but results have been good in use in Saldus, according to the exterminator ...," Valdis assured me. "Sounds good, Valdis, vitamin-pump them to death — just make sure to tell the exterminator that it has to work on *Riga* rats, not their country cousins," I quipped. Valdis nodded back conscientiously.

The following Monday, I met as I usually did, with Valdis.

"So, what's up?" I asked, with an upbeat tone.

"Not much, everything's going as expected."

"Great — I assume that that means there are no more rats..."

"Well, no, not exactly. Although, judging by certain parameters, you could say that they are a little less prevalent than they were before."

"Hunnh?"

"Well, the rat poison was placed at intervals approximately two meters apart, upon pieces of paper most resembling the plain carton paper..."

"*Valdis!* Simple question — do we still have rats?"

"Yes."

"Let's invite Ratman back then, O.K.?"

"*Khorosho.*"

In the meantime, I decided to take a look myself, between the shifts. When I arrived that evening at nine, the quiet and the cleanliness of the bakery struck me. But as I stealthily approached the section of the bakery where the baking was done, I heard some utensils hitting a metal surface, followed by the rustling of plastic bags. I looked at the table, and saw three rats, each about 8 inches long, moving around the table. As I stepped within five yards of the scene, they bolted, in different directions. One ran past the pile of turquoise blue "rat delight," upsetting the nouvelle arrangement of the appetizer.

The following day, I met with the exterminator.

"Well, it seems that the rats also abide by the rule that you should never eat blue food. Do you have any other ideas?"

"Well yes, we have another substance, an anti-coagulant of the Warfarin group, which, I have heard from colleagues, is much more appealing to the rats than the first one. The poison works on the basis of blood thinning. Furthermore, the poison is passed on through the saliva. Consequently, when one rat bites another one, as they frequently do — being that they exhibit cannibalistic tendencies —, then the second rat will also perish, and so on down the line. I've also been told that they can't resist the *taste.*" The last phrase he stated with such enthusiasm that he could very well have been selling a portion of Carre d'Agneau in Sauce Dijonnaise and potato croquettes to a restaurant customer.

"Sounds disgusting... I like it. Carry on."

The following day, I was awakened by a phone call at around two thirty in the morning.

"What's wrong, Edvins?"

"The oven's not working?! It stopped."

"Everything else is working?"

"Yes."

"What about the circuit breakers, did you try switching them back on?"

"Un-hunh."

"Well did you call Valdis?"

"Yes ... but he is not capable of working ... was sick, and ... went to the *banya[1]* this evening."

"All right. I'll think of something."

"What is it?" asked Inge, who was now also awake.

"They don't know, I'll call the electrician."

I called Leopolds and was pleased to know that Valdis had had at least enough presence of mind to call him, before passing out again. The electrician was already on his way out. As I hung up, I was wondering what we would do — it could be a week before it's fixed... hundreds of orders could be lost. I was thinking the worst when I walked into the bakery, some twenty minutes later. At the very moment that I walked through the door, the oven started up again, making the sound of a small jet engine with its first combustion. "Oh, what a be-e-yu-tee-ful sound!" I exclaimed, breaking out into a wide grin. "So, Leopolds, you solved the problem, great! What was it?"

"This—," he said as he pulled a gray dead rat, some twelve inches in length, with some singed whiskers and a blackened snout, from a newspaper he had rolled quickly into a cone. "This rat chewed through the cable. Short-circuited the wiring."

"Oh, that is just disgusting," I said, giving my thoughts free rein, "rat saboteurs, jeeez ... $%^&#**@ rs can't eat some poison ... they 'can't resist it' .. . goddamn chemistry Ph.D. They'd rather chew polypropylene cable ... Look at these piles of hot-pink *&(&^^%!! Look like go_ _ _ _n pink popcorn. Professor Rat has one more chance." Sure enough, the hot pink-colored piles of rat poison were untouched, lying in exactly the same places that they had been put three days earlier.

As I walked out, I looked up and to the right. The Aerosmith poster had been replaced by one of a well-endowed female nude. "Hmm, I'll have to talk to the brigadier about that one ... I don't understand it, I said that I *liked* Aerosmith."

The following day, I went to the bakery to ask Ligita how much marzipan she foresaw using over the next six months, so I could order it. Besides branding the substance to sound like sexual stimulants, the Danes know everything there is to know about making a world-class, flavor-enhanced and sweetened almond paste, or marzipan. Today, they are importing the finest California almonds, crushing them, mixing in various grades and granule sizes of sugar and flavorings in a sterile environment and then packaging the "marzipan mass," in all imaginable shapes, grades, and unit sizes. They then ship it throughout Europe, Asia, North Africa and the U.S., where it is used by professional bakers and baking hostesses in all fifty states — especially California. Ligita reported that she would be needing 50 kilos of Kranse XX, and 200 kilos of Bitter OO.

After taking the order, which I would then forward by telefax to the manufacturer, I walked down the stairs and to the ovens and saw Edvins, the brigadier.

"I have to commend you on your taste, there, Edvins — you couldn't have chosen a finer specimen of female — but, uh, don't you think that some members of the opposite sex might take offense?"

"Hmm... I didn't think about that... but I understand... we'll fix that."

The following Wednesday, I met again with Valdis and the ratman. Valdis now said, with a tone of voice bordering on boastful, "Well, now, Mr. Popovitzkis has a third poison, which they have used on rare occasions. It first dehydrates, and then when the rats drink water, it causes the intestines to explode. It—" "Fine, fine, Valdis — spare me the details, please — but I warn you, if it doesn't work, you're going to be sitting in the bakery with an airgun, a recording of rat mating sounds and a pot of strong coffee."

That Friday, I was negotiating the design of a new logo, with a local artist. As we finished the meeting, I got up to go to the bathroom at the end of the hall, which had heretofore been used only by the administration. I was surprised to see three of the bakers waiting in line. "What are you doing here?" I asked. "I mean you're always welcome, but isn't it a little far from the bakery?" They meekly looked at the floor, and then Nina said, like a four-year-old would explain why he went to his parents' bathroom, "We're afraid... there was a big rat floating in the potty this morning." "A *rat*?!" I cried out, a split-second before realizing that the rats would be looking for water anywhere, not just "outside the premises" as the rat exterminator had said. "Oh, I understand. Yes, well, the ... uh ... technical people are taking care of that so it doesn't happen again. In the meantime... please be my guests."

"That is just disgusting," I thought to myself at first, and then quickly realized that finally, the rat population will be decreasing. The following Monday, just when I started feeling that a hard battle had been fought... but won, I got a call from Zigrīda, in the store.

"Boriss, we can't have this."

"What is *this*, Zigrīda?"

"Three of the chocolate Danish, they've been chomped by rodents."

"Are you sure?"

"Yes, you see, they started with the edge and went straight for the custard cream in the middle. We've noticed before that they are crazy about that. They usually take a little chocolate glaze, but they're not very fond of it. It seems that two or three bites of the glaze suffice . . ."

"Yeah, yeah Zigrīda, it's clear. We've got rats again. Or at least, the ones that we had are still there. *Khorosho*, I'll take care of it."

Nonetheless, I called Valdis and told him to fire the rat man and bring the cat back. During my next trip to the bakery, I even petted the scruffy animal, while Ligita smiled jubilantly.

I couldn't really blame Valdis either — this exterminator was no doubt one of the best in the city at the time.

As a result of an "open communications" policy that I had asked for from the other partners, I learned that one had to use a light hand in controlling the work environment of the bakers. Zigrīda said that although *she* understood that a Western model meant that the supervisor controlled the environment of the worker, and that the widespread knowledge of the existence of unemployment meant that the workers complied, here things wouldn't work in the same way. She said that the bakers value their ability to determine their environment almost more than they did any increases in salary or rank. I had to admit that the idea didn't sound unreasonable. After all, the employee's cubicle is the sacred bastion of each individual worker. So, it should not have been a surprise to me when on the following day, I noticed that the poster featuring a nude, well-endowed female had been taken down and replaced by a poster of a nude well-endowed *male*, the very end of whose most private part was covered up by a "Made in Denmark" label.

Footnotes

[1]Ritual of Russian rituals. The banya is a Russian sauna. Vodka is consumed
    before, during, and after the ceremony. Those that pass out during the
    whipping with wet birch switches are taken out into the 'dining area' and
    forced to drink vodka to wake up. In Soviet times, the more deluxe the
    sauna, the greater was the prestige of the factory, and subsequently, its
    General Director. The highest honor in this informal class struggle was to
    be the General Director-with-the-most-luxurious-sauna-forced-into-
    early-retirement-with-incipient-cirrhosis of the liver. Of the latter, people
    spoke in hushed, reverent tones, not unlike the ones accorded to fallen
    war heroes of the Great Patriotic War.

11

SETTLING IN

THE FAMILY HAD MOVED INTO the city in mid-September. Markus and Eliza transferred to the new school, and a family life began to take shape. In the evenings, I would come home around 6:00 and spend time with the children, before retiring at an hour much earlier-than-any-I-had-ever-even-contemplated-in-my-existence-heretofore; like it or not, the first production of pastries had to leave the bakery at 6:45 A.M. With the kids, I wanted to make sure that the time we spent together was fun, and if they learned something in the process, then all the better. For example, at the beginning of our relationship, I played chess with Markus. I would lose intentionally, so that Markus could develop self-confidence. Then, after the fourth time, to keep him striving, I decided to win. When Markus lost for the second time in a row, he apparently felt that he might lose more often than he would win and announced that chess was a stupid game that was for idiots, and he didn't like it.

Although I'm no fan of the game myself, I tried to set the record straight for him by recounting that some of the world's smartest people play it, and the champions are almost all geniuses, including the Latvian, Mihails Tāls.[1]

"I don't care, they're dumb anyway."

On that note, the formation of a future chess champion screeched to a grinding halt. So we started reading. I read some children's books to the kids.

But that soon grew too passive, so we went back to playing a game, but we changed it. After executing selected tasks around the house, Inge would allow the children to indulge in a spirited game of "Monster." I offered to play the role of the lead protagonist. My goal was to catch the kids, while dragging my foot along the floor zombie-like and making deep guttural sounds. The foot-dragging allowed them to escape . . . sometimes. To encourage them to help each other, I added the law of "kazum," by which the monster would release the captured child if the other one "came to the rescue" by tapping the Monster strongly enough to get its attention. This had to be done before the monster counted to three. Otherwise the victim would undergo an absolutely grueling tickling. All told, it was no mean theatrical feat. When the lights were turned out *and* elements of hide-and-go-seek were added to the game, it turned into a high-intensity event for the kids. The intensity could be measured either by Markus' squeals of laughter, Eliza's shrieks of fear, or the crescendo on Inge's commentary, which followed one of two major lines of reasoning; "Now *couldn't* you *find* any *civilized* game to *play*, for goodness' sake," *or* "I have just put the apartment in order, could you *please* be more *careful* with your *stupid* playing . . . morons!" We all knew that the former was also out of the question . . . after all, zombies are *not* Miss Manners . . . or rheumatologists. After each session, I would approach Inge with a quickly contrived look of apology and say, "Aw honey, I'm really sorry about this . . . but the kids just love it. Sure I don't look like a college graduate when I do this, but the kids can only play so much chess . . ." However, the pleas fell on deaf ears — after the fifth "session," Inge placed us on a strict timeframe. From that point on, playing "Monster" was rationed out — by minutes of play — only after the completion of difficult chores or outstanding academic achievements (the kids', not mine).

By this time, all the appliances, decorations, and books had been moved from Ogre to our apartment. However, some rituals that accompanied these items were quite foreign to me. For example, one night, during the first week of October, I was sitting and reading. Suddenly, I heard what sounded like a large turbine, beginning to go into high-rev, coming from the bathroom. I thought that the turbines cleaning out the water from the waste pipes had backed up, gone into reverse . . . and were now forcing up waste through our bathroom. I jumped up, glanced quickly at Inge, who appeared equally startled, and ran to the bathroom. I opened the door, and saw nothing more than the "Riga" clothes wringer, in the final apogee of its working cycle. An object that looked like an oversized high school chemistry class centrifuge, propped on an orange inner tube, was having an epileptic fit. It was vibrating violently, bobbing uncontrollably from side to side, salivating streams of soapy water.

"*Inge*! . . . Come here, this . . . this . . . *thing* is out of control!"

Inge jumped up and ran to the bathroom. She looked in.

"No, Boriss, don't worry, it's just wringing out the clothes."

"You mean, it always does this?"

"Sure."

"Won't it tip over or something?"

"No, not unless you pack the clothes in a really lopsided way."

"Oh. What about the water being spit out?"

"Yea, I suppose it could be neater. But you know Boriss, this washer/ wringer unit is a real *defitsitnaya* item. There are waiting lists for it in Moscow and Leningrad."

Inge proceeded to explain tht this "epileptic centrifuge" was the very cutting edge of clothes-drying technology in Latvia, Moscow, and Leningrad in 1991. And the washing unit was equally in demand.

"Welcome to country-in-transition. But look at the positive points — the apparatus is simple to use, and portable, allowing for hook up to the bath faucets. Given the lack of space in most apartments, it's not a bad feature to have. One adjusts the temperature of the water by regulating the handles ..."

As I was to learn later, the wash temperature could be adjusted, but the wash modes were limited to "brutally clean" and "pretend-to-be-gentle." This machine's mechanical thrashing was expected to compensate for the infamously weak Soviet laundry detergent formulations. One could expect to find Egyptian cotton or woolen items in tatters after one wash cycle. On the other hand, the phrase "whiter-than-white" was operable here ... stains were flogged into oblivion. Finally, the wringer could provide hours of entertainment for the low-budget family — the orange inner tube bobbed uncontrollably no matter how evenly one arranged the clothes around the edge of the inside. But true to Inge's word, the clothes were virtually dry to the touch when the unit grudgingly come to a stop. In effectiveness, the two units were probably no worse than the Whirlpools, Boschs, Siemenses, and Mieles that had long since combined the two separate functions of cleaning and wringing into one unit and then were enclosed in a sound-insulated white case.

I promised Inge to finance the purchase of any appliance that didn't make the bathroom sound like it was about to lift-off, so the following month we replaced the *Riga* washer and *Centos* dryer with a "Vyatka." I was pleased to discover that the Vyatka generated no sound louder than a healthy purr. However, Inge was less enthralled by the machine's three-hour cycle and two-quart capacity, which meant that laundering was a late-into-the-night task. Furthermore, its Soviet "good-golly-gee, electricity's-free" energy consumption somewhat compromised its export potential to any country outside of Saudi Arabia.

One evening, at the beginning of October, after Markus had played the piano, Eliza had baked some cookies and the kids had been "monstered" to, Inge and I sat down on the couch. Inge asked me what I thought the kids would be when they grew up.

"Oh, I dunno, but it looks to me, like Eliza's going to be a psychologist... she understands people and how to talk to them so that they feel good. Markus is going to be a ... train conductor."

"*What?!*"

"Well, what should I have said — a baker?!"

"Oh, for goodness sakes, you are really... just ridiculous. He'll be a doctor."

"Yes, certainly... a witch surgeon."

"*Oy perestan.* Get off it. You are so critical of him."

"I am not... just being realistic."

"Sure — I can tell — you are so 'objective' whenever Eliza asks you for something. She just twists you around her little finger ... if she would have asked you, you would've baked the cookies for her, put them on a plate, and promised her to tell everyone that *she* baked them."

"Oh stop, absolutely and totally untrue... I don't know how to bake *those* kinds."

After laughing, Inge said; "Well, tell you what, Boriss — you've kept your side of the 'deal' so far... and the kids are asking now all the time... you know, about our relationship. I'm having more and more trouble explaining that you are a 'Special Uncle'. So—"

"Are you saying what I think you're saying, Inge?"

"Yes."

"I thought you'd never agree. I'd love to."

We then embraced for a mere twenty minutes.

"So... how long does it take to organize a marriage around here?"

"Oh, to get permissions and things — count on around two weeks," Inge answered. After that, there is a three-month 'cooling-off' period, to allow us to confirm our feelings."

"Seriously?"

"Oh yes, are we ready for a *Sovetskiy socialisticheskiy brak?* Soviet Socialist wedding?"

For mid-October, I had planned the second of two trips to Germany. I had planned it to coincide with my mother's long-held desire to visit Russia, the land of half her forefathers. The plan was that we would meet at our distant cousin's place in Hamburg, the starting point of a trip that was to cover five major cities, the focal point of which was Riga. I have to admit, in retrospect, that my mother couldn't have chosen a more splendid time to visit Russia, the primary purpose of her trip. The major cities had recently been freed up from the iron grip of mandatory "Intourist routes" and "Intourist hotels" and "Intourist restaurants," serving "Intourist-approved meals" to be later deposited — wholly or partially — into "Intourist-approved potties." At the same time, the Mafiya had not yet activated its legions of pickpockets, hotel thieves, and mugger-prostitutes, which it was planning to do the following year, once they had been properly trained and briefed. So October of 1992 was an ideal non-summer month to visit Russia for the Western tourist.

At the same time, in the mind of the typical entrepreneur, *any* three-day, let alone two-week absence during the first year of a start-up is equivalent to eternity and *will* spell disaster for the new company. So it was with mixed emotions that I departed for Hamburg; to rationalize the departure even more, I decided to purchase an automobile. The word in the streets of Riga had been that the appetite for foreign cars in Moscow was growing voraciously, while the Latvian border guard and customs structure was in its infancy and hardly capable of keeping semi-truck trailers of drugs and alcohol from entering and leaving the country at will, let alone passenger vehicles. Consequently any German automobile newer than six years, and the size of a Volkswagen Golf (Jetta) or larger, was a target for theft. So when I called my distant relative Bjorn to confirm my arrival date, I asked if he could keep an eye out for any small-model cars in the area.

When my mother arrived, she was in good health and cheer. Most importantly, she came prepared to restore my life to its proper rhythm, which had — most certainly — been lost in the year that had passed since my last visit with her. Unfortunately, it so happens that no matter what is intended by me, or hoped for by my mother, a primal neural reaction is unleashed every time that I know I am to be spending more than three days in her company. No matter how many presidents, prime ministers, or world leaders I might successfully have been organizing visits for or met with, any trip with my mother reduces my capacity for logical reasoning to that of an eight-year-old's.

True to form, the trip preparation from Hamburg to Sweden began with my mother's question: "So, did you take your driver's license?" It's the sort of question that drives all twenty-year-olds, not to mention thirty-year-olds, absolutely and unconditionally nuts. It's that silly, simple phrase that communicates lack of trust, and the negation of one's adult status. It was also a question that I couldn't answer affirmatively; while the wallet containing different foreign currencies, valid credit cards, neatly folded map of Stockholm and (of course) my driver's license, was waiting pointlessly for me on top of the nightstand in Riga, the wallet with my U.S. social security card, expired credit card, enough Latvian postage stamps to send a letter from Riga to China thrice and a card illustrating the letters of the alphabet in sign language was lying snuggly in my pocket. So I answered as would any thirty-two-year-old, under the circumstances, in the face of the matriarch: "What a really, really, stupid question — I mean how could you ask such a thing? . . . What do you take me for . . . an idiot?!"

"Just as I thought . . . Bjorn, can we drive to Sweden without a driver's license?"

"Sure, Aline, just as long as he doesn't go over the speed limit."

"Come on, guys, don't worry . . . in the event that we *do* get pulled over, with the help of *this* unique card, I can signal to him that I left my *valid* driver's license in Riga, and I'm sure that that'll be the end of all interrogations . . ."

"Let's go, son . . ."

And thus we drove, in my newly purchased ten-year-old Volkswagen Polo (with matching panda decals and aqua and pink stripes on either side of the car) to Sweden — obsessively observing all speed limits along the way. It took us two full days of driving to reach the *Russ* ferry, anchored in one of Stockholm's passenger ports. The trip on this boat was, thank goodness, uneventful. My mother had an opportunity to play some slot machines, and I, to prepare questions that I would ask Zigrīda, Valdis and Tamara the accountant upon our arrival. The sea was calm, which it rarely is in the fall and winter months.

Our arrival in Riga was met with great pomp. Inge and the children each brought a large bouquet of flowers. As Inge later confided, "I had to bring *lots* of beautiful ones, so that your mother wouldn't think so harshly about the 'old lady' with two kids who would be taking her son away from a bright future back in America, with all the great education that he had." But there was no need for panic. My mother took to Inge very well, even though my "great education" was lying untested somewhere in the more distant vaults of my mind.

After a whirlwind two-day tour of Riga's main sites, my mother and I were once again solo, this time on a train to St. Petersburg. Upon our arrival there, I took her to the Hermitage, Pushkin's apartment, and a half-dozen other places where we had to attach oversized pressed-wool slippers to our shoes, and shuffle from room to room, polishing the parquet floors with our feet. We later joked that the slippers must have been a contribution from the French Ministry of Culture (or possibly from Pierre Cardin himself) to the Russian one, insofar as each of the slippers would stay attached to the feet by virtue of a blue-white-red striped elastic band, and the "disheveled peasant"-style had made a comeback on the catwalks of Paris earlier that year. Besides, we reasoned that only the French were so scientifically thrifty as to have contrived a scheme that would result in one's floors getting polished by strangers while having them pay for the experience.

After we arrived in Moscow, I left my mother with a relative of our good family friends from San Francisco, and rushed to catch the next train to Riga. Although I had been gone for a total of seven days, I was envisioning that The Merry Baker had ground to a halt — its stores shut down and bakers peddling its last stocks of flour on street corners.

Over the course of that trip with my mother, I also discovered that I couldn't live without Inge. Perhaps such thoughts occur often to those adult children that inadvertently find themselves spending time with their parents. So, upon my return, I shared this fact with Inge. I then suggested that we try to push up the time for the wedding. We agreed that it would make little difference in terms of planning and guests. As concerned the latter, we concurred that since both of us had been previously married, we could dispense with a guest list; neither of us had a convenient second set of friends who had not attended our respective first weddings), whether we married within a week, or within a month, so we vied for the former. After several under-the-table contributions and pleading through contacts, we found a Justice of the Peace who would perform the ceremony without the standard three-month waiting period. I discovered, in the course of this process, that the waiting period of three months between the application and wedding date had been a ploy by Soviet authorities to prevent wedding vows from being made without sufficient forethought. However, given that the divorce rate exceeded 70 percent in the Soviet Union in the 1980s, this ploy was another shining example of Soviet social policy gone hopelessly awry.

My mother, freshly returned from Moscow, where she claimed that "people have this strange habit of buying puppies, enjoying their company until these poor creatures grow to adulthood, and then abandoning them *in my hostess' neighborhood*" — was delighted that she could preside at this wedding. The kids were happy too, apparently having concurred with Inge that I was an acceptable find. Three days after the wedding, my mother departed. Prior to doing so, she thanked me for arranging "an *unforgettable* trip to my father's homeland" and for pushing up a "wedding marked by your happiness, my son." She then swore that (for different reasons) she never wanted to experience either of them again. As to the bakery operation, she said, "Congratulations. Great job you've done so far . . . but you have a *lot* of people . . ."

Now that I had my own automobile in Riga, the onus of ownership befell me as well. The first challenge that I faced in Latvia — which could be called many things except a "challenge" in the West — was filling the gas tank. I began, naively enough, by looking for a gas station within the city limits. I got some directions and drove…and drove…and drove some more. When I was so far out of town that the lights of the city were like distant stars, I pulled into a *Benzinovaya Kolonka*, or, in Latvian, *Degvielas stacija*. To get an idea of what this station looked like, one had only to envision the most decrepit gas station on a forgotten country road in Nevada or New Hampshire, increase the number of tanks by five, take away any "service" element, and you had the *Kolonka* or *Degvielas Stacija*. I put the nozzle into the tank, and pressed the handle. There was no activity. I looked for buttons on the rusty black pump, and found a red one. I pushed it repeatedly. There was no effect. I then guessed that payment for the gas was executed in advance. I went to the window. The clerk waited. I expected him to ask me how many liters I wanted or something similar. Instead he said, in a biting Russian, "*Nu chto zhdesh kak choknutiy?* 'So, what are you waiting for, like a simpleton?'" I asked and paid for thirty liters, which is what I guessed I needed. As I was standing, humped over the gas pump, waiting as the nozzle filled the tank, one painfully slow liter after liter, I started wondering how many of these soviet gas pump liters made up one ARCO gallon. "Erggh, ba-dum, ba-dum, ka-chunk, ba-doom, ba-doom"- like sounds emanated from the pump. I understood that one justification for having the stations so far outside the city was the excruciatingly loud sounds of the pump's operation. I concluded that these noises may hold the key to understanding how many liters have just been pumped into the tank. "O.K., one badum must mean about four ounces, so after two 'ka-chunks,' that'll be one pint, maybe a bit more. After every three 'ka-chunks' comes one 'ba-doom.' O.K., so after twenty 'ba-dooms,' my gas tank should be half full … Now does the 'ergh' happen every ten liters? …" Soon a black Volga came coasting by, and parked on the pumps opposite mine. The driver looked my way. I shrugged, to communicate that this is nothing quick. But he apparently knew. After going to the window, he returned; he put the nozzle into the tank of his car with one hand, with the other he picked up a newspaper and started reading it, using the light that emanated from the naked lightbulb ten yards away to do so. After a few more minutes, I heard the final "*ba-DOOM, ba—a-a-DOOM, Ka-CHUNK*," signifying that the allotted, paid-for liters have been deposited into the tank, or wherever else you have been pointing the nozzle.

I eased the nozzle back into the pump, but the grinding sound continued. I looked in the direction of the attendant, and he signaled with his thumb for me to push something. I pushed the red button with my other hand and the deafening sound stopped. I had difficulty relaxing the stranglehold grip of my hand around the nozzle. When I finally did so, my knuckles were white; my right hand was shaking. "There must be an easier way," I said to myself, as

I sat down and gripped the steering wheel with my left hand. I concluded that in Soviet times, pumping gas into trucks had been a job for convicts assigned to hard labor.

Degviela Station, Riga — Jurmala road (after installation of new pumps)

The next time, at another station, a long line presaged the aforementioned pleasures. It needn't have been a long line, if the attendant hadn't decided to make his chess moves between customers. After my third tank-filling trip, I decided to forgo the stations in favor of one of the Soviet gas trucks, which were parked on the sides of most major roads and at some intersections in the city. They were, more precisely, nondescript olive green Soviet Army gas trucks filled with crude but effective fuel and equipped with a crude but effective pump to dispense the stuff. Most of them even boasted a mechanical gauge that was visible to the customer. The pump could only pump out in five-liter increments so "fill 'er up" was not an option, unless you needed and *knew* that you needed exactly forty-five or thirty liters to do so. However, there was an attendant, dressed in olive green or gray-black overalls, who did the work. The procedure was simple enough: park the car on the side of the truck, quickly tell him how much you wanted. He hand-pumped the desired quantity into the intermediate tank, and then pushed the nozzle into the car's tank.

Pay and goodbye. No more finger cramps. And, if you kept the window up, then no deafening "ba-dums, ka-chunks". Of course, there were no bothersome receipts either.

The only problem with this option was that the gasoline was of "caveat emptor" quality. Not a few enterprising gas truck operators mixed diesel (a cheaper substance) into the gasoline. In the cases of being filled from such trucks, the vehicle would still continue along its way, but with some additional kicks and starts, which varied in their violence. At its worst, the jerking of the bakery trucks would result in boxes with pastries being heaved onto one another. This led to not a few disfigured pastries, and one wedding cake with a decapitated couple. However, it did not take long before we found some more or less reputable tank trunks, and instructed our drivers to get gasoline only from these. We referred to the one closest to the bakery as *"Van'kina Benzinovaya Kolonka,"* or "Little Ivan's Gas Tank." The driver/attendant was surly with the customers, but he didn't smoke on the job and best of all, the gasoline was clean.

Footnotes

[1] Tals, or Tal was the World Champion in 1960. He was the youngest chess
champion ever, at that point, winning the world title at the age of 23.

12

A COLD WINTER WIND

ANOTHER THING ABOUT BUSINESS — SOMETIMES you just have a *bad* month. December was it and the signs appeared from the start. On the first Sunday of December, I decided to go to the bakery to help the bakers on new cake ideas for the Christmas season. But, after turning the water on in the shower and soaping myself, I felt that the stream wasn't getting warmer within the three-minute timeframe my subconscious had allotted for this. So, after waiting another minute, I stormed out, wondering if something hadn't blocked the flow of hot water to the bathroom. I tried the kitchen faucets. Same icy cold water. Five minutes later, dressed in a warm-up suit, I made my way to the basement. There was no light, so I went back upstairs to the apartment for a flashlight. As I reached the door, another tenant came racing down the stairs. I had seen him a few times before, replacing light bulbs in the hallway, so I decided that he must be the pseudo-superintendent and therefore best informed on the problems of the house. I asked, before the man had reached the landing of the floor below, if he knew what had happened to the hot water.

"Yeah, some 'bandits' cut out all the copper tubing and cistern from the boiler downstairs. Apparently, they just worked this building and the next one sometime before seven thirty this morning," he replied, with a matter-of-fact tone of voice, as if these things were as common as morning dew on the grass.

"What!? The whole cistern?? Jeez... any idea how long it'll take to repair?"
"I'll try to put something in temporarily, but it would be good if you could call the House of Administration."
"Sure, I'll try."

I called the "House of Administration" office[1], the repairman on duty answered, in a voice well tempered by one spirit or another, "Yes, we kn... n. .. now what the [*hiccup*] problem is, but [*hiccup*] we can't do a thing about it-s... until tomorrow." The soundpiece was pierced by giggles and the phrase "what does that pederast want?" in the background. I slammed the phone down. "Well, that's just grand — now we just sit and wait and freeze. I suppose that I can wait another day to shower... "if it'll be fixed in a day..." I pondered aloud whether or not I should just take my place on the "aroma express" that would leave for Ogre in an hour and shower at my in-law's place. Inge shrugged her shoulders, and said that it was my call, but that I shouldn't get my hopes up that they'll fix the problem by tomorrow.

She said that people termed housing administrations "houses of ill-repute," and then recounted that, "The Germans had just finished the bombing of Britain, and it was having no effect, so Hitler called Stalin and said, 'My dear friend Josef, listen, I need your help. I've just bombed London, but the city is still standing, and the English dogs aren't surrendering. Couldn't you somehow help me reduce the city to rubble?' ... 'Sure, Adolf, I can, but it'll cost you some territory." "O.K., more of Poland. What'll you do?" "If it's rubble you want, then I'll have my people smuggle in the staff of 20 Houses of Administration."

I decided on going to Inge's parents, who were pleased by the unexpected visit. Several of the residential houses on our side of the block had suffered the same fate. Apparently, the units of the Mafiya that traded in colored metal (copper, aluminum, brass) had decided to relieve over ten apartment houses of the copper components of their pre-war heating units. This involved about 150 pounds of copper per building. I suppose that it was out of courtesy to the tenants, that they did so between six thirty and seven thirty in the morning, before the dwellers would be taking their showers. Inge turned out to be right — the hot water was restored only after four days.

By the end of November, the reputation of The Merry Baker had spread to other parts of the city, and reports were coming from the store clerks that people were traveling from ten and more miles away to purchase a cinnamon swirl or custard stick. Nonetheless, our location was still far from ideal. For example, one transient had decided to make the stoop of the bakery his home-away-from-home, incessantly leaving both beer bottles and orange peels as momentos. Another heaved a brick through the front window. The store clerks had remembered seeing him earlier, in the store, protesting vociferously against the "*Nye demokraticheskiye tseni* 'non-democratic prices'" established by the bakery. His protest took a destructive form in spite of the fact that the cheap standard Soviet-era products were readily available on that street in several locations not fifty yards away.

So the hunt for retail space was on. I first approached Zigrīda about the need for finding a good location, preferably in Old Town or the Center just West of it. She replied that her sister-in-law had a honey store in Old Town, and knew *everybody* that was worth knowing in that part of town. As to the Center district around it, she said that the best bet would be to approach the city government, as it had almost all the vacant places. In fact, at this point, the key property owners in Riga were the five municipalities. We had very good relations with ours, but their territory did not include any of the high-end or even middle-class sections of the city. On the other hand, the Center municipality controlled access to several hundreds of vacant and soon-to-be-vacated locations on the five major boulevards.

We met with the representative of the department that let out vacant spaces. We were told that the municipality used a system whereby they solicited written proposals. Subsequently, a panel of five to seven council members would judge the proposals and on the basis of merit award the lease rights to the company with the best one. I met once with the director of the board of the Center municipality, and she had quite a pleasant personality. She talked up the importance of supporting the small entrepreneur and the small retailer "that is the fabric of the re-emerging nation." When all had been said, I felt that I was dealing once again with some truly progressive individuals, who cared primarily for the rational development of the real estate and retail sectors of their beautiful city, and swore by a democratic philosophy of governance. In any event, she told me that it would be a pleasure for her to receive a proposal from The Merry Baker for one of five ex-bakery locations whose fate would be decided later in the month. She told me to make sure that "it's a good proposal; we'll be judging them on merit alone." The next week, we submitted our ten-page proposal, which included details on new personnel to be employed, taxes to be paid and other elements that communicated "good corporate citizen here" for the district. Two weeks later, I was told to appear at the session in mid-December, during which the recipients of five locations would be announced.

When I arrived in the large waiting room, I felt the glare of a dozen eyes. "Another bloody candidate!" they all seemed to say. All who were not seated were nervously pacing back and forth (the result of having had a cup too much of Latvian coffee[2]), chain-smoking cigarettes, and in other ways curbing their tension in the poorly lit, air-deprived foyer with worn linoleum flooring. The number of important business personalities present astounded me. I saw Raimonds Gerkens, the Latvian equivalent of Mr. Woolworth, establishing a chain of low-price point retail stores. One representative from Skonto, a leading international trading company at that point, was bantering with someone from another large metal trading company. One individual greeted me. He was a Canadian developer of medium-sized hotels. When I asked him what he had applied for, he said that it was for a plot of land under a house that had once belonged to a neighbors' grandfather, and would make a fine site for a hotel. When I asked specifically where it was, he named one of the two public squares in the Old Town of Riga. It would have been tantamount to someone making claims on Union Square in New York City or San Francisco.

Fortunately, I was spared having to hear all the machinations being launched on the city's landmarks, as the previous session's participants exited the room, and someone announced the name of the location we had applied for. I passed through the large oak double doors, each weighing about a hundred pounds, and entered the room. There were some twenty people already seated in the chairs to the left. To the right were three tables, arranged in a horseshoe, and covered with green felt. Seated around the table were two councilwomen and two men. At the head was the Chairwoman, whom I had met two weeks earlier. They were staring intensely at documents lying in front of them, as if infusing information received in the last minutes, crucial to deciding a very important question. I walked quickly to the back row of seats, sat down, and gripped my notebook tightly. The chairwoman, a stocky woman — who in her previous life had no doubt been a member of the regional committee [*soviet*] — wore thick, plastic-rimmed, anti-designer glasses. She began her introduction with a steady, deliberate voice that bespoke great authority, coupled with absolute objectivity and fairness, "We welcome all of you today, to the session, deciding the fate of three locations in Old Town, and two in other parts of the city center. We have had several applications for each location, and we have rated each application on a scale of one to five. The total number of points earned by each of the top three applicants for each address we will announce today. All decisions are final, and based on merit alone."

There was a pause, as two of the other four council members forwarded documents to the chairwoman. She accepted them, adjusted herself on the seat, and began, "The winners from among the candidates for Lāčplēsis street thirty-four, and Kungu street number two are..." She tried to make it as exciting as the Academy Awards, but after drawing the pause out to thirty seconds, it came out a tedious, "Bread factory number twenty-nine and Kommexscheme." The winners of the rights-to-lease of the first two addresses were one large soviet-style bakery, and an ice-cream manufacturer. The latter decision struck me as being a little strange, given that these locations were zoned to be bread shops.

The third address announced was the one for which we had applied; "*Smilšu* street four . . . six candidates." After looking at the paper placed in front of her by the councilwoman to her right, she announced, "The winning proposal, with twenty-three points, is . . . The Merry Baker." I was euphoric. I stood up, and nodded in gratitude to the jury. Others in the audience were clapping. Several persons turned around and nodded to me. One lady even smiled and gave me a thumbs-up. "Won on the basis of merit alone," I thought to myself. I've done it, we're in."

As I sat back down, a gentleman in a dark blue western-tailored suit stood up and said, "Excuse me, but I believe that the honorable council board will see that the Smil u street four address was also one of the addresses submitted by Kommexscheme for inclusion in its 'total development project' of bread sales sites in Old Town."

The chairwoman did not respond. Silence descended on the room like a cold fog. The chairwoman looked down at her papers, then began nodding, at first imperceptibly, and then vigorously, as if she had found something that she had at first overlooked. Some of the other council members began shuffling the papers in front of them, as if they had failed to read the fine print on an insurance claim and were now being exposed, in an uncomfortable moment, to a clause that nullified their claim rights. The council chairwoman turned to her colleague to the right and began discussing the situation with her in hushed tones, inaudible to the silent onlookers. The other council members apparently understood what was taking place and began mimicking the chairwoman. I later surmised that their "discussions" went along the following lines:

"This one went weird — they should have seen that Kommexscheme had applied for this spot too — and you know how much *those* guys paid to this district's chairman. Oh well . . . which sausages are you going to buy this Christmas? I like the ones that they have at the third stall at Vidzemes market."

"Really, I was just going to get the usual *Doktora Desa* Doctor's Sausage from *Rīgas Miesnieks* 'Riga Butchers,' although most probably slip in a few 'jubilee' sausages if the payback scheme goes through as it should."

They were soon nodding vigorously as well. After a few minutes, which to me seemed like hours measured out with an hourglass, the chairwoman gathered her wildly shuffled papers; resumed her stately demeanor, and announced, "Please excuse the 'little misstatement,' but we must correct our last announcement. In fact, the Kommexscheme company is the winner, with a total of twenty-four points." Deaf to the murmurs circulating through the room, I pursed my lips, folded my hands over my head and dazed into the ceiling. The chairwoman then announced, "However, we would like the representative of The Merry Baker to come and see us after this session." "D__n right, I will ... if I don't get something out of this, then there'll be hell to pay for these people," I thought. Then as I reflected further, still numb from the defeat, I realized that we were quite powerless in this situation. *I* had determined that it was the company's policy to pay bribes to *no one* for any service, good or favor, except with pastries or an occasional cake. I had done so out of the belief that objectivity would soon triumph over corruption, a carryover from "advanced" socialism. Leaning on my Buddhist convictions, I had also convinced myself that giving in to bribery would result in greater retribution at a later point. Although I had been hard pressed to define what these future consequences could be, I dismissed the notion of bribery on the basis of it being morally repugnant. I reviewed what the other non-material options might be. My co-directors had no familial ties to any members of the council. As much as I might have wanted to believe otherwise, my company's products were not life-saving ones, although not a few gourmands would claim that a well-timed chocolate-almond truffle had given them a new lease on life. In fact, by the time I approached the council Chairwoman, I was quite at a loss as to what I would actually demand; I stood in front of her, silent.

"We apologize for this ... misunderstanding. Perhaps you can come and see my deputy immediately after the holidays. We'll see what we can do." I nodded and left. As I walked down Blaumaṇa iela, I experienced a bitter taste in the mouth — one that would not be lessened even by consuming one of the bakery's 'Rossini' confectioneries[3].

Had she not announced that our proposal had received twenty-three points and had it not appeared, for even that fleeting sixty seconds, that my company was to get the space, I would never have thought twice about the consequences of unwavering morality. Now, I ambled back to the store, oblivious to the Christmas decorations that graced some shops for the first time in fifty years, trying not to feel my jaw as it hit the occasional fire hydrant. I stopped outside the bakery store and looked through the window. It was three thirty in the afternoon, but already well into dusk. The salesclerk was leaning on the counter with both elbows. She was swaying gently from side to side, in rhythm to some music emanating from the radio. A customer walked through the door, carrying an object. He put it on the counter, and began saying something. Inta listened, slowly rising from her leaning position, and then shook her head from side to side. She crossed her legs and assumed the "I cannot be bothered to get out of this fantastically comfortable lean to help *you*" position of the informal Soviet codex on sales clerking. The customer grew more agitated, and started shaking his finger. Inta shrugged her shoulders.

At this point, I walked in, "Inta, what is the problem here?" "Nothing—," she replied, snapping to attention, beaming with the forced innocence of a seven-year-old who had just hit her little sister, but was sure that no one had seen it.

"This man says that the product is not as good as it was when he was first buying it."

"Yes, and—"

"He wants a …," she then moved her hands from her sides to her chest, to dramatize the word, "*refund.*"

"Yes, and what do you propose?"

"Well, I've certainly already told him that we cannot give a refund … shall I tell him to leave or else we'll call the police?"

"No, not exactly, Inta … let me talk to him."

"So, sir, do you speak Russian?" I asked, proffering the standard line of courtesy to Latvians so that they wouldn't be immediately offended and start pouting. The man nodded. "What's the problem here?"

"This cinnamon roll used to be soft. This time it was hard when I bought it. The clerk said it was fresh, and it wasn't. I paid twenty-eight rubles for it, and I want my money back."

"What if we were to replace the cinnamon roll with something else—," I asked the man, hoping not to lose a customer, "Like a golden sweet pretzel? It's twice the price … and it's fresh." The man nodded in agreement. "I'm sorry about that, I'll certainly speak with the sales staff here. All items that are a day old should be clearly separated. Have a nice evening, sir."

After the man left, I looked at Inta and said, "Now Inta, I'm not sure what you were taught during the *Velikiye Sovetskiye Vremena* 'Great Soviet Times' and quite frankly, I don't care. From now on, the client is the most important person that walks through the door." Inta nodded and kept her face frozen in a plastic smile.

"In the West, he is referred to as a 'king.' Now, would you call the police on the 'king'?"

Inta fell deep into thought, analyzing my words, the expression in my eyes, the angle of my eyebrows, the creases in my forehead, the tone of my voice, hoping that one of these would yield the correct response to the question. I repeated the question. After another pause, during which she understood that I would reveal no more clues, she shook her head, but then added, "But these clients are . . . don't yet have that 'culture.' If we keep exchanging things, they'll bring back old things, and exchange them for new ones."

"Maybe a few will, but most who buy here won't do that . . . they don't have the time to complain about *melochi* 'small change.' Now let's look at this pastry that he returned. Was his complaint factual? From the looks, you can't tell, although it is a little smaller than it should be, but that could be from incorrect *tehnologiya* 'technology.' So . . . touch it."

She did so as if she had been told to touch a pile of nuclear waste.

"Don't be afraid — we're not going to give it to anybody now, and I *certainly* won't make you eat it . . . so go ahead." She pressed with her finger. "It's still good . . . it gives."

Then I pressed it. It did give, but it was at least twenty-four hours old, most probably closer to thirty-six hours.

"Well, I see that you have gotten used to another idea of 'freshness.' No, I think that this was probably baked yesterday morning."

Inta shrugged her shoulders. I reiterated our policy on day-old pastries, which had to be kept separate from the fresher items.

"But what if they are still soft?" she asked.

I understand her question — things in the Soviet times were "fresh" unless you could break your teeth eating it, or it was covered with green.

"In Western Europe, where Latvia wants to be, if the white bread isn't baked that *morning*, then it is old. Even the night before, it's old. Think of that."

Inta smiled again, but this time in disbelief. "Morning, hunnh?" She shook her head.

"Yep."

In most cases, I found that customers reacted about the same as they would everywhere else in the West; when expectations were met, they were pleased. When our performance fell short, people were upset.

The last in my trilogy of mid-December disappointments involved one of the brigadiers. One day, the accountant informed me that the use of butter and eggs in the products exceeded the norms for production in October and November. After sharing this fact with Zigrīda, I asked her if she had noted the production being greasier or more yellow than it had been in July. She replied that she hadn't noticed any "improvements" of that type, but had a hunch that it might be something else. She had heard some rumors but wanted to confirm them before telling me what they were.

Three days later, she asked if I wouldn't be free for fifteen minutes to talk with Gints . . . about his stealing from the bakery.

"What?! *How?*"

"Very simply. He brought in a plastic egg holder, and carried out twenty eggs per day with him when he left."

"Really? Did you catch him?"

"In the act," replied Zigrīda crisply.

A few moments later I was facing Gints. I detected a small smirk on his face. He appeared unrepentant, almost proud. When I posed the question, "Don't you think that stealing will affect your future?" he replied, "Stealing? I didn't steal anything — I bought the eggs at the market before coming to work . . ." His claim wasn't worth discussing; we all knew that all markets opened only two hours after his shift had started and he was nothing if not punctual.

"I'm gonna go with Ilze [another baker] and start my own bakery . . . I'm not going to work anymore in this slut-filled place where nobody's ever happy with the fact that I'm getting all production out on time . . . or *quality.*"

"Obviously not, when eggs go home instead of into the production, we won't be happy with the quality!"

I then changed my tone, and added, using my best *Fortune* 500 company terminology, "Gints, it's *your* life that we are talking about here. Sure, I'm disappointed by your behavior, very disappointed. But it's for *your* sake that I'm saying that lying and stealing will never, ever get you anywhere." He kept his steely stare on me, shook his head and continued smirking.

After he left, docked of his last month's pay, I turned to Zigrīda, "Zigrīda, *that* is very depressing. He lied too . . . whoever hired him?"

"Uh, *you* did — *I* was against bringing him on."

At first stung by this response, I quickly added ten more layers to my skin and responded, "Well, ya can't guess it right every time. I thought that with him being an ex-military guy, he would be honest, trustworthy, reliable, etc."

"Boriss, that depends which military you're talking about — I suppose that things are different in America."

From that point on, given my spectacular talent for discernment, I decided that I should best remove myself from the baker hiring process, before I manage to recruit a serial killer and have to answer for the contents of our meat pies.

Later that week, after I had had time to nurse my wounds, a little silver lining appeared on the massive gray cloud that had formed above Avotu Iela. We received our first large order from an *embassy*. The Danish embassy ordered a series of Christmas cookies and confectionery pieces — all told, some five kilograms (eleven pounds) worth. It was a large order, and given that the items would be custom-made for the Danes, a lucrative one. Preben faxed us some recipes. Besides some gingerbread cookies, and some deep-fried bowties, they were primarily variations on butter cookies. The bakers produced some test cookies that tasted fine to me, but since we hadn't ever eaten the originals, we had to hope that this was what the embassy wanted.

On this fine Friday, two weeks later, it was four forty-five in the afternoon. I was pondering the question of which entry point in Old Town I should use to carry the crates, now holding six kilograms of cookies, to the embassy; why the bakers had not managed to finish in time for the four o'clock delivery; how we could get more orders of this type. I started out of the unfinished driveway of the bakery in my Polo. What I failed to see was that bus #10 had just taken off from the bus stop at Matīsa Iela.

The Soviet trolleybus weighs in at fourteen tons, and uses about half of the energy in the local grid to go from zero to twenty-five kilometers an hour. By the same token, it takes fifty yards to decelerate and stop. Contributing to the oil-tanker maneuverability is the fact that over 90 percent of the buses are double-sectioned, held together by an odd collection of wires, tubes and a little fence-like structure. The interior has neither functioning heat nor cooling, but *does* feature stone-hard seats and reliance on muscle-bound Afghan war veterans to open windows. The buses are painted school bus yellow, with a red stripe on the side, about once every ten years. However, the paint fades without dignity, quickly assuming tones that resembled the lighter shades of dog droppings. During the period of "Advanced Socialism," they were washed as often as three or even four times per year. These vehicles were most often seen blocking rush-hour traffic, the most opportune moment for the hooks which clasp onto the electric wires on top to flip off the wire at intersections, a result of the driver having forgotten to decelerate to a crawl ten yards earlier. In turn, this would leave the bus with no power and invariably stranded in the middle of the street.

However, at this moment, bus #13 was far from stranded — it was in its hyper-acceleration mode some thirty yards to the left of the driveway that I was using to leave the bakery. In my frenzy to get to the embassy as soon as possible, I drove the car too far out of the bakery driveway, leaving approximately two feet of the front end in the street when I came to a halt. This may have left a couple of inches for the bus to pass by, but I wasn't quite sure of that. No, I wasn't quite sure that the double-sectioned bus, weighing five tons and now barreling in my direction, would avoid my front fender. With lightning speed, I shifted to reverse gear and accelerated. My car boldly jerked forward and hit the front right side of the bus. Sure enough, I had just put the car into *first* gear. The impact sent my car turning a full quarter turn clockwise. The bus slowed to a stop, some twenty yards later, and the driver exited. The passengers chanted, almost in unison, "Book the bastard! Take his number! Make sure he never drives again!" Many were beating the windows.

The driver, now worked up to a frenzy, gestured wildly as he bellowed, "Just look at … *this!*" Apparently not sure what to do next, he started pointing to a small dent and chipped paint along a four-inch-long stretch on the front right side of the bus. This bus had a seven-year "ochre" fade on it and a half-dozen similar scratches. But the driver had found "my" scrape because it had knocked off a quarter-inch of dirt as well as some paint.

"Why, this thing'll have to … go to the *shop!* Oh this is real bad. I'll have to … I'll have to … *take* your car papers and your … *driver's* license."

I stared in disbelief — "What, a crazed bus driver with the powers of a highway patrolman? I must have come to hell . . . what about the Danish diplomat who had ordered this … their party is starting in twenty minutes — will my car start? What will they do without their *kager?* Do I have any dogcrap yellow paint I can give this bus driver? Oh my God, will I be able to start my car again? It's twenty-five degrees Fahrenheit, I'll die here of exposure … *wait, STOP.*" When I finally got a grip on my panicking mind, I replied, "O.K., I understand. I'm sorry. Would … six hundred rubles handle it?" He pretended to weigh the offer in his mind.

"Well, all right — but next time, watch what the devil you're doing!"

Besides being spared the thespian challenge of making a dramatic confrontation out of something he didn't really care two bits about, he had just pocketed a week's wages. The maddened crowds settled down, apparently heartened by my frightened, dejected look, and my handing over of something that they no doubt assumed to be car documents. The bus left. I stood there, stunned, looking at the left side of the hood, now lifted up five inches higher than it had been three minutes earlier. The left side of the fender was now suspended six inches from the ground.

Ten seconds later I was off and the cookies were delivered to the embassy, only fifteen minutes late. Driving back and remembering all those faces creased in anger, I couldn't help thinking, "And what if I had had an Audi?"

That weekend, I decided to take a break from the mind-numbing pre-Christmas work schedule and treat Inge and the kids to a Christmas concert, just like I might have done back home. However, Inge didn't want to venture into the sub-freezing weather, preferring instead to stay home and prepare the gingerbread dough for subsequent forming, stamping and glazing.

So the three of us went to the Cathedral of St. Peter for the Christmas concert. St. Peter's Cathedral is one of the two oldest cathedrals in Riga. If one divides cathedrals into their most striking characteristic, then St. Peter's falls squarely in the 'Ones-with-cool-single-spires' category. The story of St. Peter's is the story of a gaggle of architects' quest to build, preserve, and re-build its spire[4].

Tonight however, we were there not for the spire, but for the concert — the first such concert since 1943. As we entered, Markus and Eliza followed me to the pews, which were now arranged for the concert. Markus had difficulty with the uncovered wooden seats, wondering why they couldn't have been more user-friendly, like the ones at the Riga movie theater. When Markus got up to wander around and look at the family crests, restored after the Second World War and now hanging high on the columns, Eliza came alive. She pointed to the pulpit and asked, "What's that little stage for there?" I promptly explained.

"Can he fall out?"

"Well, yes, I suppose so, but he rarely does. The reverend is not allowed to drink before the sermon. He has some very important things to say to parishioners every Sunday."

"Like what?"

"He explains to people what certain parts of the Bible say, like you're not supposed to kill anyone."

Eliza then pointed out that if people can read, why in the world would they need someone to explain it to them.

"Well, Eliza, not all of them are as smart as you, and the way that the Bible is written, they could be confused. There were a lot of miracles performed, for example. But what did they all mean?"

"Oh, like Jesus' walking on water, right?"

"Yes."

"That's easy, the water was frozen there."

"But water didn't freeze in that area, it was really warm."

"Oh," she replied, and then started looking intensely at the choral singers, who were now filtering in. Markus returned and sat down. He lifted one leg and put it on Eliza's lap. "Move over, stupid."

This prompted a comment from me along the lines of, when coming to a cathedral, if nothing else, remember to respect others.

"Oh, I *do-oo* . . . she was just bothering me . . ."

He turned the other way.

Within the first six notes of "Silent Night," my eyes welled up with tears. All the grade school choruses, the junior high school concerts, the songs on the radio when I was growing up, came flashing back to me. But for Eliza and Markus, the Christmas concert was too high-browed an affair. With the exception of "*Eglīte*," the Latvian version of "*Der Tannenbaum*,"[5] the chorale works had no visible primary or secondary effect on their heartstrings.

Afterwards, we went to one of the naves, to view the exhibit of Nativity scenes. These creches, each two to three feet wide, had been collected from some forty different countries. Markus walked through quickly. Eliza, on the other hand, examined each of the first ten carefully. After a few minutes, she asked what the story was with the three old men at the manger. That was subsequently followed by the question of why the scene was so similar, why none of the Africa sculptors had, for example, added an elephant. To my convoluted answers, she responded simply, "What if there *were* elephants and tigers there, then?"

By now, Markus was impatient to leave and began throwing a fit, "All these sculptures are dumb. I'm going!" He hesitated for a split second.

"Go ahead, Markus, we'll see you outside ... don't go too far."

"Ah, I'll just go home."

"Fine, if you can't wait a few more minutes for us, then go."

I turned to Eliza, and asked which of them she liked the best.

"Oh ... I like the bright one, from Brazil the best. What about you?"

"The one from Brazil is very bright, but I like the one from Iceland the best — they've painted the faces nicely."

Eliza then pointed to the sheep in one of the scenes and said, "Why do they look like rabbits? They have such big ears." We concluded that Tahiti was a bit shy of sheep, so the artists had to guess a little.

As we exited the cathedral, we heard the thumping of concert speakers, so we went in the direction of the sound, and ended up in *Doma Laukums* 'Dome Square.' Dome Square is a cobblestone square approximately one hundred yards by eighty yards in size, next to the Dome Church. It did not always look like a stately "piazza" that one finds by the hundreds in Italy. This square had been the work of Kārlis Ulmanis, the last pre-war president of the inter-war Republic[6].

Tonight, President Ulmanis, as well as Leonid Brezhnev, would have been shocked to see the crowd of several thousand gyrating not to stirring speeches but to loud acoustic rhythms. The music was mostly Latvian rock, with one "Sleighride" thrown in, for variety. People of all ages were crowding the square, celebrating a holiday which two years earlier was not publicly recognized and listening to rock that was undeniably "anti-socialist." Two years earlier, riot police would have disbursed these people with tear gas and bullets, while the event organizers would have been sentenced to a term in prison. Tonight, everyone was just enjoying the concert. After fifteen minutes of wandering, we headed back to the apartment, to find that Markus had arrived just a few minutes earlier, and had managed to summarize the whole thing to his mother in one word — "boring."

Christmas sales were weak. A snowstorm erupted on the twenty-fourth; apparently people from other parts of town who might have ventured in simply didn't bother to.

The following week I stopped at the Danish embassy to gather the crates, collect information on the cookies and wish the diplomats a happy New Year. I was told that the party was a success. As to the quality of the cookies, I was assured by the Danish first secretary that "the *Anglakakor* were really good."

"Like home-made?" I asked jokingly.

"Oh no . . . *not* home-made," started the first secretary, with a deadpan expression on his face. "Uh-oh, now I'm in trouble, I've just insulted his Mom," I whispered.

"They were like the *Anglakakor* that my Mother *thought* she was making."

Footnotes

1 "House of Administration," or Namu Parvalde, was responsible for the administration, management, and repair of properties within a strictly defined geographic area, usually encompassing some 50,000-100,000inhabitants.

2 The citizens of the Baltic States have a penchant for consuming a lot of coffee.From my observations it was Italian-strength coffee, in U.S.-sized cups, drunk with Prussian efficiency. Although no statistics were available for Estonia, Latvia, and Lithuania at that time, Finland, the northern neighbor of the Baltics, ranked #1 in the world for per-capita consumption of coffee in the early 1990s. The Coffee Companion, Quintet Publishing Limited, London, 1995. Pg. 82.

3 'Rossini' consisted of two round pieces of hollowed and baked meringue, filled with an apricot-and-whipped-cream mixture, fused together with a sugar glaze, then coated with white chocolate. The only drawback to this otherwise ideal accompaniment to an espresso was its shape, which prompted the question from perky artists (among our more frequent customers) of what specific part of the composer's anatomy did this confectionary represent?"

4 The first records establish the existence of the church in 1209; that structure was burned down in 1215. In 1408 Johan Ruhmenschotel rebuilt the spire, in a 'high Gothic' style, again exclusively from wood. It burned exquisitely. Robert Bindeschue appeared in 1491, to replace it with a 137-meter-high spire, making it the highest wooden structure in Europe. It didn't burn; in 1666 it collapsed. That spire was replaced by something more modest, which the city's fathers kept around for seventy years. Finally, J. Wulbern rebuilt it between 1736 and 1744. Although his initial construction lasted only two years, the Roccoco spire that he replaced it with lasted a record 195. But on St. Peter's day in 1941, a German artillery shell caught the spire, and it once again burned down, taking with it the entire cathedral. Eventually, the Soviets cleaned out the burned remnants of the interior, and re-built the spire in metal, installing an elevator inside in the process. The elevator is in use today, and the view onto the Old Town from the spire is well worth the wait.

[5] 'Der Tannenbaum,' or in English, 'Oh Christmas Tree'; the original melody for this tune was composed by Richard Wagner during his sojourn in Riga as theatre conductor. The original melody, since modified, was based on Latvian folk melodies.

[6] In 1934, the area was congested with nondescript tenement buildings, which were divided only by a busy traffic and tramway intersection. The National Radio had a balcony overlooking the intersection. Karlis Ulmanis decided that large crowds should be able to gather on the cobblestone square to hear his addresses to the nation and that the massive cathedral walls should be the backdrop. He subsequently had the nondescript apartment buildings razed. He did, however, leave the tramway intersection.It took the Second World War to destroy that. The Soviet postwar leadership (in one of the few acts that could be deemed to have been of benefit to Riga), did not replace the tramway tracks in this square, or in any of Old Town for that matter, and closed all of the charming cobblestone streets to thru-traffic, making it one of the largest pedestrian zones of any "old town" in Europe.

13

DEEP-FREEZE

TWO OF THE ANGOLAN STUDENTS studying at the Latvian Medical Academy meet after a year. The first says, "So, how do you like the 'winter' thing?" The second replies, "Well the green one's O.K. — but the white one is...unbearable." This joke was making the rounds of the European community in January. The Americans were less prosaic; Riga was "nice" but suffered from having only three seasons — June, July and Winter, according to several diplomats. Eighteen degrees below zero (centigrade — 0 degrees Fahrenheit) allows the cells of meat, fruits and other vegetables to stay intact, and thereby retain their "moistness" when they thaw out. On the other hand, for a living human, it is a degree of coldness that marks the divide between "refreshingly crisp weather for skiing" and "a justifiable reason for low-level anxiety." If your car stalls in the middle of nowhere — of which there is a surprising lot in Latvia — your discovered corpse, with blood cells intact, will be thawing out over several days.

In the baking business, it meant trying to adjust output to the weather forecast. A perfect match could be assured, if one observed these simple rules:

1) On the first day of a big freeze, no one wandered outside; no sales.
2) On the second day of a big freeze, people wandered outside at the end of the day only, in small numbers, and consumed pastries and cakes in moderate quantities.

129

3) On the third day of a big freeze, people made beelines to the nearest café to eat pastries and cakes all day long, as if they had been castaways for the last three years. The economy of Costa Rica received a 10 percent surplus on account of increased coffee bean exports to Latvia one of these days.

4) In the event of a sudden warming, people also wandered outside in hordes, but avoided bakeries like anthrax-infused envelopes. Sudden warming occurred on the eve of the second day or the third day after the first day of a big freeze.

6) If it snowed, no matter what day, sales would be — as a sign of solidarity — glacial.

7) The day after a snow, people bought pastries and cakes as if they had received information that on the next day, bakeries would be wiped off the face of the earth.

8) If the weather turned warm enough to thaw snow, people's interest in pastries and cakes disappeared entirely.

9) The weather forecasts in Latvia in 1993 were as dependable as a Dotcom's future earnings were in 2000.

We had, apparently, applied these guidelines successfully, as the turnover of the bakery grew steadily over the six-month period. Nonetheless, the results of the first half-year of sales showed a small loss. It was nothing alarming, but pointed to the fact that there were problems tied to high fixed costs, in relation to the output. In spite of the fact that at Christmas time, a few customers had come all the way across town to purchase items at The Merry Baker, Zigrīda and I knew that we really needed another location. To-date, neither the official "proposals" nor Zigrīda's search — through a tangled grapevine of friends and relatives — had produced any fruit. Her sister knew the whereabouts of a number of cheap, vacant spaces, but apparently due to her having been a rat or a mole in one or more of her previous lives, the spaces were all in basements.

We finally decided to pay a visit to the same municipality that had awarded and then retracted our victory. On the third Monday in January, we went to the deputy chairwoman of the committee that assigned leases to companies. Zigrīda accompanied me. The chairwoman's deputy smiled when we arrived.

"We *really* like your products… they're quite delicious… but unfortunately, the other company had submitted a truly large-scale development plan…"

I bit my lip.

"We simply hadn't seen that they had included the other address in their proposal. However, we would be happy to offer you others. But you'll need an 'entry ticket.'"

"Fine, where do we buy one?" I asked.

She turned her gaze to Zigrīda. Zigrīda understood implicitly and asked the lady, "And how much might the ticket cost?"

"Well, it's about five thousand dollars for a really good spot."

"Are there any guarantees that the spot won't belong to a private person, a house-owner?[1]"

"None."

"We just don't work that way … what else can you offer?"

The councilwoman then began suggesting other locations. With each, I would confer with Zigrīda, to pinpoint where it was. Most were unacceptable because of their location. Others would require The Merry Baker to build its own store from the ground up. At that point, kiosks were not part of our strategy — we simply couldn't imagine how it would be possible, given the currently available building materials, to insulate and heat a little kiosk with an open window when the temperature outside reached minus ten degrees Fahrenheit. Pastries and breads were one of a few products that did not benefit from cold storage. Finally, she asked if it would be acceptable for us to do some renovation on the space prior to using it. I replied that perhaps that would be acceptable. It depended entirely on the location.

She offered us a spot on Alfrēda Kalniņa street. Alfrēda Kalniņa was currently a quiet street, bisecting two of the busiest streets in the city. The space was forty meters from the most popular park in Riga. The space was also across the street from the back of the Riga Circus. I imagined that we could expect a regular pre-show business from the entertainers.

"Yes."

She recommended that we take a look first, but that the municipality would need a response within forty-eight hours. I agreed. I walked out relieved. The City Council of the Central district had redeemed itself. So as not to lose time, I viewed the site that very evening. I noted with satisfaction the pedestrian traffic flowing steadily by on the intersecting street — what I thought was a hop, skip and jump away. The next day, we tried to get the keys, but to no avail. The administrator in charge of the buildings in the center said that it was with the "superintendent of plumbers," but that I could rest assured that the space was "first-rate." I had Valdis search out the "superintendent of plumbers," whom he finally found at the end of the next day. When we asked for the keys, this plumber-of-all-plumbers replied that the keys were at his summer dacha and that he wouldn't be able to get them, alas, until the weekend. However, he said that the space did indeed have some beautiful vaults in it, as well as a good electrical supply — twenty kilowatts. The latter excited me, insofar as my experience to-date had been that the median supply to a store was about two kilowatts. This supply of current was about enough to emulate a medieval apothecary, assuming one had plenty of candelabras and bearskins, but about 15 percent of the minimal requirements of a normal store anywhere in Europe, even North Eastern Europe. The master plumber further explained that he was in possession of the keys at this point because there was a broken pipe under the space and that subsequently, a little water had seeped into the space, but that otherwise, it was a "fine space" — perfect for a sauna as well. "Well," I said to myself after this meeting, "what the heck, a little seepage we could take care of... and this will make for a splendid summer location, so I'll risk it."

At ten o'clock the next day, we came to the administrator of the space. He smiled and prepared a two-year contract. At only two lats per square meter per month, the rent was low. I had agreed to meet with Valdis, on the following Tuesday. By then he was to have gotten the keys from the plumber. That Tuesday afternoon, the door to the half-basement was finally opened. I stepped down three steps, but couldn't go further — the water must have been knee-, if not waist-deep. Valdis surmised that it couldn't be sewage, because the water had only a slightly unpleasant odor. We also concurred that to go further, we would need rubber boots... along with a definition of "seepage."

The next day, with boots on, we walked through the main rooms. I asked Valdis what he thought.

"There's a bit of water, here."

"Really Valdis, I always thought that a 'tea room' was called as much because you waded through the tea to get to your table. Yes it's *clear* that there's water, but *why* is it here, and how come there's so much of it?"

"Don't know, I'll have to ask... it depends if it's from a leak, or from the walls. It doesn't smell like *fekaliya*, so maybe it's just seepage."

"And what does that mean in terms of renovation?"

"The entire wall has to be reconstructed and waterproofed."

I then noticed that the only item above the waterline besides the electric panel was a toilet. I envisioned how our customers would triumphantly end their meals. When the Daugava river floods or the Ķegums dam breaks, and all the basements in the city are flooded, our clients won't have to worry. They might have to wade to the counter, and drink their coffee underwater from a "Bodum" Cafetiere... *but* they'll be high-and-dry when they piddle.

I asked Valdis to find out the approximate cost of the renovation. Two days later, he gave me a full report. The problem had to do with a backed-up pipe that took all water, including drainage, from the building to the street. It apparently could be changed easily enough, but the front yard would have to be dug up. The following day Valdis inspected the street pipe, which should have carried the drainage from the building. It was also cracked, and had, he surmised, not been touched since before the war. In short, we were being asked to replace thirty meters of municipal piping that would have to take ten tons of *fekaliya* per week — out to the middle of the street. This quantity was about fifty times more than all our future customers could produce at their most regular moments.

During that same week in January, the circus' winter season restarted. During this half of the season, the circus planned to host several new acts. One included a troupe of tiger trainers. There wasn't enough space in the parking lot of the circus, so they parked across the street . . . in front of our subject building. Some gypsies decided that they should park their wooden carriage behind the tiger trucks. On that Friday, when I came to do a final assessment on the space with Valdis, I saw three circus trailers parked in front, surrounded by gypsies in brightly colored garb. As Valdis recounted to me why the replacement of the pipes would run some $20,000, four little children — dark-complexioned and dressed in tattered, soiled clothes — approached me. "A few rubles please, for food," they whined. It dawned on me that with this group of customers, we wouldn't get far; it was time for the board to meet and discard this refuse of a project.

We heard, some six months later, that the space had been rented, drained of water and being used as a safe house for one of the Mafiya gangs. The rumor was confirmed a year later when in these premises the police discovered two swollen corpses, with gunshot wounds to their heads.

Footnotes

[1] Previous (pre-war) owners or people that could confirm a blood relationship to said pre-war owners had the first rights to privatize buildings and land. Once the privatization board of the municipality accepted the validity of the papers proving ownership, no other leases could be signed between the current lessees of the space and the municipality. At the termination of the current lease, the lessee had to sign an agreement directly with the building's owner. The new landlords, in 1993, were developing a reputation for indiscriminately dumping out the previous lessees and taking on new ones even if the former had conscientiously redone their interiors and added significant value to the space. Since the longest municipal lease was for a three-year period, the situation did not inspire a great deal of confidence that investments in renovation could be recouped. On the other hand, if the buildings' pre-war owners were not going to appear before 1995 to privatize them, and the buildings had not been municipal or government-owned buildings before the war, then these municipal buildings could, at that point, be privatized by the existing tenants. Oftentimes, the latter could be done using "certificates" or a certificate/cash combination, which put the actual costs of purchase at a quarter or less of market value. In short, leases from the municipality were a big gamble, which could result either in large losses, or windfall gains.

14

TRANSFERS OF WEALTH

I TRIED NOT TO LET the difficulty in getting retail space slow the company's growth. As a result of personal selling activity I managed to get the Danish and other pastries on the breakfast buffet tables in one of the best hotels of the city. Five other restaurants also ordered the breads and cakes from The Merry Baker" or the wholesale wing of operation. Thanks to inventive use of orange and almond essences, our *Siera Kūka* cheesecake was a leading seller.

However, I wasn't able to reach the stability in production output of employees, in quality of product, and in understanding "service" that I felt that I would need to make the business viable. I was "challenged" by the personnel available. Generous incentive plans and training programs were not succeeding in overcoming problems. I was discovering, that — to coin a phrase from Voltaire — the problem with common sense, is that it is not common; in Latvia's food sector, it was employed sparingly.

For example, one morning in February, Valdis informed me that an oven had "sprouted legs." Having seen an oven standing outside the warehouse a few days earlier, I wondered if it might not have been the same that had "sprouted legs." I asked him to explain.

"Well, I had moved both ovens out of the bakery at Avotu street thirty-one, to the bakery at Avotu street seventy-six. More precisely, I had taken out one window, and squeezed one oven into the space where it was supposed to be. The other one we had left on the street. And yesterday afternoon, the oven was *no longer there!*"

"Valdis ... so what're you saying happened to the oven?!"

"Well, it was placed in front of the door, basically parallel to it ... perhaps slanting a little, but directly in front of the door ... and when we prepared to move it, you know, with my men Gera, Valdi, Ronalds and myself, well, how should I put it ... the oven was, so to speak ... *gone.* It was no longer visible — at least to my eyes—"

"Whoa, *VALDIS!* Shut up, please. You moved the oven out of the bakery five days ago. Ovens like that, on streets like this, don't become *invisible* after four days. Ovens that are put outside for five days, in neighborhoods like this — *get stolen!* Is *THAT* what happened?"

"Well, given the circumstances, it would seem that all the evidence we have at this point in time and space does appear to lead us in that general direction—"

"Right ... now, Valdis, all the evidence that we have at this point in time and space leads me to the conclusion that either you believe in extraterrestrials and their ability to make two-cubic-meter ovens vanish from the streets, *or,* that you do not wish to continue your relationship with the company by failing to take responsibility for an action of *yours.* Either find the oven, or pay for it!"

Valdis looked down at his shoes. His face reddened. He nodded his head slowly. The oven was not crucial for production at this point, but I speculated that when the existing ovens would incur problems, there would be a wild, frenzied hunt for spare parts.

On the following day, Valdis arrived to the meeting bearing his customary sheepish grin and black leather tote-all. He was in good spirits.

"I think that I have what you want."

"The oven?"

"Well no, not that. But we do have the space for the accounting department."

"Oh, really?"

"Yes, I got a signed lease from the rightful owner ... for two dollars per square meter."

"Good price, how'd you do it?"

"For a bottle."

"I don't get it."

"Well, you see, he's an *alkash* [alcoholic], and I offered him a bottle of vodka."

"But wait — a bottle of vodka, and you can get a flat?"

"No, not always — it depends on how desperate the alkie is."

Then I reflected on this business-deal-a-la-Soviet, and asked Valdis what would happen if someone were to offer the alcoholic *two* bottles. Valdis responded that we wouldn't care anymore — we had his signature on the contract.

"Right, Valdis, but what I'm asking is: are you sure that this is the only contract, or are we going to have to take this up in court with fifteen other suckers that supported his drinking habit?"

"No, no, he assured me that I was the *only* lessee."

We went to look at the space, and I was treated to a fine sight indeed. I entered a room, which had not received any renovation to speak of since the end of the last century. The room had slanting walls, adorned with wallpaper, or more precisely, groupings of wallpaper, on a wall that in other places was imprinted with a crude *fleur-de-lis* pattern throughout. The walls and floor were painted, respectively, in the official "stepping in it" colors of the soviet era — dog manure ochre and cow-dung brown. As I walked towards the other end, everyone's eardrums were dominated by the creak of old, sagging floorboards. I tripped twice over islands of linoleum that had been too well fastened to be removed by an axe/hammer. But in the corner stood the *piece de resistance* — a wood-burning stove covered with the original gray-silver paint. On it were etchings, carved throughout the decades, preserved through neglect. There was a call to arms for revolutionaries: "Crush to death all Trotskyites"; part of the first line of a revolutionary hit song: "A bullet to the head…"[1] To the left was a large Easter rabbit, sitting comfortably in a basket of expletives; next to it a banal "*Vasya* was here." The stove not only afforded the only heat in the room, but also had a convenient little shelf protruding from its side, for the placement of a tea kettle.

"Good work, Valdis, in finding it, now how quickly do you think it will be done?"

"Done?" he asked, as if I had posed him a rhetorical question.

"Yes, re-no-va-tion finished… you don't expect the accountants to work in these conditions, do you? We know they're only accountants, but still!"

Valdis was taken aback, no less than would the owner of the Ritz Carlton at the hint that his establishment was wanting in interior design. We then agreed that the space would be repainted, floor redone, and the minimal amenities added.

Footnotes

[1] "to all who seek to oppress us." This was the first verse of a Soviet song.

15

RETAILING MADNESS

ALMOST EVERY EVENING OF THAT winter, I brooded over what else we could do — besides obtaining a new location — to improve sales. In February, I had several ideas. One morning, I called Zigrīda aside to ask if she wouldn't have a minute to discuss some things that could improve sales.

"All right, gladly," she replied. I started in Russian about how shiny metal trays looked much better than plastic ones and subsequently made the cakes appear more valuable. Zigrīda noted this. Then, in one of my rare moments of overconfidence, boosted by the Latvian-strength coffee, I decided to continue in Latvian, to describe the Merry Baker "cake catalog." I thought I was saying the following:

"Clients are kings. They want to know what they are buying. When they see a pretty cake, they want to know what is on the inside. They want to know if they would *like* what is on the inside. For example, there might be peanuts inside, and a customer doesn't like peanuts. Or maybe there are poppy seeds, and he doesn't want to eat poppy seeds, because he is going to a meeting in the afternoon and he doesn't want black things on his teeth. Same with hazelnuts, chocolate, and so on — he might not like the taste. Therefore he must know what is inside the torte. *That* is why there must be a catalogue. Now, not all our products should necessarily be listed in the catalogue — just the main ones, our 'permanent' selection. And furthermore, we don't need to list absolutely *all* the ingredients of the cakes in the catalogue..."

At this point, Zigrīda burst in, "Say it in Russian — it'll be easier for you." Obligingly, I started again, but wondered why the agitation. What I was actually saying, I discovered later after conscientiously analyzing my pre-meeting notes, was closer to the following:

"Clients are stomachs! They see a pretty pastry. They want to know how the interior of the room [is decorated]. They want to see... if they have affection for these groceries. Maybe there are peanuts inside [the room], and a person doesn't [carnally] desire peanuts. Maybe there are some poppy-seeds in our [store] interior, but a person doesn't want to eat poppy-seeds. Maybe he is going to a 'little rendezvous' in the afternoon and he doesn't want black things on his sword. The same with hazelnuts, chocolate, bananas and so on. That's why he [must be] a catalog. Not all of our groceries must be in the catalog, just the 'all-time' pastries. And not *all* the [construction] materials that we use in the cakes must be in the catalog. Just the main ones..."

When I got to the point of descriptions of the cake ingredients, she interjected "What?! You mean, describe what's inside?! Won't our competitors steal the idea, steal the recipe?"

"Well, Zigrīda, we don't have to put *exactly* everything. It's natural, isn't it, after all these years of everything being hidden, that we begin telling customers things about ingredients — it communicates honesty..."

"Sure... if they believe it."

"Well, let them try a few times. After they taste this, then they will see that we write only what is true."

I then moved on to describe what might be done to improve the exterior, again getting a kick from the caffeine, and, switching to Latvian, "We want to make... place look alive... fresh. Plants work well for that." Zigrīda looked at me inquisitively. "I mean, not big ones, but little ones — different colors. You know mostly just green, but can be white, pink." Zigrīda nodded and then asked, "Who'll take care of them, for example, when the store is closed, or when they get sick?" "If they get sick, well, we just replace them." She continued, staring, and I interpreted this as a Latvian's disbelief at the foreign man's disdainful approach to plants and trees, which are sacred in the pagan backdrop of Latvia.[1] Finally, when the store clerks could no longer suppress a giggle, I asked what I had said. "Little birds,'" they humbly replied.

I couldn't fool the storekeepers and I couldn't fool Zigrīda. The merchandising could help a little, but our primary salvation would have to come in the way of a new space. In February my co-directors "found" three locations. The first location, at the *Vidzemes* market, had the sanitary appeal of a Turkish toilet in a Marseilles slum. The second so-called "fine" location was across the central entrance from a topless bar. The third location was behind the train station, next to a hotel from whose lobby emanated the mixed stench of degenerating livers, cigarette smoke and unlaundered socks, and whose rooms boasted beds of no more than five-and-a-half feet in length. That particular hotel would later be described, in "Riga-in-Your-Pocket" — one of the more frank tourist guides, as a perfect residence for unwashed thieving midgets, who could hear when the next train was coming, to better make a quick getaway.

Zirida Auza. Director of Retail Operations. Personnel.

The three of us then went to assess a bakery in Yuriy's former factory site. It was located on the side of a building that faced the industrial park entry road. The current lessee of the bakery complex was leaving. During the course

of the lunch hour, not one person walked by. I asked Valdis, if he didn't think
that this lack of walk-by traffic might have something do with the fact that
the nearest residential area to this industrial complex was over four hundred
meters away on the other side of a large, muddy, construction site.

"Yes, perhaps you're right, but what about the internal clients?"

"What about 'em?"

Valdis turned to the *brigadirs*, who was showing us the place. She was a
stocky woman, with wrinkles in her face that bespoke an endless suppression
of any instinct that might have allowed her to smile at some time before the
last ice age.

"Well, Irina Jakovlevna, how many people are still working here?"

Her face remained motionless. At the same time, her eyes were shifting
nervously from left to right, as if to say, "Why bloody hell, what's it matter to you?
And if I say the wrong number, then you'll probably tell the boss, right? And then
he'll call me in and say, 'Irina Jakovlevna, how come you gave *disinformation* to
these good people, my friends' — or else he'd say, Irina Jakovlevna, why in the
world did you tell these strangers how many workers actually remain here? Who
are these people? If they were *spies*, would you then tell them where we are
sending our hydraulic moving stairs? Perhaps you would give away all secrets...
let them poison the water wells, would you?"

So Irina replied in a half whisper, with fits and starts, "Well, there is still
that division... making the stairway mechanisms — how many people is that,
Vladimir Ivanovich? ..." throwing the question back at Valdis.

"Maybe three hundred now ... O.K., one hundred fifty ..."

"Then there are the stores... I don't know how many people there are —
look for yourselves."

I ended the information-extracting session as quickly as possible by
calculating out loud that 250 persons did not constitute a client base unless
they purchased twice a day, "each and every one of them."

"But Boriss, have you looked at the equipment — it's quite... productive,
isn't it? They appear to be making a high-quality bread," he added, sizing up
the French-made equipment, which was churning out some four hundred
baguettes at that moment.

"Yes, Valdis ... but then why is he leaving the business?" He dropped his
gaze to the floor and shook his head, "I can't tell you why."

Once again, we left with nothing. But I proceeded, naively, to trust that luck
would come our way soon. That night, I shared my concern about not finding
another location with Inge.

"I understand. I wish I could help you, but I have no ... connections. You know, Boriss, I know it's hard, trying to do what you do without bribing people. I ... I just wanted you to know that I respect you for that. It's not the way things work here now, but they *will*. I don't know how to say this, but ... I think that you're doing the right thing ... Really."

"Thanks, Inge, thanks."

I decided that the next best thing would be to literally knock on the doors of the shops in areas that were desirable and inquire as to the status of the location. I asked my secretary, Viya, to accompany me, as to make sure that there would be no language problems. At the same time, I felt that by going together as a young couple, we would also disarm some of the more suspecting people, whereas if I were to go alone, I would once again be perceived as a foreign capitalist. By now, post-Soviet slang had evolved enough to include foreign businessmen. The term was *firma* 'firm,' and by it was meant that like any firm, we had capital. Some individuals were hell-bent on convincing us to part with it, for one reason — such as a *velikolepnaya* 'great' investment — or another, such as fear, as the kind that could be generated by holding weapons in front of the *firma*[2]. As we walked down *Bruņinieku iela* 'Knights' Street,' I noticed two new convenience stores, a film development store and a lingerie boutique amongst the myriad of Soviet shops, which were still in the throes of the better-look-like-a-tombstone-dealership-in-a-ghost-town-than-a-store-that-might-attract-customer-vermin Soviet merchandising ethic. The former four had painted door and window frames. They also had brighter lighting outside; one even boasted some window decorations.

But we weren't interested in these finished, rented spaces. As we arrived at our first destination, a space that was in the process of being renovated, I asked the security guard for the construction foreman. The latter was a thin, gaunt fellow with a piercing look. Viya started.

"Hello I noticed that you're finishing this space — do you know where I could find the owner?"

"No."

"Is there an owner?"

"I ... No, no. Yeah, there is an owner ... but he comes only once in a while."

"Do you know if he's already rented this space out?"

"I dunno ... ," he said as he looked down on the ground, "but he says that there's gonna be a store here."

"Yes? So he's looking for someone to make a store here?"

"Yeah, he keeps saying — pretty undergarments, pretty undergarments ..."

"Oh, I see. Well, if he hasn't yet rented it out, perhaps you could leave him my card."

As we turned onto *Čaka* street, I saw the first indisputably "enticing" establishment in the entire neighborhood — the *Ali Baba Casino*. As I looked down both sides of the street, I also counted four photo development stores, and two more lingerie boutiques. I wondered why I hadn't noticed those before... anyway — "Well, Viya, you'll certainly have no shortage of places to recommend for your boyfriend to buy you that 'little something special.'" "No," she said as she lowered and then shook her head, smiling, as if I had uncovered an amusing secret. In fact, by the looks of it, there were enough "little something specials" for every woman, man and child in the city. Our next stop was an old soviet scissor-sharpener's shop, which seemed completely preserved, with even the twenty-year-old sign intact. As we walked in, the old store proprietor looked up without raising his head more than a quarter of an inch. Viya started, with hesitation in her voice, "Hello, sir... we... we were just, uh, wondering about the premises—"

"The lease is expired, the owner took the building back, and it's going to be some camera store. What more do you want to know?" he barked.

"Not much, just... how do you know that it's going to be a camera store?"

"They said a camera store... Phooey, Phooey, Phooey."

I turned and asked Viya if that sounded like more cat belyashi to her.

"No, in Latvian, that could be Fu-I, or F-u-u-i, or F-u-j-i."

"Thanks Mr. Goldmanis, good luck at your future location."

We then walked further along *Bruņinieku street*. We noticed a barbershop whose doors had closed, and a sign that read, "Closed for remodeling." We saw someone moving around inside and waved through the window. "This is a guy — go ahead, Viya, ask him what's happening."

"Hello, we were just wondering, is this going to be a barbershop as well after remodeling?"

"Naw," said the unshaven security guard. "Gonna be a bar . . . and a fish store."

"Wait, Viya . . . a bar and a fish store?" I interjected. "Yeah."

"In the same space? He's gotta be kidding..." I whispered, while trying to unravel the logic of this combination.

I asked her to confirm, assuming that I hadn't understood something precisely. She asked again, then turned to me and confirmed that we had heard correctly. It was going to be a bar together with a fish store. As we walked out, Viya said that it seemed an odd combination for her as well. I then tried to envision that combination, and to what end. I imagined a man going to the store on assignment by his spouse, "Get some salmon for the family and fish for the cat." Aha, but you can get salmon that is lightly smoked, hickory-smoked, lightly salted, and Leslie-salt-barge-salted — a tough decision. As concerns fish for the cat — there's the *Putasoo* and *Renges*[3]. The former would need to be thawed out and boiled but the cat wouldn't eat *Renges* cooked. It's clear, poor hubby would need a stiff drink before making *those* decisions. One wrong choice and the wife would be screaming at him about how he's a useless loafer, always coming back drunk and *never* bringing back the right fish — better prepare for the worst. Viya was amused but not terribly convinced that my interpretation was correct. I decided to ask Valdis about this later.

The results of the day yielded no available space, except for a handful of basements and . . . a space on the "first floor" that required so many stairs to walk up that it was a veritable second floor. I was amused at the possibility of drawing a square on the sidewalk in which our treasured customers would stand, to receive their previously ordered torte from a height of fifteen feet: "Ready, steady, Mrs. Littledeer, here comes your German Chocolate t-o-r-t-e . . . hmm, not such a good catch this time. Well, good thing you didn't order a five-kilo torte, have a nice day now!"

Inge had been called upon to attend a reception sponsored by the WHO, and the kids were in Ogre with the grandparents, so I was alone for the evening. I didn't mind much, as I was exhausted. Perhaps out of frustration, I ate more than half of a shepherd pie, along with two tomatoes that had been snagged from refrigerator-induced wet rot at the last possible moment, and settled into the couch to start watching another episode of *Men's Hour*.

"Fish and liquor . . . what next?" I thought to myself. The soldiers in fatigues doing training exercises around a wooden tank were failing to hold my attention and I dozed off.

But over the next few days, I couldn't shake my curiosity about this obsession with photo shops, gambling casinos and lingerie shops. I asked people about this over the course of the week and they obliged me with several different theories. The most believable one concerning the photo development stores was that color prints were a novelty. In Soviet times, most shops developed only black-and-white pictures, and even that was done over the span of three days. Color picture development was done in only a few places, was exorbitantly expensive and the results quickly faded to a sepia brown, which looked worse than black-and-white photos. Furthermore, one of Hungary's richest entrepreneurs had started his accumulation of vast wealth with a chain of photo development boutiques[4]. These factors, along with the absolutely minimal manual labor or merchandising know-how necessary for automatic film developing, apparently encouraged entrepreneurs from all walks of life to open up photo boutiques.

The gambling casinos turned out to be about the best method of earning windfalls, for those with more starting capital. In the absence of an uncorrupt gaming commission to guarantee the pay out of a certain portion of turnover in winnings, this venue also turned out to be effective in laundering money.

The lingerie stores were purely a money-laundering tool of the Mafiya, with the added perk of providing a source of "gifts" for mistresses. Prices in the stores were astronomical, but the goal was not turnover or even sales of *any kind*. In fact, the more customers there were, the more of a headache for the owners, was what one World Bank specialist later told me. The goal of having a money-laundering retail operation was to be able to prove to the tax authorities the capability of generating a good turnover on the sale of a relatively few items. In that way, the tax authorities couldn't prove the necessity of having a high monthly turnover by linking it with something so patently absurd as ... customer traffic.

As to the bar and fish store, Valdis chuckled when I asked him the question. He answered, "Well, Boriss, how can I say this. In our part of the world, after a good *vypivka* 'drinking session,' nothing is more natural to consume, than a nice salty fish. Some say that herring compensates for vitamin loss ..."

Footnotes

[1] Tree worship is a fundamental aspect of life for this Indo-European people. Pagan ceremonies continue to be enacted to this day. For example, hugging an oak tree while facing another one across the road is supposed to bring positive cosmic energy. It is a tradition for every newlywed couple to plant a tree for the family. The couple must visit the tree on an annual basis during the course of their married life. Especially common are oaks and linden trees, with the former representing the men of the family and the latter, women.

[2] At about this time, one German radio correspondent was rudely surprised by the appearance of masked gunmen at the front door of his apartment. The gunmen relieved him of all his cash and spare valuables. The apartment building had two armed security guards at the time.

[3] Putasoo and Renges are two common fish found in the Baltics, the latter being a genus of mackerel.

[4] By 1995, Gābor Vārszegi, the president of the Fotex company, was the wealthiest entrepeneur in the retail sector of Hungary. But tales of his transition from rock musician-to-retail-mogul had spread throughout Central Europe well before that.

16

RIGA GOIN'WEST

INGE HAD MANAGED TO GET a very impressive posting, by local standards, with the World Bank in Latvia. As assistant program administrator, she was responsible for a good deal of the program administration, designed to provide loans to the country. She was delighted with her new job and now made me promise to speak only English at home. In fact I was a bit weary of trying to communicate all the time in Russian and/or my dismal Latvian, so I welcomed the opportunity to slip into English.

Outside of home, new opportunities surfaced as well. In 1992, the only English-speakers that I met were part of the diplomatic corps. I hadn't met anyone like myself. Unlike Moscow, which positively teemed with Englishmen and Americans at that time, Riga didn't seem to have any anglophiles. Walking along the street, one would only encounter Latvian and Russian languages, with an occasional smattering of Swedish. Towards the end of March there was a reception at the ambassador's residence, for members of the budding American business community. The topic was about the needs of the community, and whether or not the embassy could be of assistance in filling those needs, and the establishment of an American Chamber of Commerce. Just speaking my mother tongue would have been incentive enough for me to go, but as the embassy had also ordered goods from The Merry Baker for the reception — including some very pricey "Napoleon Hats" and other marzipan-based confectioneries — I was *definitely* going to attend. The reception was held in the drawing room of the ambassador's residence. Comfortably seated around the periphery were fifteen more men — most in their early thirties — and one woman. We were invited by the ambassador to take a glass of wine and some of the hors d'ouevres before sitting down. He subsequently delivered a brief introduction and opened the floor to questions and concerns that we might have, in our roles as entrepreneurial trailblazers. J.C. Cole, the director of a property development company, started the discussion by saying that the issue of not being able to obtain a long-term visa is rather serious. "More precisely," he stated, "I cannot seem to get a work visa, although they have waived infractions of overstaying a tourist visa, and don't seem to have a problem with the fact that I am working while having only this visa. However, I'm uncomfortable with the uncertainty of it." The ambassador, an American of Latvian descent, replied, "I think that this is an issue that may be troubling several of you. Jay[1], would you be able to follow-up this week on the request that we had made for a regularization of procedures for the working visa." "Yes, certainly. I've contacted Mr. Ozoliņš about it, and he promised to get back to me at the beginning of next week. But, if you were to provide us, uh, with a list of those American employees in your companies, we can focus the government's attention on the, uh, authenticity of the issue — and that we're not talking about an army of workers." All were visibly pleased that the embassy had been so proactive on this issue. Attendees mentioned another few inconveniences and they were duly noted by the Chargè d'Affaires.

Then Arnie, a Russian who had emigrated in the '80s to the United States, spoke up, "Yes, I hev one beeg prooblem — ven I go to restaurant here lest veek, some civeel guard man held masheen gun to my hyead — sed me thet I must get out of cauntry. I don't understand, there eez police, there eez army, but what is zeess 'zemessargs'?!" A stone silence fell over the crowd, including the ambassador. Everyone stared at Arnie. While most others were dressed in Brooks Brothers suits or their equivalents, Arnie was wearing a heavy leather jacket in which he was perspiring effusively — judging by the beads of sweat on his forehead. Furthermore, he was sporting Ray Ban sunglasses and enough bulky gold rings to make a stout woman swoon with envy — and render a slender one incapable of lifting her forearms. Unlike the previous comments, *his* did not elicit any empathetic head nodding. An embarrassing silence ensued. After about thirty seconds, Rob, a fast food entrepreneur, broke the unnerving quiet by saying (with a tone of voice that one might have used in defending an establishment when faced with complaints of overdone steaks),

"Folks, you can be assured that this won't happen to you when you come to *our* restaurant." The crowd erupted in laughter and a smile of relief spread on the ambassador's face.

As to food establishments in Riga at this time, Sol Bukingolts' and Rob Ross's "American Fried Chicken" restaurant had much to commend it. Although the restaurant was fast food at its simplest, with less chrome and far dimmer lighting than one would expect from an equivalent American establishment, it offered a crispy fried chicken and a very respectable *gumbo*. Yes, it may have paled in comparison to what one might find at Brennan's, but to encounter anything even mildly spicy or crispy in Latvia was a miracle. Of course the service was carried out with the aforementioned post-Soviet enthusiasm and courtesy, which meant that one had to be very knowledgeable as to what one wanted; ask no questions; order food with lightning-quickness and above all, order no more than two items at a time. In not fulfilling one or more of the above requirements, by the way, one would receive an "Oh God, here's another one of those idiotic customers who can't even understand what's in the @$@*%!! pictures — when do we start passing out formaldehyde for the brain-dead ones?!" glance. The interior also lacked ventilation. Since it had two-meter high plate glass windows, one could combine lunch with a sauna when the sun was shining, even on the coldest days of winter. But all-in-all, the establishment was a radical and welcome departure from the standard post-Soviet greasy-porkchop venues.

For those who were dying for a hamburger, two variations could be had in Riga. One was the *Pārsla* burger, at the train station, which was somewhat more like a good meatloaf, together with ample tomato sauce and a bit of lettuce between two buns. The burger was satisfying to the palate, but had a tendency towards a short half-life; specifically, it would go halfway down the digestive tract before coming back up. Mine made its reappearance when I was viewing one of the German situation comedies that were received by satellite antennas now available in Riga (so it took me a little while to realize that it was the burger that was inducing nausea). The booth was located on the main artery of customer traffic walking through the station, so the company no doubt made quite a fortune on first-time customers and even a handful of repeat ones.

The second variation was *Viking Burger*. This restaurant was glitzy, highly chromed and had a solid burger/fries/soda offering. However, the burgers were invariably cold, old, or slow in making their [announced] appearance. The second problem was that the burgers were served with condiments found in *no* hamburger establishments that I had ever frequented in the past. The establishment offered a runny, tasteless tomato sauce and Soviet mustard. For those that haven't experienced the latter, it is strikingly similar to the green *wasabi* horseradish that is served with sushi in other parts of the world. Any first-timer who has tried too much of it — any amount greater than what can fit comfortably on the end of a toothpick — can recall the searing pain that the tongue had endured, and the contortions that the mouth had undergone afterwards, as it repeated the exclamations: "ah, ahuHH, AHUHHH, HHNYEE, Uwahhh."

The *Viking Burger* fries were "home fries," fried at low temperatures in a cubic ton of palm oil, just the way the doctor or a good nouvelle chef would dramatically emphasize *not* doing. Napkins were also a *defitsitniy* 'in short supply' item, so one was given a glossy 3 ½ inch by 3 ½ inch square of very thin paper, coated with something waxy. As a result of the coating, the napkin was as efficient in absorbing grease as smooth Italian slate marble. I was invariably caught in the situation of asking the cashier for more napkins, or, when I was in a hurry, cleaning my fingers on a pair of pants or a worn-out tie. Furthermore, seeing the grease falling from the burgers and the fries of fellow diners at the stand-up tables hearkened a return to Neanderthal times. I half-expected, the few times that I went, that one of the fellow diners would come over to my table and try to steal my burger with the explanation, "Muffa hungry, want *EAT!*"

Besides boasting four fastfood restaurants, Riga was taking other significant steps towards rejoining the Western community of nations. For example, the Ministry of Culture applied to UNESCO with the purpose of asking that Riga be awarded the status of a "World Heritage Site" city. The Ministry took this initiative with confidence. To understand why, one needs only to see Riga's houses for one hour, when the early afternoon sun illuminates them. Mind you, in the winter, one hour is about the extent of afternoon sun that is to be had. But when it illuminates the Medusa's head or the lithe nymphs on *Elizabetes* Street, or the howling husky on *Skārņu iela*, or the man-sized gladiolus flowers adorned with a gold leaf on the corner of *Ģertrūdes* and *Čaka* streets, one cannot help but marvel at the imagination of the architects of that time. One of the more prolific and creative ones designing the art nouveau facades was Mikhail Eisenstein, father of Sergei Eisenstein.[2] He designed an entryway, framed by Jonah the whale opening its jaws, on *Tallinas iela*. On *Alberta* Street, he had drafted the blueprints for several buildings, some of which boast sphinxes, medusas, and Venuses the likes of which can be found nowhere else in the world, particularly on the house where Isaiah Berlin grew up. For two brief decades, the inhabitants of Riga said that they were rich and tired of the neo-classical styles that had dominated Second-Empire France and Italy, not to mention the utilitarian styling of old German merchants' houses. Consequently, in the span of twenty years, the city lost its Hanseatic appearance and acquired a Nouveau one.

'Elizabetes Street, 10 (Architect-M. Eisenstein)'

As luck would have it, Riga was all but unscathed by the First World War, as well as the Second one. This preservation of its architecture was about the only benefit accrued from the lightning-quick occupations of the city. Furthermore, this luck continued after the Second World War, ironically, as a result of the planned obsolescence of the city's center by the Soviet authorities. No one bothered tearing down "unfashionable" buildings and replacing them with post-modern ones. This unplanned blessing allowed the city to gain acceptance to the vaunted list of World Heritage Sites in 1997. The UNESCO Council wrote that "It is generally recognized that Riga contains the finest concentration of Art Nouveau buildings in Europe."

Footnotes

[1] Foreign service officer working on economic issues (not his real name).

[2] Sergei Eisenstein is considered one of the founders of modern cinematography. His most famous works were 'Alexander Nevsky,' 'Ivan the Terrible,' and the 'Battleship Potemkin,' which was a re-enactment of the Bolsheviks' storming of the Winter Palace.

17

REFUSE

Now there was one aspect of life in Riga that took a great deal of time for me to get used to. I saw it for the first time a few weeks after arriving in the city, when I was walking down a street to get to the apartment. I noticed a group of people ahead of me, loitering. At first, I was apprehensive. It was dusk, and a few of them were sizing me up. I've been in "situations" in New York during my studies at Columbia, and I had developed a sense for potentially dangerous groupings. But as I approached nearer, I saw some baboushki in their midst and a couple of men who were wearing *tapochki* slippers. If they were going to mug me, then fleeing quickly away afterwards was not part of the plan. These people were radically different from one another. It was as if a mental hospital had just brought out the patients they had involved in a "cross-section" study and told them to wait on the corner. As I approached within ten feet, a few of them looked at me, but most looked well past me. Then, as I passed between an old babushka and a nervous young man in a sweatsuit, they mobilized. These people bent down, and each one of them picked up a plastic bag, a plastic bucket, or a metal box, and then grouped up next to the curb. I heard a massive roar of motor behind me, as a garbage truck pulled up.

The garbage truck made its rounds everyday in Riga, just like in all modern cities. In fact the Riga trucks circulated *several* times per day. But with this, all similarities to garbage collection in the West ended. The history of this social

154

phenomenon is worth recounting. Prior to 1981, there were trucks, and they would collect containers. Just like the ones behind the restaurants in any downtown alley, these bins would be filled by inhabitants, and then lifted up and the contents would be dumped into the back compartment of the garbage truck, or into a separate truck. However, the medium-sized bins probably shouldn't have been filled as high as they had been with garbage. The unruly [advanced] socialist masses kept exceeding their norm of one-half of a cubic meter of refuse per week per household. This they did in spite of making a concerted effort to flush as much organic material as possible down the john; to recycle their glass bottles at the "glassware acceptance" booths; to use their *Pravda* newspapers as toilet paper (with or without reading beforehand); to save old clothes as rags to be washed judiciously and passed on to future generations. These activities did not suffice — the bins continued to overflow and attract rats – the gargantuan Norwegian varieties. At the same time, the slouches at the *Nizbny Novgorod* sheet metal factory #3 were not meeting their quotas of model NN-3-C city trash bins, and even if they did, the Central Planners had probably calculated reserves only for Leningrad and Moscow. They couldn't even be bothered to send replacement tops for the bins in Riga. In any event, the rats kept partying on mounds of trash, in the process growing fatter and more libidinous, like late Roman emperors.

Alfons Rubiks, the Mayor of Riga in 1981, changed the system of trash collection altogether, and so decimated the city's rat population. Overnight, it became the individual's responsibility to throw what he needed into the garbage truck. Ten years later, the procedure had been turned into a science; brown and sky-blue trucks would turn down a particular street, and stop every forty to fifty meters. People, who had been waiting tensely with their pails besides them, would run or walk briskly out and dump their garbage into the back of the truck when it pulled up. When I first saw it, the whole process reminded me of a "good humor" truck when it rolled down the street on hot summer days in the '60s in America. Only, in *this* case, pensioners took the place of the children, screeching brakes passed for the bell and a foul stench replaced the smell of ice cream. Furthermore, there was remarkably little glee or humor to be found surrounding the arrival of the truck. Although this ritual might have given an opportunity to chat with neighbors, most people were so tired of idle gab with their communal apartment neighbors, and so concerned with keeping their garbage a private matter, that they just quietly waited in discrete groups near the entryway to their buildings. Those that couldn't — either for reasons of possessing poorly developed biceps or overly developed senses of smell — hold their pail next to them, placed it on the sidewalk and stood a few steps away. When it rained, the people would take shelter under an awning or if the building had one, an archway. Those people who could afford them had plastic bags to put their garbage into ... but would take the plastic bag back home after emptying it. For this reason one often saw inverted plastic bags hanging on clotheslines above the bathtub in people's apartments. One popular rock star had a reputation for recklessness. This reputation was partly founded on the fact that "he enjoyed the feeling of throwing the entire plastic bag into the truck ... while everyone else watched on."[1]

One could pick out the more discreet garbage depositors relatively easily; they would cover their pails with a newspaper. They would wait until the rest of the dumpers finished emptying their receptacles into the back of the truck. Only then would they approach the back of the truck on tiptoes, and empty their own pails into it as quickly and forcibly as possible. Then, as if they had just tossed a grenade in the truck, they would sprint back to the sidewalk.

Others judged their neighbors' upward mobility by the remains in the pail. I saw two people once "sneaking a peek" at the empty Coca-Cola and imported liquor bottles (that marked a rise to the next socioeconomic class) of another apartment dweller. This was done with the discretion that would normally be reserved for watching a member of the opposite sex get undressed.

After the last depositor left, the garbage man who had been riding on the back of the truck would inspect the deposits, pull the lever to start compaction, and then resume his post on the back of the truck. Alternatively, this "riding" garbage man would signal to the driver, who would start the compaction from the panel in the cab. The trucks were referred to as "Rubiks-i." On account of the fact that the garbage men didn't so much as get dust — let alone garbage — on their [white] gloves, some expats termed this protocol the "immaculate collection."

What made this procedure ultimately user-friendly was the fact that of all the times of the day the truck circulated, only one of them was even vaguely suitable for working people with day shifts. On our street for example, the truck circulated at 11:00 A.M., 4:30 P.M., and 7:00 P.M. — three workdays per week.

The system was also the catalyst of my first parenting conflagration. We had agreed to share the tasks of the household. During a collective family "division-of-labor" session that we had had in January, Markus had been assigned the garbage duty, on a twice-per-week basis. He was assigned this task mostly due to the inconvenient timing of the "Rubiks" pick-up for Inge and myself, and Eliza's inability to pick up a full trash pail. On this particular day, I was to recall many times later, I was home earlier than usual, and at that moment tied up trying to light the fire in the wood-burning circa-1930s heater. I had piled up the small logs and below them laid what resembled a nest of small branches, interspersed with pieces of paper. The result, I reasoned, would make a scoutmaster's heart sing. I lit it, and it burned heartily, filling the hallway with a dense gray smoke. I closed the door, saying to myself, "Now *that's* done." Five minutes later, I opened the door, to see five or six of the small sticks charred, but the logs only lightly blackened, and the fires definitely, indisputably *out*. I needed to find the flue. I looked next to the door, then up and to the right. Finally, after more than two minutes of searching up and down the white, sporadically cracked pre-war tiles, I found a small metal knob on the side. I pulled it forward and then backward, with no results. I pulled it to the left. A gust of freezing wind hit the back of my leg. Having hit paydirt, I carefully proceeded to place the rest of the small sticks under the logs. Since they were stacked precariously at best, I moved with the precision of a Swiss watchmaker.

At that moment, I heard the screech of the garbage truck brakes. "Markus, the truck is here!" I belted out, without turning my head from the stove/heater door. After half a minute, I heard the shuffling of slippers. A second later, one of the logs fell, threatening to upset the whole balance of my incendiary architectural wonder. I grabbed the two logs that I felt were the foundation of the structure and stabilized them with two wads of tissue. I then looked around to see Markus putting on one of his shoes — which he was doing as if it were made of glass, with spider's silk laces.

"C'mon, Markus, hurry — the garbage truck won't be here forever!"

"Can I just leave my slippers on?"

"No, definitely not, we've discussed that before ... now hurry up!"

Markus took the second shoe, and with the speed of an inchworm after a feeding frenzy, wiggled his foot into it. In the meantime, I was inserting the last of the papers into the construction, which I was still holding with my other hand. I glanced behind me to see Markus picking up the overstuffed garbage pail; jerking it in the process. The top two inches, containing newspapers, banana peels and a *Bounty* wrapper, came sliding off. He bent down slowly and started studying the banana peel, as if he had never seen one before in his life.

"*MARKUS!*"

"Yeah, yeah."

The door slowly shut behind him as he left. Sure that there were no more drafts, and that the pile could stand on its own, I straightened myself and slowly moved my hand to the flue. I moved it to a half-closed position. I struck the match, and by the movement of the flame, could see that there was a sufficient, but not overwhelming, flow of oxygen. "Victory at last," I thought. I kept the door ajar, and saw the small branches slowly catching on fire.

Markus came through the door at that moment. He was carrying the garbage pail, which was just as full now as it had been two minutes earlier. "The truck left before I got to it," he said as he slowly plodded back. Now livid with rage, I said, as calmly as I could, "Markus, you missed the truck on purpose. This just shows an 'I-don't-give-a-damn' attitude towards the rest of us!" Markus shrugged his shoulders and put the garbage pail down. I then bounded across the floor, picked up the boy, and in one fluid movement laid him prostrate on the floor; I lifted my hand well over my head, and brought it squarely on his still rear end. I couldn't recall whether I hit him on the butt three or four times — but do remember timing it elegantly to the sentence: "You cannot live [whack] like a prince [whack] and have us slave [whack] for your majesty's pleasure [whack]." I then lifted him up and just as unexpectedly for the stunned boy, said: "You're a good boy, Markus, in principle ... but you just act very badly sometimes." I may as well have been telling someone sitting in the electric chair that his *real* judgement will come afterwards. Markus silently went to his room.

I struggled with what I had done for the entirety of the following day. When I returned home from work, I felt uneasy. I noticed that the garbage had been taken out. "Markus, you've done well," I said as I passed by his bedroom later. Deep down, I knew that I would feel quite uneasy when face-to-face with Inge, who had just returned from another trip abroad. At the same time, I didn't feel that I should be defensive about the incident. Yet, when I walked into the kitchen, I could sense that Inge was distressed. She put the plates forcefully on the table, and snapped, "*Why* is the *table still DIRTY*?!" at Eliza, who apparently hadn't wiped it beforehand. "Uh, oh," I realized — the word is out. After dinner, over which a morgue-like silence presided, Inge asked me to stay and talk. As I prepared the hot beverages, the minutes seemed like hours, the atmosphere thick and impenetrable, like a London fog on a warm, humid day. Shortly thereafter, we were each sitting on our respective sides of the table, one of us holding a mug of hot tea, the other of hot decaffeinated coffee, last of reserves smuggled in from Hamburg. I felt like Kasparov, up against Karpov.

"Umm ... Boriss, I don't know how to say this—"

"Is it about Markus?"

"Yes, of course. We had an agreement." She waited until the solemnity of the phrase reached me. Her voice was quivering, "Why did you beat him?"

"I spanked him ..."

"Whatever you call it. Eliza told me everything."

"I spanked him, because he continues to act like a king on a throne ... we are *not* his servants..." I seethed out, feeling the anger rise again to my cheeks.

"Yes, but there are other ways to deal with the situation, like explaining to him that his conduct is not right."

"Yes, I did, remember, last week, three times — but he still acts like this, disregarding others..."

"Then explain again—"

"And again, with no effect, until we're bobbing around like puppets. Is *that* right?! It's useless."

"Well, if you don't want to, then ... I think that it leaves no choice, but to part ... it'll be hard on us, but we'll move back to Ogre."

A painful silence followed.

"Wait, Inge, can't we resolve this another way?"

"I don't think so," she quietly said, as she got up and went to the bedroom, shutting the door behind her. I got up and walked, stopping in front of the fireplace. As I approached the door, I heard gentle, heart-stopping sobs. Realizing that my reasoning would not carry the day, I volunteered to leave. I told Inge that I would move out of the apartment, until an unforeseen time in the future, when clearer heads prevail. I took my bags, went downstairs, and hailed a cab that took me to the Rīdzene Hotel.

Footnotes

[1] From the conversation with Indra Samite, Latvian-American trailblazer in Riga and Minister of Finance, 1995.

18

EXILE

DURING THE RECEPTION THAT FOLLOWED the meeting at the embassy the previous week, I had invited Jay, the U.S. Foreign Service Officer, to go out for some drinks. I decided that the following evening would be as good as any, so I called him. He happened to be free and we agreed on a meeting at the Ala bar. It was his suggestion, and since I hadn't gone to any bars in over a year, I had no alternative thoughts on the subject and welcomed the opportunity to see something different. I figured that if I were to get into a barroom brawl, I wouldn't see anyone besides my work colleagues for a few days anyway, and bruises would be small change compared to the toothless mouths and severe head injuries that they had seen throughout their careers as Soviet managers. The Ala bar was found deep in a basement at the end of a dark alley. The thirty-four stairs down were steep, steep enough to be non-negotiable for someone in a less than perfectly sober state. The only solace for one who tumbled down was the chance of falling, at the bottom, into the lap of one of the thirty or so "Best-of-Barbizon"-beautiful coeds lining the walls and surrounding the grand piano in the center. The bar itself was approximately fifteen yards long. The grand piano, in deference to Liberace or Clayderman, boasted a large candelabra. However, the other lighting was surprisingly bright, so the candles were merely for decorative effect. Jay was already there, flirting in an animated manner with one of the coeds. However, when I arrived, he cut short the conversation, she left with her drink, and we greeted each other. He ordered some drinks, and we started talking. As we started chatting about the American Chamber's inaugural meeting, I could sense that he was preoccupied. He did not want to appear impolite, yet his eyes were roving madly along the wall behind me. Intermittently, he cast a steady, sober gaze at me. But the distraction of the back wall was overpowering — soon after we started the conversation, I had trouble following his train of thought.

"So Jay, you say that the economy now will proceed to grow at an accelerated pace?"

"Well yes, Boriss, you see, the production curve has yet to meet the demand curve . . . speaking of curves, do you see the curves on that brunette, standing third from the left?" I didn't even need to look at her to understand that she was a brick house. Instead, I started looking around for a plate to put under his eyes when they fall out.

"But the demand will most probably have to be met through the import of items that are not produced domestically, which will unleash a negative balance of payments —"

He then looked at me [or through me] as he interrupted, with what sounded to my amateur economic ears to be another accurate assessment of the macroeconomic situation, and a sideways glance at another beautiful coed.

I was thinking that this bar should be providing lead-lined vests to some of these girls to avoid X-ray burns.

I turned the topic to the future of the Latvian economy; "But, back to the production as I've seen, most goods cannot be produced domestically, which will force the importation of consumable goods, as opposed to those that will be used in production."

"Right, but they still have enough industries alive at this point, which export their finished products to Russia — enough to smooth the transition over the bumps. But any successful transition will also depend on a surge of the middle sector, so to speak, between services and finished materials production, the sector of raw materials export like lumber and peat . . . ," he trailed off as he caught sight of another attractive coed.

"As if I hadn't noticed — don't let me stand in the way here . . . ," I thought, now beside myself with a mixture of frustration and impatience. "That's right, I don't blame you, you've got good taste . . . she's a looker —," I continued as I checked out a Kate Moss lookalike that had moved up to the bar.

"But why did you say that information and services will not necessarily be imported, like they are in Russia?"

"Because there are some signs that these sectors are developing rapidly here, fast enough to offset imports. For example, software-programming capabilities here are high. With the imported hardware, they have been producing software for IBM. They have a four-million-dollar contract with Boeing."

"Impressive."

I offered to get the next round of drinks and then left to chase down one of the barmen. I found one twenty feet further down the bar. In the process of making the drinks, he held the juice bottle some two feet above the glasses. The falling streams of vodka and juice hit the already-poured contents with enough velocity to spray the drink onto the bar, onto the hair of the girls who were sitting at that spot, onto my tie and heretofore-white shirt. The barman smiled radiantly, as if to say "Hey, ain't I just Tom Cruise?!" I returned the smile and said [in English, knowing that he wouldn't understand], "Totally *awesome* — you've just conditioned this girl's hair with vodka, ruined my tie and made my shirt *bubonic* with just one *deft* movement — *cool*!" He held his thumb up and smiled jubilantly — he understood.

When I returned with the drinks, the attache was again flirting, using every muscle [and not a few hormones] in his body, with what I — heart-lustfully — had to admit was a stunning dark-haired girl of what I guessed to be eighteen or nineteen. Jay turned to me and said, "Hey, I'd like you to meet 'Lolita' (a name that, I found out later, was not at all uncommon in Latvia)." This was the first time in my life that I had met someone bearing this name; I couldn't help grinning as I greeted her. She returned the greeting with a shy, short smile. Her eyes were focused on my freshly poxed shirt. "Don't worry, your dress won't get infected by my shirt — it's too small," I wanted to say, but didn't. Instead, I decided that I had nothing to lose, and asked if she hadn't read the book. She answered with a stare that would compare favorably with the expressions found on the faces of Warner Brothers cartoon characters after they have been hit squarely on the head with a cast-iron pan. I wondered if it was the "*Lolita* [is the title of a book]" or the "do you read?" part of the question that was throwing her for a loop.

Jay seized the moment.

"So-o-o, Lolita, what are you studying?"

Sensing that I was now little more than an extra on this scene, without a line or a purpose, I quickly finished my drink and parted. "Catch you later, Jay. Just choose well," I mumbled, already an unnoticeable dust speck on his cognitive screen.

As I exited the bar into the pitch-black courtyard, I lost my bearings. Then, upon hearing the sound of liquid streams against a hard surface, I looked to the right and saw the outlines of two guys leaning against the wall. I immediately understood that the exit must be towards the opposite side, for such well-bred gentlemen who, in sub-freezing weather, volunteered to support the walls of this old building while relieving themselves, would not have performed the latter act near the entrance to the courtyard — that would have been *gauche*. Although open-air urinals were a rarity in most parts of the Western world, the continued existence of such fixtures in provincial capitals of France made it all the more chic here in *Mazā Parīze* [Little Paris][1].

As I walked quickly down Aspāzijas street, I was wondering why I was so frustrated. I should have been fine after having consumed the two screwdrivers. Was it because I hadn't gleaned enough information from this source ... because I hadn't made a connection which I could call friend ... or because I hadn't joined him in picking up one of the coeds now that I was — de facto — a single man. "I can't ... I'm still married ... Well, I was until yesterday ... maybe we'll clear it up ... ," I thought to myself as I braced against a chill wind that drove the temperatures to minus 30 Fahrenheit. I recalled that not uncommonly, people in Soviet times froze to death in the parks after a good drinking bout and a misstep. The emergency room or *ātrās palīdzības nodaļas* workers alluded to this when I had visited them two years before. When I asked one doctor why these are considered cases of "natural death," he assumed the air of a Soviet propaganda pundit and replied, "What could be more natural than distilled grains and some fresh air."

I walked slowly up the sloping, ice-covered path past the Chinese popcorn booth — one of the few surviving relics of the seven-hundredth anniversary of the City of Riga in 1901. I crossed the cast-iron footbridge over the frozen canal. The ducks below had turned themselves to face the wind, thereby reducing wind resistance. To the right was the spot where wreaths and bouquets of flowers had been laid a few weeks earlier. The flowers were in memory of Andris Slapiņš, the reporter who had been shot dead on this spot by Soviet sharpshooters on January 21, 1991. A few candles, miraculously protected from the wind, illuminated the fresh-frozen flowers. They appeared freshly picked.

I hurried on, shivering, trying to envision what had happened on that night, in this corner of Riga. Judging by the number of Latvians that had been killed or wounded in this park, there were at least two sharpshooters involved. They had been shooting from the second or even third floor of the Ministry of Justice building, now fifty yards in front of me. The explanation given afterwards was that they were "defending" the *OMONtsi*[2] in the street. The latter, however, were in no need of being defended. They had mounted their machine guns atop the cars parked on the street (with the Latvian drivers still inside them) and spraying the park entry with gunfire. I heard later from the Chairman's chauffeur that their task had been to create a "diversion" while colleagues from the KGB evacuated the Chairman of the Supreme Council, who was dining in the restaurant two floors above. The restaurant was relatively well-insulated for sound and together with the band, this effectively prevented anybody from hearing what was happening one hundred feet below, on the opposite side of the building. The maitre d' approached the Chairman and told him that another client of the restaurant needed to speak to him about an urgent matter. The Chairman was then led to the kitchen, where a KGB officer handed him a waiter's vest, and told him to go outside. He did so, using the employees' entrance; a car — not his own — was waiting for him. At this very point, his own car was being used as a mount for a fifty-caliber machine gun. In the meantime, the front steps, which I was at this very moment clumsily attempting to climb, were covered with several other well-armed commandos. When they saw curious onlookers on several of the interior balconies of the hotel, they charged inside and pumped some rounds into the walls and through the glass barrier around the central stairway. One American diplomat, sent to observe the situation in the Baltics, was coming downstairs from his room on the upper floors to see what the commotion was about. As he and one journalist reached the third-floor landing, shots rang out around them and bullets whistled by, which prompted them to start "eating carpet."

The Chairman had been evacuated quietly. That he was being set up (by the Central Committee) to play some key role on Moscow's behalf was a subject of debate long after the events were relegated to history[3]. That he was the founder and a stalwart member of the "Latvian Way" political party — which was to remain in power for at least eleven consecutive years after this day — is indisputable fact. "The right man in the right place at the right time," I concluded, as I passed the plate of glass neatly perforated with a 9mm round.[4] Ironically, one of the stray bullets hit the Freedom statue, entering it at thigh level on the left side (if facing the statue), and traversing the interior before hitting — but not penetrating — the opposite side. As a result, there is a "pimple" that is visible, just below the armpit.

Once in my room, I recalled how this hotel, by now just one of several which accommodated foreigners at a *respektabl'niy*[5] level, had been the first one in which I had stayed overnight in Latvia two years earlier. I remembered the strolls in Old Town or Vecrīga (pronounced "Vetzriga"), and passing by the barricade that had been constructed on Jēkaba street to block the access of Soviet tanks to the Parliament building. I recalled the euphoria that swept Riga, when I arrived for the first time, just two weeks after Moscow had withdrawn the Soviet troops. The people that I met in February of 1991 had been euphoric; they had something now, which they hadn't had before —

hope and expectations for a life such as their cousins across the ocean were leading. They looked forward to developing their careers without interference from Moscow, eager to see the world beyond the Iron Curtain, and optimistic about their childrens' futures. For the country, this revolution was the ticket to get back on board the train that was going down the "fast development" track — the track from which Latvia had been derailed in 1940.

I wondered now, while rummaging through my toiletry kit for after-shave that would be potent enough to reduce the odor of sewer fumes emanating from the bathroom, whether those people's expectations were being met or not, now two years hence. I looked out the window towards the Ministry of Justice and then tried to close the drapes to shut out the blinding light streaming from the new hydrogen street lamps three feet below. The task was Sisyphean in scope, as the two-yard composite width of curtain could not cover the three yards of window width, no matter how the three drape sections were arranged. So I stopped moving them from side to side, lay down on the stern narrow mattress, looked up at the fire alarms-that-I-had-always-assumed-were-microphones (I was to discover, seven years later, that I was being unduly suspicious of the fire alarms. In the fall of 1999, on the top floor of the Hotel Riga — one of three Riga hotels that had been designated for foreigners in the 1980s and early '90s — Nils Students, a U.S.-born member of the new hotel administration, discovered a room containing relatively sophisticated listening equipment. The equipment was still operational and could surveil most of the rooms in the hotel, but only through the radios . . . not the fire alarms.) and sighed, thinking to myself, "Guess it's back to square one with the relationship."

Footnotes

[1] A popular analogy, made in the late '20s, perhaps when Riga was at its peak as a city. City council members repeated this analogy occasionally in the post-emergence period, in moments of grand delusion.

[2] Other specialists referred to the OMON, or Osobiy Militseyskiy Otriad, as the 'Black Berets', and they were a paramilitary operation whose primary purpose was the restoration of order in times of unrest. They were also employed as SWAT Teams and execution squads, depending on the need.

[3] For a more precise analysis of the politics surrounding the re-declaration of, and struggle for, independence, I recommend Anatol Lieven's The Baltic Revolution (Yale University Press, 1993).

[4] The hotel, in deference to those that had defended the barricades, kept the glass intact until 1999.

[5] Respektabl'niy — should not to be confused with 'respectable,' as the two words are distant cousins. When referring to individuals, 'respectable' in the West connotes a person who might be an active member of his church or temple, a contributor to society and an exemplary family man — a 'pillar of society.' 'Respektabl'niy ' refers to someone who practices the entertaining of call girls in saunas, the consumption of large amounts of hard alcohol in one sitting, and the driving of large black automobiles at dangerously high speeds a hair's breadth away from large crowds of pedestrians. Consequently, these staples (prostitutes, saunas, large arrays of hard alcohol, and secure parking spaces for large black cars) were the ones that the *respektabl'*niye hotels concentrated on providing — along with a more-or-less stable supply of hot water for bathing. Other amenities were not considered necessary. Courteous, Western levels of service — not to mention the South East Asian dream-like one — were apparently considered fluff.

19

PURGATORY

THE FOLLOWING MORNING I WAS one of the first ones in the dining room. I picked up my plate and headed to the buffet. Upon looking at the pale pink-gray hotdogs and watery porridge in the chafing dishes along with cucumber slices, shredded cabbage and carrots tossed in an oily sugar dressing in the glass bowls on the buffet table, I remembered why I had been so determined to supply this city with Danish. "'If you can't find 'em, bring 'em in, I sez to myself.' No luck. 'So if you can't bring 'em in, bake 'em yerself'" was the motto I emphatically professed to swear by, when I was in the company of English-speaking expatriates "but never, *ever* give in to the naked wiener-and-cucumber breakfast," to the approving nods and "hear-hears" of the listeners.

I decided that I would call Inge on the second day of my self-imposed exile. I reasoned that cooler heads would have prevailed by then. In the meantime, I had to get a message to Preben. The machine that this master baker had sworn was the mainstay of any professional bakery, and had subsequently become the first foreign equipment purchase for The Merry Baker, was now gathering copious amounts of dust in a corner of the production floor. The bakers had claimed that it was nice, shiny and "imported," but that it was more time-consuming to use than their simple rolling sticks for the same amount of production.

A second question involved crust. Preben had taught our bakers to bake bread with crust, as they did in Denmark. And, in defense of the bakers, they were doing so. But this innovation appeared to have a negative effect on sales. The thickness of the crust on *our* bread was a point that was playing directly into the hands of the large Soviet factory-bakeries. Because the ex-Soviet bakeries used no steam, their breads never developed crust. In Western Europe, this soft crust was a dead give-away to the fact that the bread was more than twelve hours old (so why bother with it?). This explains why most Western Europeans still relied on the corner bakery, or a bakery unit inside a large store, for their daily bread. And to make sure that it was fresh, they examined the crust. Latvians examined the crust as well — however, upon finding that it did not give with a gentle nudge, they immediately concluded that the bread was at least four days old. I once overheard some pensioners wrestling with this paradox: "On one hand, it smells like fresh baking. On the other hand, the crust is hard..." In some cases, the customer pushed the crust with his or her finger, until the crust was broken. The pressure applied would propel the finger deep into the bread. After the finger was retracted, the bread looked like it had been chewed or stomped on one side. In other cases, the crust was crushed completely, and, if the hands had not been terribly clean, it looked as though the loaf had been tossed under an approaching car's snow-tires-with-cleats and then retrieved for sale. Finally, we implemented a policy of having one "sample" (read "mauling") loaf to demonstrate freshness; during the inspection it was to be covered with paper. This tactic served us well for a while, as people got used to the concept that crusty can be fresh.

Nonetheless, by the middle of January, the bread sales to stores began declining precipitously. I understood that without implementing some revolutionary concept, my bakery would go the way of the dinosaurs. And Grigoriys' "variations on post-modern bread rolls" were not doing the trick.

I subsequently asked some of the foreigners in town what they thought. I approached some French people, who insisted that the French baguette was the sole item worth baking, besides croissants "wheech nopody ken mek ze wey eet shuuld pee." I consulted others. The Germans insisted that broetchen and multi-grain breads would guarantee success. Several Americans claimed that bagels would be the key to economic salvation. My Northern California roots made me seriously consider San Francisco-style sourdough bread. However, all of these "solutions" ultimately appeared dubious, on occasions when samples were passed around — the conservative habits of the rye bread-eating populace discouraged experimentation with newfangled breads. But sensing that our rye bread and half-rye bread variations would soon be emulated, I had to ask Preben for other ideas that might be worth implementing.

So I went to the International Telephone and Telefax Center and took my place in the line of expatriates who were trying to make a telephone call that would cost less than the standard $4.00 per minute to Europe being charged by the hotels. Of course, anything was preferable to the alternative, which was the "place-an-order-on-your-home-phone-and-pray" technique. If one wanted to make a phone call overseas from one's home phone, one had to call the number for the placement of international calls, and a rude, impatient middle-aged lady would take the "reservation" for the call. When a line opened up — anywhere between one-half hour and two hours after the "request" had been placed — the lady would call back, announcing in an "answer-quickly-or-be-damned" tone of voice, *"Amerika?!"*, or *"Francija*?!" or whatever the location was. And heaven forbid that you should try to reserve more than two calls back-to-back. The operator would roar back, that you were being a shameless line-hog, depriving others of a rare opportunity to speak with loved ones/bereaved relatives/winning lottery-ticket salesmen. But if they acquiesced and made the connections for two calls, then one could be sure that the operator would mix up the two destination countries, which made for amusing opening repartees: "Bjorn, how ya' doin?" "I don't know heow Bjohrrn eez doing — I guess zet Bjohrrn een retayaarement eez doing well, *le cochon*, selleeng eez underweahrs! You 'ev called Jean-Phillipe in Pareess." To avoid these inconveniences, anybody who had anything to communicate quickly would be coming here, to the "Center." A modest sign, atop a large but otherwise nondescript door, marked the spot. If I hadn't been taken there the first time, I would never have found it.

The line was relatively short this day, with only five people in front of me. The first person in line was a heavy-set bearded missionary, spreading the word of the Gospel on behalf of one of the Florida communities. Behind him was a Frenchman who was thoroughly enjoying the experience of flirting with his interpreter. The remaining three were dressed like local people — worn jeans and a shirt that reminded one of *American Graffiti*. The young man in front of me was sending out a letter, written in some very unique English, to a Swedish "assosiasion of orienteers." "Deer sirs, I wood like to get the informasion on your meeting who will be taking the plase of Maij in a Malmo for all-world orientationing societies..." I caught myself reading before remembering that it was probably rude to read other people's faxes. My mind began wondering: "Why did he decide to spell 'societees' with a 'c' in the middle; he seemed to have been doing quite well without that letter until then... What if there are 'moose madames' along with the 'deer sirs'? ... Will they be offended? . . . Will the month of 'Maij' whose place the meeting has taken, be pissed off? Does that mean that there won't be a May in Sweden this year? How many 'Malmo's' are there in Sweden? What is a 'Malmo' anyway? . . . sounds like 'mammal' uttered by someone with a speech impediment . . . . Yeah, Inge *has* done well with this crazy language."

It was finally my turn and I gave the number to the clerk, who took it without looking up. Irina was one of the stunning beauties that were regularly seen in the telecommunications field. She made it a rule never to smile or look even vaguely interested in what she was doing or in the customer. She changed her drop-dead-serious countenance only when she handed back the change, at which time she looked up and smiled glowingly, as if she had just finished having great sex with a new lover. By doing so, she removed all suspicion that she could possibly have shortchanged the hapless male customer, which, in fact, she did regularly. The call went through with no problems or delays. Preben seemed as eager to come back to Latvia, as he had been to leave seven months earlier. The date was set for the end of February. I was happy. Irina's smile made me feel even happier; I later discovered that, sure enough, I'd left with a Lat less change than I should have.

As I walked down the street to the best spot for catching a cab, I recalled that I had been invited to attend a meeting of the "7G Club" that evening. One of the two local councilmen who had been instrumental in renewing the bakery production site lease, even after Petuhov's 'Trust' had been liquidated, had invited me. He had described the club as a small group of enlightened professionals and local politicians who are interested in doing some social re-engineering. They had formed a club, which clearly worked along the lines of a Rotary, but on a Latvian scale. He also said that he wouldn't explain what "7G" stood for, except that it had nothing to do with those "wealthy donor nations" — I'd have to attend a meeting to find out. I agreed, as it would be good practice for my Latvian. It would also help prevent too many depressing thoughts from creeping up on me, making me feel like a leper . . . infecting other people with a slimy propensity to reach out and beat kids like Mr. Hyde.

That evening, when I arrived, there were nine people sitting behind desks configured into a horseshoe shape. Seven candles were glowing on the "table." It reminded me of some kind of an initiation rite for a school child's secret society. They greeted me enthusiastically, which surprised me. Why they accepted me into their club to begin with I don't know. Although their professions varied, they had all been active members of the National Front, and as such, had played a key role in the restoration of Latvia's independence. Gints, the local councilman who had invited me to this meeting, was a physicist who had been working in a radiation laboratory, not two years before, alongside the current prime minister, Ivars Godmanis. I understood right little of what was being discussed that evening, but did have the opportunity to sip some good coffee around a candle-lit table, and watch normally phlegmatic people raise their voices, wave their arms, and impersonate Italians. But in fact, my thoughts were far away from this room — every thought of mine was about my wife, whom I had abandoned for three days.

Later that evening, I called Inge. "Inge," I said, as if the next word would unleash a ten-megaton explosion. "Hello." I had expected something cold in return, but there was nothing, so I continued, "I just...I...I miss you." I waited for what seemed like an hour in an ice storm before Inge said, "I miss you too."

20

RETURN OF THE PRODIGAL SUN

PREBEN HOBBLED THROUGH THE doors of the passenger exit at the arrival gate of the airport. He was much thinner and more haggard than when I had seen him last, seven months before.

"Great to see you, Preben. How have you been?"

"Oh all right," he said with what seemed to be relief.

"How's the little woman?"

Preben looked at me oddly, and smiled. "History, I'm afraid."

I stopped in my tracks. The two of them were no longer married.

"What happened?"

"Well, she turned out to be pretty emotionally cocked-up, and she couldn't stand living with anyone."

"Oh."

I had to concede that the latter makes for a tough marriage. I filled him in on the progress as well as the "regress" that had taken place in the bakery in the course of the past six months as we drove to the tall, Soviet-built *Latvija* Hotel in the middle of town. It was one of two post-modern metal-and-glass skyscraper structures in Riga. This one featured grayish aqua-blue panels, below the windows. The Latvija Hotel, termed "the Blue Whale" by local residents on account of its coloring, reminded me of a Kenner *Girder and*

Panel set structure. With the help of this remarkable toy, I had built and deconstructed several skyscrapers in my childhood, during my flashes of megalomaniac rage. The Girder and Panel set consisted of miniature plastic gray beams, which would fasten to one another with a dovetail groove. Upon the girder structure, one attached little red or aqua-blue plastic panels. A child with initiative could build a skyscraper, place floors inside and antennas on top, but not much else. The Latvija Hotel looked like a Girder and Panel structure that had been "finished" with the aqua-blue panels. And, without such fixtures as airconditioning, fire escapes, hotel doors that locked securely and *working* (as opposed to *show*) elevators, the Latvija Hotel's functionality was not significantly better than that of the Girder and Panel structure. The other problem was that when the mayor-of-the-moment's megalomaniac rage ended, he couldn't dismantle this structure as I could mine. It stood more than thirty floors high, the "Blue Whale" of Riga. For the Mafiya, it was soon to become a "cash whale," as they discovered ways to infiltrate it with their prostitutes, their robbers and their barmen, who had no moral problems with pouring contraband alcohol into Stolichnaya bottles. But at this point, if one didn't mind climbing a goodly amount of stairs, stayed clear of the self-employed call girls and avoided flaunting large wads of money and diamond rings in front of the hotel staff, then the hotel was quite acceptable. The deciding factor for me was the drive-up parking area, which always had space even for my non-black automobile, which I now parked, before accompanying Preben to the check-in desk.

That evening we went to the bakery. "Edvins, ole boy, howya doin?" asked Preben. Edvins smiled and replied in Latvian, "O.K., little-by-little moving forward."

"I heard that the pastry break is giving you problems," Preben said as he pointed to the decommissioned piece of equipment.

"Yeah ... nicht gute," Edvins replied, waving his finger. "It's too slow. We work much faster with the wooden sticks," he explained, picking one up and demonstrating the lightning-quickness with which a roll-sized piece of dough could be flattened.

Preben chuckled. "Is that so?" Then he shook his head. "Boriss, ask them when they'll be forming the next batch of sweet dough." It was in ten minutes. Preben jumped to action, uncovering the machine for use on the next batch. As the dough came out from the mixing bowl, it was placed on the table. The brigadier cut the twenty-pound chunk into smaller pieces, which were covered and laid to rest for another ten minutes. Preben then took eight of the pieces, while Edvins and the other bakers looked on. He laid the pieces on one side of the roller in the middle, onto a canvas white sheet. He pressed down on one side of the lever that was in between the two white sheets, and the dough pieces were sent through the two rotating metal rollers in the middle. The pieces were deposited on an identical white canvas sheet on the other side of the rollers, but now two millimeters flatter. This action he repeated four times, in both directions, until the items reached exactly their intended flatness and size. "You see, it's a snap, easy as one-two-three," Preben blurted out. He didn't need to say anything, though — the bakers' eyes were wide open. Their heads were nodding in acknowledgment, like the little dogs in America's car rear windows in the 1970s. They realized that they had just saved *ten minutes* of work. When Edvins recovered from his reverie, he said, "I see, yeah — we didn't know that you could do *eight* pieces at a time."

Throughout the night, Preben was patiently giving tips and helpful hints. "and don't forget to cover the dough ... it's like a baby, that wants to sleep ... the dough must be worked now that it has risen, let's go ..." and he promptly picked up some pieces and started forming them. Others quickly followed his lead.

The following day, we met to brainstorm some ideas.

"So Preben, what do *you* think we should make?"

"Oh, maybe some more marzipan pieces — they're very popular in Denmark. That and a 'Horn-a-Plenty.'" He gave several more dubious-sounding suggestions, after which he shrugged his shoulders.

"O.K., what else? I mean, you believe in the business, right?"

"Sure, Borisss ... and I believed in it in Limerick, too — it was the 'Danish Viking.' Didn't I tell you about it? On opening day, I dressed up in a Viking outfit — and handed out the wienerbrod to the people passin' by. A lot of Irish gals showed a lot of interest in the pastries ... or in me, I couldn'a tell. Of course I weighed less back then ..."

"O.K., Preben, so ... are you saying I should dress up like a Viking?"

"No, no, don't bother ... Hey, what about pizza?"

"I think I'd look better as a Viking."

"No, dummy, how about makin' pizza?"

"Yeah, maybe ... I've thought about it. But my partners aren't too keen on the idea. You see, we have pizza in Riga, Preben."

At this point, since we were both hungry, we jumped in the car and drove to the only Soviet "pizza" outlet that I knew of.

When we arrived, the windows were steamed over. This was a good sign — there would be customers inside. As we entered, we were nearly bowled over by the colors of burning bacon and onions, combined with degrading livers and the stench of unwashed armpits. Nonplused, we walked up to the counter, which consisted of badly painted pressboard. One could see it was pressboard through the three holes where someone had nailed sample cups to the counter at some previous time.

"We'd like a pizza, what kinds do you have?" I asked the serving lady. She was wearing a turquoise-colored apron, which she was also using to display the deposits of twenty or thirty previous pizzas.

"We got ham, lard, and jubilee."

"Great... what's a 'jubilee'? She then gave a look that reverberated — 'You some moronic dumb-ass coming and getting your highs from asking me what a 'jubilee' pizza is?!"

"It's with 'jubilee' sausage [*duh*]."

"Oh, jubilee sausage, hunh?" I turned to Preben. "That's a bit like salami.. . and a bit like a chewable doggy treat. Today, I feel like having a good chew, so that's what I'll have."

I turned back to the lady: "Would you have any vegetable pizzas?" She started wagging her head from side to side and turned to the right, to someone we couldn't see, behind the barrier. "Lena, this guy is asking for a vegetable pizza [can you believe your ears?!]"

"Tell him we can — we got plenty of onions — onions are a vegetable, aren't they?" The serving lady then turned to me; "You heard her — we can give you onions [you *putz*]."

"Hmm, I'll think about it. So, what'll you have, Preben?"

"Just those three choices?"

I nodded and he started laughing.

"Just a ham. Gotta mind the teeth, mind the teeth, aye, but we better order it now, otherwise she'll come after us with that knife there," he said, pointing to a kitchen knife with an unfinished wood handle and a blade that was thoroughly spotted with rust, "and we die of tetanus."

"Right... hello, ma'am, we would like one ham, and one jubilee, please."

"Whaddya wanna drink?"

"We'd like something that's cool." Her eyes flashed daggers once again. "Khorosho, khorosho, some *limonad*[1] please." She slammed two grease-smeared *granyenka*[2] glasses on the counter and started filling them from an unmarked plastic bottle.

We sat down at a table with a grease-smeared brown laminated top, by the window.

A few minutes later, the lady re-emerged from behind the barrier, threw two plates on the counter and shouted, "One ham, one jubilee!" I picked up the two pizzas and brought them back to the table. They met the rigid specification of pizza, insofar as they were round and had cheese on top. In fact, the cheese covered the ingredients completely, so we had to poke a little before we could tell which was which. Although they were no more than seven inches in diameter, they had crusts that were two inches wide, leaving three inches in the middle for cheese and other contents. After taking a bit of the crust off, I bit into my pizza, and along with the "jubilee" sausage, tomato sauce and cheese, I felt a distinct fourth texture. It could have been cooked cabbage, but as I chewed the mystery mass longer, it appeared to be something else. Preben asked me if I was having problems with something. At that instant, I tasted the fat. "No, Preben, no, they . . . uh . . . just gave me a free piece of . . . lard in mine," I mumbled. "And some free hair in mine, I see . . . ," Preben replied, while pointing to a thick black hair, running along the edge of the cheese. "So a free surprise with every order, I see. Aye, how thoughtful of 'em."

Two men, with disheveled hair and modeling grease-stained overcoats, walked through the door and bellied up to the counter. The first one made some sign with his fingers. The counter lady pulled out a half-liter bottle of vodka from under the counter, and poured 100 milliliters (about four shots) into two *granyenki*. The two customers downed them on the spot. Preben laughed and said, "Maybe that's how you have to prepare for eating these pizzas."

"Yeah, Preben. Guess so. You know, I thought of making pizza, but I tell you, the co-directors and Ligita were so against it, you'd think that I was proposing to set up a slave-labor camp."

"I see why."

Although it was clear that foreigners would love a normal pizza, Preben agreed that as there still weren't more than a couple of hundred semi-permanently residing in the city, they comprised too small a market to make it worth committing the full production to. Nonetheless, we agreed to start with a pilot production of real pizza which would be made available in the store, and thereby test the market first.

Preben helped out for a couple more days before departing. At the airport, as Preben was waving his last good-bye, I looked past him and saw, sandwiched between two sheets of dark gray-purple clouds, a dull yellow-orange sun, sending its healing rays Latvia-ward 299,792,458 meters per second. It was now April and I finally felt better.

My relations with Inge were quickly back on track. I committed to spending more time with the kids in the evenings, which with Preben's arrival, I had not done. We looked for a piano for Markus, after he expressed an interest in playing it. My mother sent us the *Great American Songbook*. Soon we were singing a dreadful version of "Amazing Grace." We started playing a myriad of

family board games. These included a Swedish version of "pick-up sticks" —
featuring plastic objects ranging from swords to pitchforks to flintlock rifles
— *Parcheesi*, and Clue. When the kids wearied of these, I would tell stories
about imps, headless horsemen, and Michael Jackson.

I also swore to make a mad dash for language comprehension during this
period, so that I could communicate better with the kids, who — unlike my
co-directors — were not terribly conversant in Russian. One element of this
"mad dash" took the form of attendance at another meeting of the 7G Club.
For this meeting, I had been invited to give a little speech, because I had been
the first American that they had ever met. I also committed myself to delivering
it in Latvian — at least until I got stuck beyond the point where I could extricate
myself from the mental block that accompanied speech-making in
impossible-to-master foreign languages. At that point I would expect my face
to turn various shades of red, my eyes would start bulging and in other ways
my body language would communicate, "*Help* me, *please*." More observant
listeners could then offer to change languages — they seldom failed to.

When I entered the room, everyone was surrounding Ilze, one of the lady
members who — in contempt of the accepted etiquette governing winter
behavior — generated an aura of joy and optimism, through a charming smile
and a full-throated laugh, worthy of a 250-pound opera singer. The chairman,
Ruta, announced that it was time for everyone to take his or her seats. She
introduced me, but then interjected, in Latvian, what I thought was the
following; "But first, we are ... to have Ilze among us today ... She had been ..
. bloodied ... by some ... heavy drinking." "An alcoholic?" I thought to myself
for a second before realizing that that couldn't be. She was the Director of
Social Services in this section of the city and she had a well-earned reputation
as a workhorse. Besides being a serious manager, she made it her mission to
improve the lives of the pension-age residents of the city.

"The story please, Ilze." The chairman of the club waved his hand. Ilze got
up and approached the front of the tables. She remained standing, smiled
from cheek-to-cheek, and began; "Well, I was sitting on . . . chair . . .
reading_____. I heard ... hitting_____door_____ opened and ____ man,
with an _____. He was covered ___ red_____ He was drunk_____ said
that he was in a tent____ " I was straining for every word of this description. I
knew that it must have been a hell of an incident, because everyone else was
in rapt attention, which I had not seen at the previous meeting. In short, I
understood something about axes, and some police with Kalashnikov
machine guns. But after that, I stopped trying to understand what was being
described and knew only that she ended with: "second in critical."

The group broke into random conversation while coffee and pastries were served up. Ruta then approached me and asked if I wouldn't say two words about life in the States, my first impressions of Latvia. I agreed, but asked if it wouldn't be easier for everyone involved if I were to speak in Russian. Ruta agreed, saying that it wouldn't be a problem. I then approached the last speaker:

"So Indra, if I understand that scenario correctly, this guy with an axe hit somebody?"

"Yes, in fact, he killed a friend he was arguing with — hit him over the head with the axe. Then he hit his girlfriend too — she's in critical condition. All three were alcoholics," she said, smiling and shrugging her shoulders.

"And this was in *your* apartment building?!"

"Yes, my next-door neighbor, in fact."

"Oh, my God!" I couldn't help blurting out. "But *where* were the police? I understood that they *did* show up."

"Yes, they did — twenty minutes after I called — and armed to the teeth. Each one had a *Kalashnikov* and a billy club. They were scared too — when I opened the door, one of them grabbed his club and the other pointed the *Kalashnikov* at *me*!"

She let out another throaty laugh.

Even after the coffee break, I couldn't shake the images; they had been described with a nonchalance that might be apropos had one been describing the making of oatmeal in the morning. It was now my turn. To borrow from Oscar Wilde, my presentation would now be the "sorbet which followed the side of beef." I started in Latvian — "My grandparents came from Russia, Estonia and Slovenia to Western Europe. My parents came from there to America in the early 'fifties. I was born in California. Now, about America —" At this point, I switched to Russian as the Latvian words that I had been lining up seemed fraught with erogenous double-meanings. I started by explaining that I didn't exactly bump into witnesses to double axe-killings on a daily basis. I then switched back to Latvian, explaining as best I could, which socioeconomic barriers tend to prevent raging psychotics and alcoholic degenerates from waking up nuclear physicists, computer programming Quality Control managers and directors of big-city social service departments during the night with their random killing sprees. Furthermore I explained what comprised the "Great American Dream" and other facts of economic life in the U.S. I ended with the statement that any twenty of the two hundred wealthiest people in America could buy every share of every company, all oil reserves in Ventspils, Ventspils itself, all ships in the port of Riga, and every showcase piece of property in Riga at their current prices. I noted some nods, as well as troubled expressions on some of the listeners' faces. I smiled, and quickly added, that the audience shouldn't worry, as the investors wouldn't do so on account of the risk.

"What else is the hardest thing for you to get used to here?" asked Guntis, the ex-nuclear physicist from the local council. I thought for a second, and then answered that I find it troubling that people here were so distrustful; it seemed that every time I asked something, the person answering was wondering which of five ways he was going to answer the question . . . and that was just for street directions." When some people laughed, I felt more at ease, and started with the part of my talk that I had memorized in Latvian, about a comparison of the weather in California, to the one here. After a few more questions, I excused myself and wanted to say why I had to run out so early, but judging by the looks on the faces of the 7G members, I must have said that I had to beat somebody senseless with a parboiled egg noodle.

When I got back, Inge asked me how it went. I recounted the story of the axe murder. Inge appeared nonplused; "Yeah, that could very well have taken place . . . ," as she glanced at the edge of the door that had just swung open and added something to the effect of "too many of the wrong people have axes around here."

The following evening, Inge and I were sitting, watching as Markus and Eliza played chutes and ladders. The two began quarreling over whether it was possible to go down the ladders. After five minutes of bickering, Eliza got up and left.

"Well, that's that," I said.

"Yes, but don't worry — let them work it out."

"Of course I will . . . but maybe we could do something that would be helpful in getting the two to cooperate on something . . . like an animal of some kind."

"Yes, that's a good idea, Boriss, but which kind?"

"A dog or a cat or even a fish or something."

"Fine — I don't like small dogs . . . fish don't do anything . . . how about a kitten?"

We agreed, and our offer received a heartfelt response from the two.

I went out to the apartment of a friend of one of Inge's colleagues. There was an adorable, sand-colored kitten, climbing the furniture and making daring lunges at the drapes. "*Sure*, sure," said Eliza, beaming with joy. So we took the light rust-colored kitten home. There we proceeded to enact all the rituals of first-time cat-owners, starting with the bowl of warm milk, ending with the alarm clock laid next to the creature when the children couldn't stay up any longer to play with it. The next day, a newspaper trail was laid between his bed, his play area, and the milk bowl. The kitten was encouraged to read avidly.

However, the kitten's story ended sadly. A few weeks later, when we had finished with our evening rituals, I noticed a meowing outside the door. I ran to the door, opened it and saw a creature that only resembled our kitten in some abstract form. One eye socket was bulging so much that the kitten looked like a cyclops with fur. The kitten had been kicked or beaten so hard by someone, that it had lost the use of its right rear paw, which it was dragging along behind itself. The creature was meowing madly, and couldn't find relief from its pain. We took turns keeping it company through a miserable night. In the morning, I took it to the veterinarian. The veterinarians looked at it, and said that they could take the eye out, and the paw would heal, but they feared that its internal organs had been dealt a severe blow. After administering several medications, they let it go, but with the admonition that he had about a 50/50 chance of surviving.

For five days more, under the care of Eliza, the kitten seemed to improve, recovering its spunky form and tremendous appetite. Then it stopped eating completely, for no apparent reason. The following day, it started meowing uncontrollably, so we took it to the veterinarian for the third time. The vet examined his gut, which sent the creature into a spasm of meowing, then shook her head, "I'm sorry to say, but the kitten has an underlying condition — it appears to be a tumor on his stomach or intestine. I'm afraid that he's … unlucky." Eliza started sobbing. I hugged her. I gave a five Lat bill to the vet and asked that the kitten feel no pain, and then I joined Eliza outside for a good cry. After a few hundred meters, I turned to her and said, "You know, Eliza, The kitten just wasn't destined to live. Even if he hadn't been kicked nearly to death, he would have died within a month from other problems — that's the way it goes sometimes … the Buddhists have a word for it — karma … But Eliza, we shouldn't be so sad — but pray that maybe he'll come back again in the form of a 'surviving' kitten."

The bakers started making pizzas, as Preben had showed them. But there was one hitch. The few customers that wanted a pizza wanted a hot one. When we accommodated them, the entire bakery smelled of pizza and our cake sales fell drastically. As a compromise we ended up offering small and large pizzas wrapped in plastic wrap. These could then be microwaved on an as-needed basis. The compromise seemed to work, so I decided to introduce another savory baked item for sale in the store — quiche. I wrote down the recipe and gave it to the bakers. The next day, I received a sample. The crust was dark brown and one-half-inch thick. The filling was topped with a burnt brown layer of cheese, which, in turn was crowned by several square chunks. It looked like a few personal trunks had been thrown from the ship as flotsam and washed onto a crude oil-covered beach during a shipwreck. I cut a slice, and took a bite. It tasted of pork fat, a mass of Crisco and scrambled eggs. "No, not quite," I said quietly.

"Well, we followed your recipe, precisely as it was written."

"But you used cream instead of the half-milk, half-cream mixture, right? —" There was silence and "you got us" looks on their faces.

"And you used ham instead of bacon, right?" The bakers nodded slowly. "Right, O.K. I'll be back tomorrow with a sample."

That afternoon, I gathered all the necessary ingredients and started setting up production in our apartment kitchen. I kneaded the dough — lightly, so that it would be flaky, the hallmark of any really good quiche. As I put the dry beans into the pie shell, Inge walked through the doors. I slipped the shell into the oven. I took the shell that the bakers had baked earlier and tipped it upside down. I then shook the beans out of it.

"Hi ... what are *you* doing?"

"Quiche."

"Quiche ... *mishe?*"

"What's that?" I asked, as I finished extracting the last bean from the shell. "It means 'everything all mixed-up' in Latvian."

"Hmm. Yeah, I guess you could say that."

"Un-hunh, sure is," she quipped, after examining the 'flotsam on the beach' version of quiche.

"Yeah, that's what I received from the savory bakery today — so I decided to make the real thing — wanna help?"

"Sure, why not? By the way, look what I bought."

She rotated me towards the counter. She reached into a bag and pulled out two enormous forest green avocados.

"Oh my God — *avocados.*"

"Do they seem good to you? ... I wouldn't know, but I figured that *you* might have seen them before."

I hadn't seen any in over two years. When Inge asked how they should be cut, it took me a second to remember: "With those avocados, just cut them in the middle, so that there are two oblong halves." Inge did so as if she were cutting a diamond. We then sat down to eat them, with a Latvian mayonnaise-tomato sauce topping that I whipped up in a frenzy. The avocados were as hard as soap, an eternity away from ripeness. Nonetheless, after consuming the bulk of it I scraped the inside of the outer skin until the shell was black as night.

After the avocado, we ate the quiche — Inge thought it wonderful. She couldn't understand why Latvians hadn't come up with the idea of combining readily available ingredients into something as good as this before.

While Latvians were incessantly surprised by the "creativity" of new recipes, the "daily grind" experiences succeeded in keeping *my* life in a state of constant suspense. The oil change, a primal aspect of car ownership, gave me my next opportunity to experience a different cultural attitude towards cars. I drove my little Polo-with-Panda-bear-decals to the "Auto Formula" garage. The gentleman who owned it was one of Latvia's first automotive entrepreneurs and collectors. He had been fascinated by cars since youth, and in the 1970s came upon the idea that the vintage cars decomposing in potato fields or in sheds throughout the Soviet Union could be restored to good condition and exhibited. In fact, the Soviet Union had been a veritable treasure trove of classic vintage cars — old Deusenbergs, Bugattis, BMWs, Audis, Fords, Chryslers — as well as some very unique Soviet ZIL's, ZIM's, ZIS's[3], that had been acquired, used, and in some cases, maintained by individual owners through the 1960s. The oldest ones — those that were not in private collections in the independent Baltics before WWII — had been collected by the KGB as they ransacked the brotherly socialist states and Germany after their capitals came under Soviet control. Under Stalin's orders, the KGB collected almost one hundred fifty thousand automobiles that had been the property of Romanian, Hungarian, Czech and German middle class, nobility or the industrial elite on the eve of the war. Most of what had been in the hands of the Nazis had been destroyed by the bombing, but Hermann Goering's twenty-foot-long Hoetsch — one of only five models ever manufactured — was also found intact, and returned to Moscow in 1945. Viktors Kulbergs, this collector, had had the idea that the cars — those that had not been transformed to scrap or rusted away — should be collected, restored, and one day, put under one roof. He started realizing his idea in the 1970s, and though some officials frowned on this activity as being a "bourgeois endeavor," he received Brezhnev's full backing to complete his project. By the mid-1980s, he had — in his words — "collected the cream of what had been available," including Goering's car. He convinced the local authorities to establish a museum, and under these auspices, he built a structure adjacent to the old *Biķernieku* racetrack and started placing his automobiles inside. In a few short years, he was able to acquire some of the gems of Brezhnev's collection and by 1992, established the most eccentric vintage car collection north of Mulhouse, France[4]. Even the front of the building was designed to replicate a Rolls-Royce grill.

Viktors Kulbergs also attracted some Latvian-Canadian investors to support his bid to acquire the Audi and VW franchises for Riga. In partnership with the expatriate entrepreneurs, he opened up the first Western-style auto dealership and service center in Latvia. The garage had quickly developed a reputation for thorough work, a large array of spare parts for foreign cars, and rapid access to parts that were not in stock. When I arrived, the "compound"-like feel of the garage section of the building struck me, which was on the ground floor. The access was from another entrance than the majestic one used to enter the museum and Audi showrooms. I parked in the parking lot, and walked through the front entrance. As one entered, one faced a booth with a sliding glass window, not unlike what one would see in a bank. The attendant greeted me gruffly with the phrase: "Do you have an appointment?" When I replied that I had, he didn't ask me my name, only the make of automobile. He took my documents and confirmed the appointment. He then told a second attendant to bring the car in. I was instructed to drive the car up to the automated gate. I did so, pulling up next to a 600-series shining black Mercedes with tinted windows. Once my car was stationary, a large, burly attendant walked to the gate from the inside. Spools of razor-sharp barbed wire ran atop the twelve-foot-high cyclone fence. The attendant looked at my license plate, and ducked back inside. The gate started sliding to the right, at about an inch per second. I felt nervous — I was about to gain access to Blofeldt's inner sanctum, where I would have to place listening devices that looked like used spark plugs into a toolbox near the front desk . . . But I was mistaken. As soon as the gate opened wide enough to let him through, the attendant walked to my car; he gestured to me, with fire in his eyes, that the driver is not permitted in — the attendant would be taking over at this point. Since his forearms were thicker than my thighs, I found his argument terribly persuasive. He pointed me back to the entrance of the office. It was now clear to me no car owners were allowed behind the sliding gate. As I glanced back in the direction of the car, I noticed some white wires running along the periphery, on the fence on the inside. As well as being tall enough to keep out giraffes and most pole-vaulters, the fence was electrified.

Once inside, I was directed to the left, beyond the reception booth, to a "waiting area" about twelve feet wide and twenty feet long. A double-paned, soundproof glass wall separated the "waiting area" from the garage work area. Some outdated automobile magazines were scattered on a coffee table in this area, along with the latest brochures from VW-Audi, featuring the new

Audi 80 and 100 series cars. Men in thick, dark leather jackets and burgundy-colored sport coats were nervously pacing up and down the area, stopping every few minutes to peer through the window. Two others, who jerked their heads violently in the direction of any sitter who rustled a newspaper, or cleared his throat, followed one, in a forest green jacket. I sat down and started reviewing an Audi brochure, as if cramming for an exam. My concentration was interrupted by an outburst: *"KHRENA NYE PONIMAYUT! Chto blyat smotryut blyat pod mashinoi? Ya skazal chto zazhigatel' pizdetz, nye rabotayet! Yesli on mnye opyat skazhit chto nuzhen amortizator, v zhopu evo, blyat' sunu!* 'THEY DON'T KNOW WHAT THE HELL THEY'RE DOING! What the #$(#(@& is he doing looking underneath the car?! I told him the *ignition* wasn't (&*^&%^&% working! If he comes back and tells me again that I need a shock absorber, &*(^&^*&$$##@, I'm gonna stick it up his ass.'" Like the initial barks of the howler monkey brood leader, which triggers dozens of heretofore dormant monkeys to scream like demons on speed, this expression triggered a whole slew of "He better not screw up on my wheelbarrow's" and "I'll kill that $#%@%%&$# scum . . . on the spot's." After a minute or so, the mafiya howlers quieted down and calmly resumed doing what they had been before, as if nothing had occurred two minutes earlier. Only the pacing continued. One neck-less man stepped on my toes and blocked the light three times in a ten-minute period. As he approached for the fourth time, I almost jumped up and shouted, *"Sir*, your Audi 80 just gave birth to a *VW Rabbit!*" But his flattened forehead conveyed the fact that the joke would have been lost on him, and subsequently, my front teeth would be lost on some of his knuckles. Ironically, at this time in Latvia, men were not even allowed *entry* into the obstetrics hospital until five days after their child was born; at that moment, they could venture as far as the reception desk, where they could greet their wife and see their child for the first time.

Footnotes

[1] Limonad was an artificially flavored, lemon-lime soda beverage — if one could imagine the Western (Lem-o-lime) equivalent with half of the sugar and 90 percent of the taste removed [for safety's sake — in case somebody actually started developing a fondness for the drink], one would be close.

[2] The granyenka was an eight-ounce drinking glass with 14-facet design. It was the common man's shot glass throughout the Soviet Union. The glass was designed by Vera Mukhina, the same sculptor who had designed the collective worker and kolkhoznitsa statue in Moscow —the symbol used on all films produced in the Moscow Film Studio. She was born and raised in Riga, on Turgenev Street near the market.

[3] Zavod imeni Lenin — The Lenin Factory. Zavod imeni Mayakovsky — The Mayakovsky Factory. Zavod imeni Stalin — The Stalin Factory.

[4] The car museum of Mulhouse houses the collection of the Schlumpf brothers, an outstanding collection of vintage 1930s and 1950s European automobiles.

21

SQUATTERS

Spring emerges, in Latvia, with fits and starts. In fact, it is more appropriate to call it an exercise in faith, than a season of the year. In common parlance, spring begins on March 1. It is true, that in Latvia, the sun makes its reappearance, punching its way through the thick cloud cover, sometime during the first two weeks of March. Nonetheless, the temperature remains in the low 20s, well into the month. By the end of the month, there is invariably a severe storm, and the country is plunged into a thick snowfall at the moment that most people are getting accustomed to the idea that there is sun to be had in the country.

The first two weeks of April bring with them rains, and during the last two weeks, something wonderful happens. All the warmth that steadily accumulates in more Southern climes makes an equivalent caloric deposit during the last week of April or first day of May. Every inhabitant of the country will gladly give an account of "that May-Day parade in [choose year], when it was so hot, we were a) sweating like pigs, b) dying of thirst, and c) undressed to our underwear [said with a coy smile]." And they have reason to remember, because it is a ruthlessly humid eighty-five-degree heat, coming on the tail of four weeks at just above freezing.

However, the first two weeks of May, whether sunny or rainy, are undoubtedly the coldest two weeks outside of November and winter. There is inevitably a biting cold wind, or even a slushy rain. It is an inescapable reminder that one was living on the 57th northern parallel, just about two hundred miles south of the Arctic Circle — where grizzlies feel good. It is the kind of weather that could only please a pastry and cake merchant.

By this time, I was making a few strides in Latvian, which were truly hard won. One day I couldn't help complaining about it to Inge; I had attempted to tell the co-directors where we need our store to be located and one would have thought that I was telling the funniest joke in the world, they were laughing so hard.

"*You* had problems, what about *me?*"The boss was talking something about there being a 'bare' market here for the next two years. I didn't understand a thing. He knows that our markets are full now with produce that we would never even dream of having two years ago — I even saw a pineapple yesterday."

An explanation of bear market ensued. To the question of why must it sound the same, "To catalyze brain lesions in Japanese linguists" and "to drive beautiful coeds into the arms of the nearest proficient speaker of the language" were as good reasons as I could find.

"But still, in English, when someone says, 'I'm going to walk to the store,' it's clear. When I say it in Latvian, my co-directors laugh, and I *know* that I'm saying it correctly."

"Say it again."

"Sure — *Vinsh iet veikalā ar kayam.*"

"Hmm, that's O.K. Could you please repeat it slowly?"

"*Vinsh ee-yet vei-ka-la ar kaa-yam.*"

She giggled. "That's why… it comes out, 'They're walking their seagulls to the store.'"

"Oh well … that explains it, doesn't it? … When I go to the store, I only take pelicans with me."

I had never realized before how painful the acquisition of a language could be, later on in life, when one had to manage people through the perception of competence… I must have kept coming across as a blithering idiot.

"By the way was it green, or brown?"

"What?"

"The pineapple that you saw at the market."

"Both, I think."

Although my becoming conversant in Latvian was not among them, the summer was promising to bring with it new opportunities. For one, Inge was taking her first extended trip overseas, to the World Bank headquarters in

Washington. I had mixed emotions about the trip. On one hand, I was immensely pleased for her; on the other, I couldn't help asking myself, "What if she meets someone . . . who's not working in this dreaded sphere of 'food service'?" I then realized that there was no sense losing sleep over the question. Besides, at least now, I could concentrate fully on completing systems implementation in the bakery . . . and the Song Festival.

For *Jautrais Maiznieks*, the first summer opportunity was to be the *Dziesmusvētku* Song Festival, an event unique to the Baltic countries. The Song Festival involves over twenty thousand singers, of all age groups, to join in singing choral pieces that are from one to one thousand five hundred years old. In fact, in 2001 UNESCO would propose dubbing the Latvian one a major contribution to the world's intangible cultural heritage, meriting inclusion on its "Intangible heritage" list[1]. To accommodate the Song Festival event, the Riga City Council built an amphitheater in the 1930s. The amphitheater was nestled amidst the tall trees of "*Mežaparks*." The event involved, depending on the year, between 11,000 and 15,000 choral singers. When one considered the peripheral activities tied to the event, such as the children's parents sewing folk costumes, driving the kids to rehearsals or getting involved in other ways, then it was estimated that this festival mobilized over 100,000 Latvians on the performing side alone. Another 200,000 people would view the event as spectators, over the course of five days. For a country of 2.7 million, pulling such a concert off was no small feat. In sheer scale, the equivalent event in the United States would involve approximately 1.2 million singers and 20 million spectators, of which 7 million would be coming to attend the showcase concert. In other words, this event would equate to about 17 Woodstocks. It did not take long for the board to decide that The Merry Baker should participate in this event as a concessionaire.

The first step would involve getting the right space. I found out who was responsible for the rental of selling space, and scheduled a meeting with the man. Evalds Eberhards, the director of the *Mezaparks* recreational complex, was a soft-spoken man of short, stocky build, who sported a neatly trimmed beard. The office was about four hundred square feet in size, with two couches placed in the middle, facing one another. The walls were lined with large framed photos of the previous song festivals, as well as architectural sketches of various buildings and a resplendent marina. I introduced myself as being from The Merry Baker. The man smiled and nodded in apparent recognition. He then started speaking in broad generalities, about the future of the *Mezaparks*; how some Germans were moments away from investing twenty-five million deutschemarks in a marina and water entertainment complex on the shore of *Ķīsezers* (a lake pronounced "Thcheeshezers" for all masochists who wish to learn the Latvian phonology), which abutted one side of the park; how the children's railroad — currently consisting of one rusty track and a rat-infested train car — was going to be restored. One could not help but be awed by the artists' renditions of the plans, framed and looking very official, now adorning the walls of his office.

Valdis then started describing the Song Festival itself — how many people would be attending, and what opportunities were available for companies "that showed initiative." He subsequently instructed me to walk around and return with a preferred site specified. To make sure that this was not another exercise in futility, I asked if there was going to be a *konkurss* 'competition' for any of the spots. Eberhards laughed and shook his head, but added that priority is given to the renters that take the most space, and those that sign up the fastest. "For such a company as yours, we would like to offer some booths. Please take a look at the map... these locations are taken... but this one — the VIP parking lot — is still available, and promises to be good."

After our meeting, I surveyed the wooden cabins, each about 160 square feet in size; each was equipped with electrical outlets and lights. There were fourteen such booths on the grounds. About five of them were located in what could be called prime space, near the main arteries of circulation. The booth in the V.I.P. parking lot that Mr. Eberhards had recommended for us could count on having about a hundred well-fed drivers as customers . . . at only the last of the four three-hour concerts that promised two hundred thousand spectators — a proposal about as exciting as being offered to cater to the SWAT unit at the Super Bowl. Of the fourteen booths, about five were situated on the arteries of spectator circulation. And one of them seemed to be located both close enough to the stage *and* to the benches to be a sure bet.

I was going to call Eberhards to make a bid for the spot, when I got a call from one of the American Chamber members, asking to know if my company was going to participate in the Song Festival. I replied that we were thinking about it, but hadn't decided yet. The Chamber colleague then offered for The Merry Baker to be a concessionaire. I replied that it sounded interesting and then asked for more details of the offer. I then heard enough "unique advertising opportunity's," "be a part of the best location in the Song Festival's" and "there are going to be *thousands* of people streaming past this one spot's" to last me a decade. Finally, when Dan Keen was audibly winded, I asked, "And so, you've secured all this space?"

"Well . . . just about — we have one more meeting with Mr. Eberhards, to seal it up. Wanna join us?" How could I resist such an offer?

The meeting took place the following week, on a Tuesday. When I arrived, Dan and another of the American Chamber directors were already there. They were dressed slicker than Manhattan investment bankers on the day of an IPO, wearing "power" ties and sporting perfectly groomed hair. Mr. Eberhards, on the other hand, was wearing a nondescript Soviet-tailored[2] gray wool suit, with a crocheted folk tie. The latter reminded me of the 'Home Sweet Home' crochet on Grandma's couch cushions. I arrived in the middle of a very aggressive monologue, being delivered by Dan Keen. "So, Mr. Eberhards, we are not *changing* anything — I am asking for us to close this deal that you had verbally agreed to three weeks ago — rights to use the inner periphery of the seating area, during the concert." As soon as this was translated for him, Eberhards looked at them with a sheepish expression, and quietly replied, "But you're asking for us to do the impossible . . . we have never offered the selling of items from the inner perimeter of the Song Festival. I'm sorry, but I must have misunderstood you in our earlier discussions."

"But we had already offered, and you had agreed to accept, payment of several *hundred* dollars —"

Eberhards replied defensively, "But that was just for the use of the house in the back, where the high-level delegations would be. We hadn't mentioned the boys and girls selling Coca-Cola at our *National* festival among the stands . . . nobody has ever done that before . . . this festival goes back hundreds of years. It represents our heritage and national awakening. People simply would not *understand* if there were salespeople running around between the seats. People don't eat during the concert."

Having understood that the plan was to have a pizza-and-coke selling concession in the VIP section of the stands, I was caught between admiration for the entrepreneurial spirit of my fellow Chamber members, and shame that fellow Americans could denigrate a near-sacred event to the level of a wrestling match. Another representative of the American Chamber, whose pizza the boys and girls would be selling along with the Coca-Cola, said, "Mr. Eberhards, this is how things are done in every civilized country in the world at concerts and national events. Now you wouldn't want that Latvia falls further behind the rest of the civilized world, would you? Besides, with your receiving our agreed-upon percentage of the turnover, you stand to make several *hundred* more dollars on this venture . . ."

Dan followed up, "Evalds, what we are giving you now, is a *great* opportunity. It's not the opportunity of making a few hundred dollars more or less . . ." He paused solemnly, and then with an intonation the Baptist minister leaves for the crescendo of his sermon, concluded, "It's about the opportunity we are giving *you* to keep that which is most sacred to a man in business . . . his *word*."

At this point, Eberhards was quiet. He cast a forlorn glance at his desk. Then he raised his head, looked straight at me and asked, "Could *you* tell me — should I do this?"

I was caught completely off guard by the request. "Well, let me say that I.
.. uh ... don't have all the facts in front of me, so it would be hard to judg ..." I
quietly took in the fierce gazes of my Chamber colleagues. "Furthermore, I'm
not really a mediator here ... I just came here to see what was being offered in
terms of selling opportunities. But having said that, and now that I *am* here,
let me ask you guys a few questions, if you don't mind."

"Sure, go ahead," Dan said. He relaxed the heretofore-constricted
expression on his face. I got up, slowly stretched my arms, then crossed them
deliberately, and made some other movements that I had no need for, in an
effort to buy time, so that I could formulate some intelligent-sounding
response.

"Are you saying that you want exclusivity of both front and back of the
stage area?"

"Sure are."

"And how far in front of the stage?"

"Just the first hundred meters."

"And are the salespeople expected to circulate along the periphery, or go
between the benches and call out that they have beer and pizza and coke?"

"Definitely between the benches up and down — I am looking for *deep
penetration*," he said, while moving his clasped hands back and forth.

"Un-hunh, yes, I'm sure you are ... and in back of the stage?"

"Now, that would be our staging area, and all the VIP receptions would
also be handled there by us."

"Mr. Eberhards, how many people will be in back of the stage?"

"Oh, yes — this is where visitors from foreign countries will be ... as well
as all the singers and dancers who are taking breaks ... and there will be over
fifteen thousand of them —" I quickly made some calculations while he
continued his description, and came to the conclusion that they stood to
generate $70,000 from this placement alone.

When Evalds finished his clarification, I turned to Don and Sol, "Guys, I
think that you should give Evalds here a break. He obviously hadn't
communicated clearly *what* he had offered you in front of the stage. We're
talking about a sacred festival. At the last Song Festival, they just about declared
their country's independence. I mean, do you want to turn it into a baseball
game? These people will be singing national songs for the first time since the
country regained its freedom." I wanted to add, "Do you really think that the
spectators, the diplomats listening will want to hear, 'Get yer ice-cold beeya
heeya'?" but refrained, instead just stating that in my opinion, they were getting
a great deal here, what with exclusivity in back.

"If you add the boys and girls hanging out at the periphery of the seats, then you have a *fantastic* deal...I honestly don't think that you guys are losing anything here."

The Chamber board members turned towards one another and began discussing between themselves. They then turned to Eberhards and Dan said, "O.K., that'll be good enough for us...*this time.*" Dan then tried to sell me on the placement of a banner ad on the trolley bus which would drive people from the park entrance to the amphitheater.

I was relieved that my first-ever mediation role between my fellow countrymen and a Latvian Park administrator had ended successfully. I also wondered why that role befell me. I didn't even *know* this Eberhards guy.

That evening, I told the story to Inge. She said that I did well, adding, "It's certainly *not* in the mores of Latvians to have food *brought to* their seat during musical concerts...even eating at one's seat is frowned upon here. But if this 'Eberhards' guy goes around making commitments by phone like that, then he *deserves* to be taken advantage of." In turn, I had to admire the business acumen of the Chamber directorate members — even a run-down fiberglass-seated people mover would become a bright bold advertising vehicle.

That evening, we watched a new comedy show, *Imanta-Babīte*. A couple of actors, who had apparently seen some western *Saturday Night Live*-like sketches, decided to do the same here. It was a welcome contrast to the documentary-historical synopses of Latvian independence, dry news broadcasts, and programs featuring farmers showing off their prize-winning pigs or sharing the secret of why their particular strain of strawberries can survive frosty mornings. These two comedians enacted variations of the world's worst jokes, and captured the zeitgeist of the first group of Latvians who had traveled freely in Western Europe, unencumbered by KGB officers. "So, Imants, you traveled to Amsterdam. Did you like it?" "Yeah, interesting place." "Did you bring back anything?" "I dunno ... I'll go to the doctor and find out." During another show they were making a spoof on some of Latvia's first television commercials. Admittedly, they had a considerable stock of shoddily made, brain-numbing commercials to choose from. These included everything from beauty salons that gave every one of their pale-as-a-sheet, pasty-faced customers a Twiggy-style cut, to those that advertised loans — "Don't worry about collateral, we'll work something out" [like sure, sign over the company and receive a kick in the head ...]. These comedians targeted one company that was selling electrical supplies, as well as lamps and small electrical appliances. The original commercial, repeated with nauseating frequency, featured someone with a James Earl Jones-voice, saying, "Electrical supplies [rebels?]? *Remember "ELEKTRO MONTAZH!"* The Imanta-Babīte team repeated the oppressive voice while simulating people electrocuting themselves with the various household appliances featured in the commercial.

On May 30, at eight at night, I heard a knock at the door. This was a late hour for anyone to be "popping by." Upon opening the door, I was greeted by the sight of our landlord, the lessee of the apartment. "Good evening, please come in." The man nodded and walked in. He started looking around the apartment.

"*Kak mogu bit'lyubyeznim?* 'So what can I do for you?'" I asked.

"Tell me when you're moving out," he said as he pushed his greasy tinted glasses back up on his nose.

I was taken aback by the question. "Well, I can't say right now, but definitely by the end of August."

"We didn't agree on that."

"Wait, when we sat down four weeks ago at the table, and I said that we planned to stay through the end of the summer, you nodded."

"I did not ... Well, I may have nodded, but I didn't say that you could stay through the end of the summer."

"Then what did you *think* that you had said?"

"If I nodded, then that meant I'd think about it."

"Right, and now since three-and-one-half weeks have passed since that conversation, I assumed you had thought about it and decided that that would be fine, so you didn't bother contacting us and saying that you don't wish to extend or renew the lease ..."

"No, I never agreed."

"So what do you mean by that? How long are you letting us stay here then?"

"I expected you to be packed by now."

"Wait, let's get something straight here. Our daughter has exams this upcoming week, which will decide whether she continues in her school or not. And you're saying that we have to move *now*, when four weeks ago we had specifically discussed our staying through August *AND* you did not even pause for a second when you said all right?!"

"My daughter also has exams, and according to the contract, you have to move out by tomorrow night."

"You're being *completely* unreasonable ... we just can't do that ... you understand, we have no place to move to, nothing packed ... you're not going to dump us in the street, like street bums, are you?"

"Isn't that what you would do where you're from, at the end of the contract?"

"Certainly not. The landlord first confirms with the people that they are vacating the space ... and not renewing their contract ... or, or he tells them that he will be needing the space for his own use *well in advance.* I mean *these* things are agreed to first in a civilized manner."

He looked down at the table, shaking his head. Then after some deep thought, he asked, "How many days do you need?"

"Well, we can move into this room by Saturday — that's two days. Then we need, I dunno, maybe seven more days to find another apartment and move into it. Of course we'll pay for those days —"

"*Khorosho,* I'll let you all move into this room here on the right. I'll give you till next Friday to move out. In the meantime, the wife and kids are already in town, so we'll be moving in on Saturday morning." With that, he turned on his heels and bounded out the door, slamming it shut as he left. "We love *you* too!" I thought, as I turned to face Inge, who had just caught the tail end of the conversation. "Inge, darling ... ," I started, "Don't worry, we'll work this out. But now, let's start planning our apartment search." Inge nodded slowly, her eyes tearing up.

Two days later, on Saturday morning, the family moved in. They brought their old Soviet washer and television set, a clothesline, a samovar, two unwashed daughters, a hyperactive scrawny black mutt — some unlikely cross between a giant poodle and a schnauzer — and a toilet seat. With the latter they definitely re-established their dominion over the space. Inge was in a state of shock for the better part of the night. She caressed the children's heads. Markus and Eliza were frightened. I felt that in some perverse way, we were re-living the drama that took place between July 14 and 17 of 1941, when in the same manner thousands of "bourgeois" families had been given less than a day to gather their belongings and leave their apartments before being deported to gulags in Siberia[3]. I kept reassuring her not to worry. "Inge, please, don't worry. This too shall pass ... "

"Why did we leave Ogre? Why did we *ever* leave Ogre?"

As luck would have it, on the following day, Inge found an ad in the newspaper for an apartment precisely one block away. She called, and to our relief, it was still available. The apartment was 60 percent smaller than our current residence, but would tide us over while we found a permanent location, which we had decided to do immediately. The apartment had only two rooms, and a much smaller kitchen, but it was available precisely at that moment, and didn't require the tedious "registration of inhabitant into address" routine. "We have to find something permanent, Boriss, you understand."

"Yes, lovely one, I know . . . this one is just temporary." But it was quite fortunate for us that we had found an apartment; starting from late Monday afternoon the hosts indulged us with hardy carousing — replete with old Soviet sing-along's like *Katyusha*[4], a crowd of red-nosed revelers, and an atmosphere designed to put-off the hardiest of apartment-mates. Whether this debauchery was designed to relay the message, "Don't even think for a *moment* of squatting here," or whether it was a soul-felt re-christening of the apartment space that they had given to desecrating strangers for nine months, I couldn't say. However, when one houseguest, in the twilight stage of consciousness, fell against the door of our room and exclaimed "Dear God, how difficult it . . . ish . . . to . . . where's the dawg . . . move around . . . on this . . . shlippery floor!" The dog, rallying to the call, started running across the parket, producing a sound like sixteen pieces of chalk scraping a blackboard. Inge and I held each other closer than we had ever done before. It was 1:35 A.M.

Little did I know that our plans for an orderly move would also suffer a severe setback, when I opened the door to the apartment on Lāčplēša street.

"So, you're Vasiili, yes?" I asked.

"Yes, that's me. I'm so glad that *you* had answered the advertisement. It's so hard to be certain these days that the right people will read it. Could I possibly offer you a cup of tea?"

"Well, actually, I was just stopping by on my way . . ."

"Please, do not offend me . . . it is a good tea."

"Well, all right, then."

He led me through the corridor. We turned into the first room on the right. It was no more than five feet by ten feet large. The floor planks shone through many places in the linoleum. The window afforded a narrow view onto the courtyard. There was a small gas oven on the right and some cabinets immediately above it. The only furniture was some shelves to the right of the oven, a small sideboard that had been painted hospital green, and a table in the corner. Unlike with our previous kitchen, only three people could sit around the table. Only one person could maneuver around the kitchen and the most sophisticated dish that could be prepared would be a BLT.

He sat down, and he asked where I was from. I responded, "Estonia." I did so almost instinctively to all Soviet Russians that I met without formal introduction, on account of their extreme attitudes to Americans; these two attitudes being either "*Wow*, it's a real live, honest-to-goodness *amerikanets!*" which would be followed by shameless fawning and wild drinking, or the "*Great*, a rich @$#!^!^^ *amerikanski kapitalist* — I've got to get him to some quiet place, hit him over the head, steal everything he has on him, and leave the capitalist to freeze…" Being blonde, I could pass for an Estonian. I figured that so few Russians had bothered learning that language, that no one would ever call me on my bluff.

"So, although I had explained some things to your wife [about this apartment], I'd feel better explaining them to you." I said nothing, but nodded in acquiescence. "Firstly, in the kitchen, the stove is a little funny. It doesn't always light in back, at least not at first. You must allow the gas to be turned on for a long time before it catches on the right back burner."

"Uh-huh."

"Now, the table shakes a little, but not to worry, a crushed matchbox does nicely in stabilizing it. The front right leg, of course."

"Yes, of course," I chimed in, looking down to see the edge of a matchbox sticking out from under the leg. I started wondering whether this man was a little delusional, or just overeager to please.

"Now this closet, I'm afraid that I can't let you use," he stated firmly, before opening the door to a "cold closet," the pre-war Latvian predecessor to the refrigerator. In the back of each of these closets was a window, approximately the size of a sheet of paper, which was used to regulate the temperature; opening it fully in the winter would have provided enough cold to keep the items in the back frozen. "It's full of records and newspapers that form … the foundation of my early life …" he continued, as he opened the door. I saw a closet so crammed with records, magazines, and yellowing newspapers, that it redefined the word *inaccessible*.

"So, you're saying that we shouldn't use this closet," I confirmed — a question as redundant as asking a California highway patrolman if it should be preferable not to use one of the overpasses above the Santa Monica freeway as a drop-off point for larger varieties of watermelon.

"Right. O.K., if you want to listen to a few records, go ahead. In fact," he said as he walked inexplicably across the front foyer to the living room, "I've been listening to a few myself." About ten record covers were scattered on the living room floor.

"Have you heard this one, by the way?" he asked, as he pointed to the cover of a *Melodiya* Recording Company record with a faded, misprinted photo of a mod black group riding a rocket towards a large round object which was, I supposed, some planet. "Von vey teeket to za *bloo-ooz*."

"Oh, yeah, Boney M. They're great. Not so popular in Am— Estonia, but my high school sweetheart brought the record back from Finland . . . great sounds."

"Von vey teeket, *von vey teeket*," he repeated as he danced from side to side, impersonating (to my untrained eye) Rudolf Nureyev with a bad case of flu. "Hey, how about we drink one hundred grams?" he said, as he gestured with the two-finger to the throat sign, which signified, "by obliterating our livers with alcohol in each other's company let's pretend to bond in a *real* way but really not at all because as every idiot knows, anything-that-you-do-or-say-while-drunk-is-readily-excusable-the-following-day."

"No, really, thanks for the invite . . . but I have to run to a very important meeting. Maybe next time."

"Too bad, I'll have to drink by myself."

"Now, Vasiili, when do you think we can move in?"

"Tomorrow, at this time, the place will be *yours*. The train leaves in three days, and I am staying with a friend in the meantime, so after I clean it up a little, it shall be at your disposal. After all, I am a writer for *Sovetskiy Komsomolets[5].*"

"*Khorosho*, so if I come by tomorrow at one in the afternoon, I'll be able to get the keys, right?"

"*Certainement.*"

"Good. So have fun taking this trip down memory lane and I'll see you tomorrow," I said, as I jerked the door open and geared myself for a fast trot to the bakery office.

The following day, so as not to appear indecently eager to bump the leaseholder from his flat, I showed up at 1:15. I rang the doorbell, and was greeted by a jovial but tonally modulating, "My *Estoonets* is here," from the other side. I chuckled to myself. But as Vasilii opened the door, his breath reeking of cheap vodka, my smile faded. Behind Vasilii, who lunged at me with open arms, I saw not only the same record covers that had been piled on the floor the day before, but they had acquired another two layers.

"Tovarisch, how about the 'Rolling Stons' — zey za best, no?"

"Yeah, yeah, they're good and all, but Vasiili, you promised to have the apartment ready for us to move in to *today!*"

"Oh this, why that's absolutely no problemo . . . two, maybe . . . hic . . . three minutsh work, that's all.

"Come, let'sh have shome tea," he said, once again hitting his neck with his index and middle fingers." Vasiili saw me shaking my head, and then added,

"Besides . . . hic . . . there are some important . . . uh . . . thingsh that I forgot to mention about the bathroom."

I raised my eyebrows, and then said, "Well, all right, but I hope that this is going to help things along quickly."

"*Certaine-ment.*"

But as I walked into the kitchen, my doubts grew. The kitchen was more disheveled than it had been the day before. Pieces of a dried *kambala* fish, the telltale sign of a drinking binge, were scattered all over the table and floor. It looked like the fish, or several of them, had been desecrated by a voodoo witch doctor, with fins and tail pulled out first and thrown in a circle around the table, followed by heads and skeletons, extending in concentric circles outwards. "Vasilii, it looks like the kitchen needs some work too!"

"Yesh, yesh," he retorted, fervently nodding, "now come *ye* along, while the water ish . . . hic . . . boiling, lemme jesh show you how . . . how . . . oh yeah . . . how the water heater worksh."

I was led into the bathroom. There was one standard Soviet-issue, chipped enamel, rust-stained bathtub, with several pipes protruding from it. Next to it, or more precisely, overhanging it and dominating the entire back wall, was an apparatus measuring some 2 ½ feet by two feet and three feet high. Above it was an exhaust hood.

"Now, it izh important ta begin . . . hic . . . with the water running. It musht be flowing . . . at a light stream," he said as he opened the faucet midway, resulting in a hefty flow. "Turn thish lever to the left . . . Light it." He did so, and I was momentarily deafened by the sound of a jet engine. "When it is lit, and going voom-*voom-VOOM*, twist the . . . uh . . . lever to the other shide, bypassing the middle . . . hic . . . position. Thish musht be done quiggly, ta avoid getting it shtuck . . . hic . . . in the middle. Cuz if you . . . get shtuck in the meedle . . . ha-ha, *no* bathy-wathy."

"Right. Seems to be no problemo. Now how strong does the water need to be to keep it powered?"

"Oh, a very li-luh, a trickle," he said as he turned the level down to what apparently was the minimum. I looked and the "very little" equated to about four gallons per minute — a "trickle" only to a beached blue whale.

As we left the bathroom, I thanked him for showing the system, and then asked, in a tone of voice that I made as matter-of-fact as possible: "So, Vasilii, when are you going to let us move *in*?"

"Pleeeeease . . . go ahead, I jusht have to call my friend, sho that I can stay at her place tonight."

"Yes, but Vasilii, you have these records all over the place, and the books piled up, along with your clothes in the closet..."

"To-mor-row... my train... sheuh... leaves, 'toot-toot'... and I musht be on it. Affer all, affer all, I *am* a... hic... editor for *Sovetskiy Komsomolets*, and they *neeeed* me."

"No doubt as role model," I thought, but answered coolly, "Can I help with something?" trying to lessen the irritation I felt on the edge of my voice.

"No, no-o, I wouldn't think of it."

"O.K. I have to run. I trust that you will keep your word and that tomorrow we can move in, Vasilii!" He smiled, clicked his heels together, and saluted with the pioneer's salute, "No problemo... *Vsyegda gotov.*"[6]

The following day, one-half hour before the designated time, I decided to stop by the apartment to make sure that the vagrant apartment holder was gone. A knock on the door produced no results. I palm-slapped the door. No sound emerged. After putting my ear to the door, I heard what sounded like a groan. At this point, I imagined that disorder would still prevail, but that some things would at least have been stuffed into the cold closet. I tried the handle — the door was unlocked. Vasilii was passed out on the couch, having made no visible progress either in cleaning the apartment, nor in moving himself towards the train station. After sitting him up, I cajoled him into telling me where I can find his friend's telephone number. On the other end of the line was a female, one of the high-strung Soviet types who can make the purchase of a local cheese more strenuous than a full day's shopping safari in Bloomingdale's women's department. This I took as a good sign, as these types of ex-Soviet women were anything but complacent.

"Hello, my name's Boriss, we're the ones that have agreed to rent the place — but it looks like Vasilii passed out."

"Oh dear."

"Yes, perhaps we should coordinate our activities... or it looks like he'll lose a job, as well as rent for his place."

"Yes, yes, I'll be right over... I can only ask for you to excuse his conduct. .. he has his... moments."

We agreed that she would take charge of the clean-up process and expulsion. Within two hours, she packed all the bags, while Vasilii started regaining consciousness. Finally, to the accompaniment of a stream of "excuse him, he's not usually like this's," I helped her load his bags and pour Vasilii into my car before driving both of them to the train station.

Prior to moving into that place, we kept the windows open for two days. At the same time, the kitchen furniture Inge repainted a bright yellow. The kitchen finally looked like it would have been "Vincent's kitchen in Arles" if he would have bothered painting it. To further mask the smell of stale cigarettes and incipient-cirrhosis breath, we wiped all surfaces with a lemon-scented cleanser. Finally, the bathtub was soaked in a vinegar-water mixture. I then asked Inge if it wouldn't be a good idea to buy a canary and a cage, with the assurance that if the bird survives, then so would the kids. She laughed, but quickly cut the laughter short and moaned, "Oh Boriss, we've got to get our *own* place."

Footnotes

[1] However, in this August 2001 meeting, the proposal lost by one vote. A Lithuanian cast the deciding vote against. He explained that, although the Song Festival merits inclusion in the list of World Cultural Heritage activities, there was no reason to single out the Latvian one.

[2] Soviet tailoring. It was about ten years behind the styles in the Western part of Europe. Caught in the "too old to be trendy, yet too recent to be stylish or eclectic" abyss of men's fashion.

[3] Accounts of atrocities differ, but records show that at least fifteen thousand people were deported from Latvia in one week's time. Most of them were ethnic Latvians, but records show that over thirteen hundred Jews and six hundred Baltic Germans were also included. It is estimated that 1 percent of the population of Latvia was deported during twelve months of Soviet occupation (Bilmanis, Alfred. History of Latvia. Princeton University Press, 1951.) Their households were immediately assigned, with all furniture, fixtures and finery intact, to Soviet Russian ofitseri. The officers were joined later by their spouses from the Russian hinterlands.

[4] Katyusha. Perhaps the most popular post-war Soviet song, about a young woman waiting to receive a letter from her loved one at the Front. It is the rallying song for pro-Soviet Russians when they are feeling indignantly patriotic.

[5] Soviet Youth — A journal that a few years earlier Komsomol (Committee of Soviet Youth) members and aspiring young communists had to devour. But in 1992, this had been the first newspaper to turn from a pro-Communist stance to a somewhat more objective one.

[6] "Always at the ready!"would be the best translation. The salute was the standard flat-handed to the forehead, with forearm cocked at the elbow. For the "Young Pioneers" the hand was raised higher and further to the left, above the head, instead of covering just the forehead.

22

MĀJA SWEET MĀJA[1]

The issue of more permanent dwelling space for the family dominated our conversations in the following week, culminating in a "if we can't get our own place, then we're moving back to Ogre!" ultimatum from Inge.

"O.K., O.K. we can't have *that* ...," I retorted as I envisioned myself wilting in the "aroma express" to Ogre, "so where do we start looking, Inge?"

"City Center, or ... *Mežaparks* ... what do you think?"

"Well, I'd like it to be in the center of the city ... but *Mežaparks* sounds ... O.K."

I had been there only twice before, and felt that it was beyond the pale of fervent activity, but at least it would not entail a train ride to get to. "Mežaparks" (pronounced Mezhaparks) or "Forest Park," had been a stylish section of the city before the war. In fact, it was Europe's first suburb, started in 1901. Built by Baltic Germans for the elite of society, it was the first planned project of houses on large plots of land which boasted trees, native shrubs and landscaping, while at the same time being accessible from the center of the city by a horse-pulled tramway. The nearest equivalent to it in the United States would be the Garden District of New Orleans.

"So what's the next step?" I asked.

"What do you think ... how would you do it in the United States?"

"Well, I suppose that ... I'd call a real estate agent or, or look in the good old newspaper."

"Well then — we'll do the same thing *here*," replied Inge with a quickness that belied a complete lack of knowledge about said procedures. The following evening, Inge began poring over the newspapers that featured want ads. Want ads, in 1993, were only crudely divided by category. "Apartments, garages, house supplies," was a typical order. "O.K., there's an apartment in Imanta ... a lawn mower in Pļavnieki ... a toolshed ... in Vecāķi ... What?! Replacement rings for a Zhiguli — what's that doing here?" I heard as Inge applied herself to the task at hand. Every night, the night-table would be covered in ads that had been cut out, for easier assembly, insofar as the relevant ads were often several pages from one another in that section of the paper. But Inge's tenacity paid off. Within a week she had found three "available" apartments. One in the nice part of the city center, another in *Me aparks*, and the third across the river, in Pārdaugava.

We lost no time in visiting the apartments. We started in the prestigious Center neighborhood of Riga — the section in which the most prominent citizens had lived before the war. The neighborhood boasts the most concentrated collection of five- and six-storied Art Nouveau buildings in the world. The apartment we went to view was located on the fourth floor. That particular day when we viewed it, the sun was streaming in. As we knocked on the door, we were greeted by the bark of a massive, angry dog. The commotion of the owner putting the dog away somewhere, then the opening of the door a crack, and the series of chains — to be released one by one — subsequently followed that. "Shades of New York, how pretentious," I thought. We were greeted by an ebullient elderly lady, "Yeah, you're in the right place. Come on in. Look at the view ..." The apartment was on the fifth floor of a building with whose floors each boasted twelve-foot ceilings, so this was a commanding height from which to view the hustle and bustle of street life below. Unfortunately, the only view it afforded was that of a massive parking lot hemmed in by the back sides of an equally tall building; one had the sensation of having been assigned one of the low-rate rooms in a large hotel — on the side away from the majestic view. "Well, this view is ... impressive, but I'd probably prefer the bay, or even this river, if I had the choice ... ," said Inge. We then began the "tour" of the apartment, going from room to room, giving positive statements whenever possible. "We want five thousand dollars for the place," the old lady announced, before returning to watch her television program. When we stopped in front of the Plexiglas cage, in which the Doberman pinscher was jumping wildly, frothing with desire to tear us apart, we looked at each other — "Seems to have the wrong karma, *vai ne?*" I commented. Besides the dog-borne filth to take away any charm that the apartment would otherwise have had, the fact that four of the five rooms were connected in the form of a ring, proved to be impracticable; this flat was an oversized corridor more than a Western-style apartment. "Horrible," whispered Inge, putting an end to all conjecture. She then turned back to the old lady — who was watching Santa Barbara as if her own son were in the show — and said, "Thank you, but we won't be taking it … we're looking for a few more bedrooms." The lady didn't even look up.

We then went to visit the place in *Mežaparks*. The house featured a round balcony with a balustrade on the second floor. A button, attached to partially-exposed wire, dangled next to the door. We took turns pushing it but heard no sounds. I knocked on the door,— this must have been the fifteenth coat, applied without so much as a light sanding of previous coats. To my eye, untrained in detecting the intricacies of previous generations of paint, the door looked like the surface of a sesame-seed bun painted the color of a turquoise pendant. Finally we heard someone descending a staircase. A lady, looking to be in her mid-fifties, opened the door. However, I didn't jump to conclusions, as I often erred on this point — she may well have been in her early forties. She welcomed us with a brief smile, and asked if we were the ones that had called earlier today for the meeting. Two of her front teeth were missing. The others were streaked brown. Her coiffure looked like it had been arranged with the help of a broken bottle. Her dress was soiled. Inge smiled, nodding affirmatively. The lady led us up the staircase to the apartment. The corridor, which is the only thing one saw from the entry, was about forty feet long, and abutted a multi-paned door. The kitchen was a space of approximately twelve feet by eight, only slightly larger than the space we had now. Immediately to the left of the entryway into the kitchen was a cast iron sink, partially coated with enamel, but mostly bare rusting iron; a circle had even been worn through the ceramic at the bottom, around the drain. To the right of the kitchen entry, successfully blocking any rapid movement along the right wall, stood a heating system or more precisely, a circa-1939 gas-powered heater. In the left corner of the room was a small cold closet. As we made our way to the back wall of the room, we saw a doorway to the right. Behind it, along the windows, was another space of ten feet by six feet. This space was the cubby where the maid once slept, in the pre-WWII era. Now, this room — where the master of that time would never set foot — was the dining room. The space allowed for one forward/backward, and two lateral movements, but not more, unless they were cha-cha steps. This couple had put the dining table in the maid's chamber. The net effect made the space look even smaller than the glorified closet that we currently cooked and ate our meals in. "Gosh, this apartment must be minuscule, if they have to do that …,"I inadvertently thought to myself.

Then we were shown the rooms. The living room was not spacious — it was royal. Alone, this "parlor" took up 600 square feet, with folding doors separating what must have been the dining room from the sitting room component of the space. A solid oak herringbone parquet covered the floor of both rooms. A room that we were not allowed to see was a mirror of the sitting room component; we later deduced that it had to have been another three hundred square feet in size. By Western standards, this was a large apartment, at what must have been fourteen hundred square feet, for a family of three in a city of one million population. By Soviet standards, it was a *gargantuan* apartment for the family of three that had inhabited it in the 1970s — not to mention for the two that remained. To understand our surprise at seeing a nothing-out-of-the-ordinary-in-the-West-sized apartment inhabited by only two people, one needs to think beyond Tokyo-scale small, and return to 1990-Soviet-scale small.

On the 21st of June 1945, the Soviet Latvian Supreme Council published decree #2765, which stipulated a new standard allowance of minimum square footage per head-of-household. This minimum was *nine* square meters (about one hundred square feet) per person. Now, that was assuming one person, living in a room. Additional family members would be treated to a resplendent four square meters (forty-five square feet) each.

By 1960, few Latvian families in Riga occupied more than one-third the living space that their grandparents had before the war. And by and large, these parameters were enforced until 1991. In 1990, in Riga's center, most people lived in communal apartments — the result of the nationalization of space. I often imagined how this decree would have left today's real estate agents frothing at the mouth. Imagine, people forced to retreat to one-third of their current house or apartment, leaving the remaining two-thirds available for rent! I could just envision the scenario.

"Hello Mr. Bērziņš, I'm from the Joseph Dzugashvili Real Estate Agency. I hope that I didn't choose a bad time."

"No, you didn't, please come in."

"Now I have a w-o-o-onderful offer for you today!"

"What could that be, we are wanting in *nothing*."

"Exactly…I am sure that as good Socialists you are wanting to be *deprived of it all*."

"Socialist? *All*?"

"Why yes — of all of your old petty-bourgeois baggage and lifestyle. But no, all that sacrifice won't be necessary from you on *this* particularly bright, shiny day! No, I have a more, shall we say, suitable offer for you. Here it is — you can choose any two rooms of this *won-der-ful*, turn-of-the-century apartment with glorious twelve-foot-high ceilings, that you'd like, and continue, living in them *from this moment on!*"

"Well, yes, we know that it's turn-of-the-century, with high ceilings and we chose it for those two rooms and those two rooms and *those* two…"

"Ha-ha-ha, how terribly amusing. Now seriously, I see a study … overlooking the quiet, stately courtyard… very nice, certainly no tramways to bother you on this side."

"Yes, no tramways, but you should hear the cat's meowing on summer days —"

"An orchestra of natural sounds, Mr. Bērziņš, you sweet man — you look so much like an animal lover. Now, you'll agree that this kitchen has all the modern conveniences — even a beautifully molded niche for a houseplant. Simply love-ly!"

"We know that it's '*seemply love-ly*' — we've been buying the 'conveniences' over the past ten years. But we still need an asparagus peeler. …As for the houseplant my wife changes it every three months…"

"How absolutely *cha-a-a-rming*. Well, that homey touch won't be lost on the new co-tenants — one of them was just released from the Archangelsk prison and I'm almost sure that they didn't change the plants *there* four times a year."

"From where?!"

"Now, I understand that your preference then is for this bedroom on the left and that 'study' next to the kitchen, right? Let me just say that in *my* humble judgement, you have made an ab-so-lutely su-*per*-lative choice."

"Bu … wha … WAIT, what are you doing, what, where will we go to the bathroom?!"

"Why in the toilet, of course, what a peculiar question. Just that now, you might have to wait a little on some mornings, when there's an eensy teensy little queue … but not to worry, the urologists at the highly esteemed 'Lenin-Is-So-Great-I-Faint-at-the-Mention-of-His-Name' Hospital in Petrosvinsk have determined that waiting to go to the potty is good exercise for the bladder … keeps the muscle walls stretching. Any other questions?"

"Wha … ? Wait, *hey*, did you say 'other people'?!"

"Yes I did, and in fact I have to rush down and meet with them just about now, so if you don't mind, I'll be running… oh, just a helpful little hint — your new socialist comrades won't be moving in for half-an-hour, so please feel free to move in a bed or two in place of the massive oak desk-with-those-little-iris-curly-cue-highlights that you currently have standing there. The beds probably won't be as ornate, but they'll be a little more comfortable to sleep on. So bye for now ... oh and do keep up with that changing-the-plant routine, it'll simply be what Marx had in mind when he said 'from each according to his means,'-something-or-other."

So, in the context of this decree, 130 square meters (1450 square feet) was up to ten times more than what most every other couple in Riga else lived in. To paraphrase one of my college friends, this apartment was "Soviet real estate porn." It had been constructed by a wealthy civil engineer. However, it had not been cared for in ages, and bore the tell-tale signs of late-night parties — cigarette burns, the scratches left by high-heeled shoes the heel pads of which had come off, and pickle-juice stains.

Nor had the apartment undergone any significant improvements or renovations since 1940. As we returned to the main hallway, I noticed that the pre-war plan of separating the toilet from the washroom had not been altered. One used the toilet, then exited the space to wash one's hands in the next room. The toilet space was approximately four feet deep and three feet wide. A plastic tank holding the water was mounted on the wall, two meters above the potty. The plastic had faded to yellow. Hanging down from the tank was a chain, at the end of which was a black plastic handle. The only element of the toilet-room that hinted at comfort was the fact that the toilet had a seat, although this seat was the most basic lacquered pressboard, barely contoured, "we-sit-but-we-don't-dawdle" model — in the winter one gritted one's teeth before sitting down. However, nothing had prepared us for what we were to see in the adjacent "bath" room. In the middle of the eight-foot-by-five-foot space was a free-standing bathtub. At one end of the bathtub stood a contraption most North Americans, myself included, would have mistaken for a whiskey still. It was cylindrical and about six feet tall; it had two tubes sticking out at the top — one went to the kitchen, the other to a rusty blue metal pipe, about five inches in diameter. The latter pipe presumably went to the next floor up. On the side of the apparatus which faced us was an opening, about twenty inches square, into which one placed pine, birch, or peat, whatever was at hand to heat the water. A thin, chromed faucet, approximately one-half inch in diameter and twelve inches long, protruded from the side. It should have extended out at an angle perpendicular to the apparatus, but it was cocked at a strange one — the result of having been used once too often to optimize balance — which ultimately sent the water towards the side of the tub. The bathtub was a stand-alone, cast-iron, chipped enamel model. The enamel had mellowed, with time, to attain a beige-yellow tint. This was an ideal container for the moonshine. The only items that suggested "bathroom" were a dirty mirror, and two toothbrushes lying atop a small wooden stool. Blue paint clung — in hopeless desperation — to a few parts of the stool, which was now largely gray. The toothbrushes looked as if someone had crushed a white centipede with his boot and then lodged the carcass on top of a blue plastic holder. A bare twenty-five-watt light bulb, suspended from an intertwined cord turned yellow-brown with age, provided the sole illumination in the room. The scant lighting reinforced the impression that this space was dedicated to an illicit activity of one type or another. If this had been Tennessee in the 1920s — whiskey; New York in the 1980s — crack; in Soviet Latvia of 1990 — personal hygiene.

The man, Yevgeny, commented that this wood-burning water heater had been quite a remarkable innovation in its heyday (some sixty years earlier). Although this one was undoubtedly more modern than a 1920s still, the thirty years of constant use since its installation appeared to double its age to a neophyte on these contraptions such as myself. "How ... quaint —," I said to the renters of the flat, when I could speak once again, ". . . and how noisy," whispered Inge, as the wind from outside stirred up the flames in a threatening manner. Inge was visibly mortified. To prevent the silence from appearing insulting, I turned to the couple and said, as if describing a perfectly normal procedure which we ourselves executed daily, "So, one need only stoke the furnace for thirty minutes, with firewood, and voila, out comes piping hot water in whatever quantity needed, as long as it doesn't exceed forty liters (fifteen gallons)..." The lady of the house nodded. Judging by the time allotted to the description of this 'still', I made sure to feign awe, "Of course, I agre an apartment with all these, uh ... *modern* comforts will certainly fetch its price, of that there can be no doubt."

We returned to the sitting room, where by now, two seats had been brought out by Yevgeny. As we sat down, I noticed that the surfaces of the cabinets were crowned with various paraphernalia, both whole and broken, which reminded me of the limited opportunities for the pursuit of hobbies in the Soviet Union. These included lamps whose bases were constructed of matches and driftwood and a plant pot made from what looked, to my untrained eye, like toilet seats glued one on top of another. But the item that occupied the place of honor on his shelves was the most bizarre ship model that I had ever seen. The model was of a tall-masted two-hundred-year-old ship; this replica was about two feet long. It was constructed of canning jars, clothespins, and piano wire, as well as uneven pieces of wood. I was tempted to ask if this model ship, painted sky blue and crowned with a rum bottle label, was actually seaworthy, but modesty got the better of me. Instead, I commented on how interesting this ship looked. The man, who had been heretofore eyeing me suspiciously, relaxed his sitting posture to a slouch and said, "I did that myself…" After taking a slow, deliberate drag on the cigarette, he continued, "took me two years." "Impressive," I replied.

The ladies returned and sat down. Inge and I looked at each other, with must have been baboon-like expressions, as we had no clue what to say next. As we were sitting, nervously waiting for the next awkward moment, I distinctly heard the older couple sizing us up, "They're such a young, handsome couple…" Then the lady turned to us.

"We have another pair that really wanted to take this place. They already came here with the kids and all."

"Well," I thought to myself, "we can bring the kids… and the grandparents… if that's their criterion."

"And they're offering a place in the *Purvciems* district in exchange for this apartment… what can *you* offer?"

"Well, since we don't have an apartment, we can offer you… any location in the city that you want," said Inge. She was hesitant — it was clear she was uncomfortable with bargaining. The couple looked at one another, and once again started whispering between themselves. Then the lady turned to us.

"What do you mean, anywhere? Don't you have an apartment to exchange?"

"We're from Ogre, so we need to exchange with someone from the city anyway… so we mean *any section of town.*"

"Well, we had been thinking either Maskavas iela or Pļavnieki."

"That would suit us just fine—"

Yevgeny then added, "We wouldn't mind living near our daughter in Imanta …" She looked at him with anger, and whispered something quickly. He waved his hand at her and then turned back to us, "But now, let's have a drink."

Unsure of what to do next, I turned to Inge and asked if I had missed something, but that they hadn't mentioned anything concerning the compensation they want for transferring their lease rights to us. "No they didn't … what do you think, should we wait?"

"No, let's tell them now… so that we can adjust our offer."

I turned to the couple and asked, "By the way, we haven't talked about the price of the apartment…"

"The other couple also offered money."

Inge smiled and then said, hesitantly, "We can offer you three thousand five hundred dollars cash, right away, plus the new apartment, which will certainly cost a good deal."

The couple offered no response and just looked at one another, as if we had just explained the formula for determining quark size. After what seemed like a full minute, she said, "Oh, let's have another drink — for *friendship!*"

When we left the apartment, a few minutes later, Inge said, "Oh, I want this apartment so-o-o badly."

"Yeah, I can understand why . . . but could you just tell me what went on for the past hour? I don't know whether we've clinched an apartment, we're on a 'waiting list,' or that we've been chatted up by a couple of people who are bored with each other and have found a cheap way of attracting interesting strangers who will try their hardest to compliment a really sorry array of interior decorations. If it's the latter, I admit that it's a pretty good ploy — with *this* apartment, they've made sure that the people that arrive go out of their way to be nice.

Inge finally answered, "Oh I don't know . . . I have no idea . . . but I'll call tomorrow." We went out the front door, and passed some bed springs that had been mounted on two metal pipes and painted turquoise blue; the bed springs served as a gate into the garden. We turned around and looked up at the window — the couple was there, waving their hands. "Did you catch his name? Didn't it sound like Perkinsovitch, or something?"

"What?"

"Nothing, never mind."

The following day, while I was checking on the production going to the Metropole Hotel, I heard the sounds of bakers talking, but without the usual accompanying hum produced by the bakery machinery. I went to the production floor tables, around which I saw the bakers in various stages of sobriety: partial; sober-if-concentrate-on-it, and keep-away-from-the-propeller-mixer drunk. On the table were no fewer than three empty bottles of Riga Champagne, two bottles of *Beliy Aist* 'White Stork'[2] brandy, and one bottle of *Pertsovka* 'Pepper' vodka. Apparently, this volume of liquor was needed to wash down the open-faced sandwiches. I realized that they were celebrating another birthday . . . or worse yet, a name's day. Valters' face was red. I opened my mouth, took a breath, and was preparing to say something to the tune of "Hey, hey, this is your workplace — this is *not* a party room," but before I could utter the "H," Valters squeaked with a shaky voice, "Please, don't be a stranger, come join us!" "It's his *name's day*, he's just too shy to tell you," said Olga, smiling. As she turned to him, he shrugged his shoulders and smiled. I was touched by this scene, so I just quietly said, "Thanks for the invite . . . I guess a *little* of Riga's best won't hurt anyone." I couldn't understand much of the conversation after that, but I did understand that the tone had changed from "let-it-all-hang-out" bawdy to "the-boss-is-here" bland. Shortly after gulping down a shot of champagne, I excused myself and went to the cake bakery below. There, the bakers were experimenting with some fillings for a new chocolate cake, whose primary ingredient, besides chocolate, was going to be *Captain Morgan's Rum.*

I got a call at the bakery. It was Inge — she was elated. "You can't believe it — they want us to go again!" As the notes of "Private Dancer" broke the background silence, I shouted, "Great, I guess that we've made the next round. Let's talk it over at home." As I walked home, I contemplated my options as to the Name's day celebration. "Well, I could fire all of them... right away... say that that is not the order we expect here... and then start baking myself... I could lecture them on the dilatory effects of alcohol. No, I'll sound like Charlton Heston: "Thou shalt not covet thy neighbor's wife"... I could pretend that I didn't see anything — or more precisely, saw and tacitly approve — Namedays are sacred! ... Right — and there are now more than thirty-five employees -- most have different names and different birthdays ..." I calculated, slowly and methodically, that up to 20 percent of the year would be spent carousing in this manner. I stopped in my tracks, and decided to consult with Zigrīda as to how to curtail this practice.

By the time I got home that evening, Inge had already "schemed" the house. "Boriss, Boriss, darling... they want us to meet with them again... I agreed for tomorrow... and I'm taking my parents with us, because my father can talk a wolf out of the forest."

"Hunh?"

"Well, you know how they said that the other couple came with the family — we'll come with *ours!*"

"You mean, seriously?... and what does that mean... if another couple comes with their grandparents, children, *and* their aunts, uncles and cousins, then *they'll* get it?!"

"NO, no, but you know, they'll feel better about their decision."

"Alright, whatever you say... should I take a sleeping bag?..."

"This is no joke!"

"Well, at least a good pan — something that communicates, 'Hi, we're *ready* to move in!"

Inge was not amused. After giving me a sideways glance, she continued, "Definitely the kids, and I'll dress them up... oh, they'll have to give it to us."

"Fine, so when do we go?"

"Tomorrow at six."

The next day, we showed up with flowers — and I brought a bottle of local black currant liqueur. We were once again greeted by Lena at the door. She apologized for her husband, who, she said, had fallen ill, and would be joining us later. She then laid out a full meal, with salad, potatoes and ham and *gaileņu* [chanterelle mushroom] salad, and shot glasses — the eight-ounce variety. Then she started with a description of the details of the house, "You'll like the garden . . . just beware of the downstairs neighbor ... Vukina."

"What's her name? Raisa Vukina. She's a colonel's daughter ... she'll turn your water off if you don't listen to her."

"Well, we'll have to be very cordial to her, I suppose," said Inge.

Unexpectedly, Jevgeny appeared. He was clearly suffering from a hangover, with the token signs of unshaven face, unkempt hair, and a raspy voice. The wife murmured something to him. He then said,

"Yeah, so we would like to live in Imanta," near our daughter ... we even found someone who's giving up the apartment."

"So, you're saying that you're accepting our offer?" "Yeah, yeah," he said, with a tone-of-voice that communicated, "Yeah, yeah, I promised, so I gotta follow-through ..." With those words, the process of "moving" started.

Now, moving somewhere in the post-Soviet Union was about like teaching a dozen hippopotami synchronized swimming. To begin with, nobody could move out of anywhere unless they had a place to move into. Furthermore, the apartment that they would move into had to be of a sufficient size that the minimum space norms were met. Of course, this meant that a suitable space had to be found for every party involved. I found out later that ours was a particularly easy and straightforward case, as the people that were moving out were going to move into an apartment that someone else was freeing up then and of the two couples with whom we would be swapping, only one had any grown children. Nonetheless, the exiting parties had to sign out of the jurisdiction of their 'house of administration,' out of the police department and off of the electrical service company roster of clients. When all of these documents were obtained, then one could begin the process of signing "into" the new jurisdiction, the new police department and the new local electrical company roster. Besides dealing with short, often coinciding and erratically observed opening hours for all said agencies, one had to be prepared for an interrogation explaining motives for the said move. Furthermore, birth certificates and identification documents were scrupulously checked. An absence of any such documents, duly registered in their respective agencies, would bring the process to a grinding halt. To make the game more exciting, short time limits were placed on the validity of "extension" documents.

Finally, as an additional challenge, Inge was currently "signed into" an apartment in Ogre. She did not have the right to "sign into" any space in Riga, unless she came from a residence in Riga.[3] A "Catch-22" took effect here — officially, all state-owned living spaces in Riga were "signed into." To circumvent *this* law, we had to stage a convoluted shadow dance of legality. Inge was to purchase lease rights to a private apartment or house — of which there may have been no more than a hundred, in mid-1993. Since there were so few of these, it was necessary to hire a real estate agent to find one. After two weeks, the real estate agent found a house, located on the edge of the Riga region — the house had no sewage disposal pipes (euphemistically referred to as a "dry" residence), no windows on the second floor, and half a roof in place. We were to be "signed into" this palace for seventeen days. In fact we never saw it. The couple into whose apartment we wanted to "sign into," had, firstly, to be "signed into" "our" apartment (the newly found hovel which we never laid eyes on). As has been mentioned, officially, there was no such thing as a vacant state apartment . . . *ever*, in Riga. Consequently, the apartment leaseholders of the apartment that the Slukhovs were planning to "sign into" had to first "sign out of" their apartment. The next-to-last exchange would have to put us into the apartment that would be traded to the Slukhovs.

Each of the sign-outs required the stamps and permissions of the "House of Administration," the police, and the utility companies. In short, our simple little exchange, which would have been handled in the West by our agreeing on a price and move-in date, would here require a total of five "sign-outs" and four "sign-intos." As each step in the process involved the stamps and permissions of the three institutions mentioned, the entire process required twenty-seven separate trips to these institutions. Needless to say, "signing into" and "signing out of" operations were executed by different *sections* of each of the institutions *and* the petitioner had to be physically present. Due to the fact that our process involved one private house — the one with half a roof — and one couple was moving out of Latvia (and agreed to acknowledge that officially), our process was a straightforward — nay, *amoebically* simple one, in comparison to most others.[4]

Our procedure began with a false start, when the Slukhovs found a seemingly suitable apartment, approximately two hundred yards from their daughter's apartment, in a district across the river. We visited it, together with Yevgeny, and saw that he was quite satisfied with it. The real estate broker was to prepare the papers. However, Yevgeny had failed to do his homework, for his daughter had no intention of allowing her parents to live within a stone's throw of her apartment. Upon hearing his "plan," she threatened to move to Liepāja — about 150 miles down the street. The older couple rethought and vied for a place either in the Maskavas District of town, or in Pļavnieki, which was on the exact opposite side of town from their daughter's neighborhood. I could only deduce that they had taken their daughter's threat to heart.

Along with being located in this section of town, another key requirement of the apartment that they would move in to was that it had to be no higher than the fourth floor, because according to Lena, "The lifts usually break down." Furthermore, it should be in a "119"-series Brezhnev-era high-rise, which boasted a better floor plan for apartments than "283"-series house. The latter were apparently acceptable only for dullards from Donetsk.

An apartment fitting most of these criteria was found at the very beginning of *Maskavas iela* 'Moscow Street,' the main thoroughfare of the "Moscow" district. The couple currently occupying it was moving back to Russia, where the husband had been offered a job in computer engineering, the wife could get closer to her siblings, and the prize-winning Bedlington Terrier could get dates with some equally purebred bitches, which — the couple explained to us — "were mighty sparse" in Riga. The couple demanded a price of $3,500 for the leasehold rights to the small but well-kept apartment. The master of the house (more precisely, the man, not the master, for it was the dog that ruled this roost; when he was allowed to join me on the couch for biscuits and tea … he had the biscuits, I had the tea), pointed out that the toilet alone had cost them three hundred rubles and three months of work to finish. Although it was furnished with the same standard Soviet light blue toilet with submarine display shelf, the walls had very nice copies of Dutch delft blue tiles, and the toilet seat was off-white and actually contoured to conform to a human rear-end. The Slukhov couple were in visible awe of the handiwork, which did compare favorably to the ship models produced by Yevgeny. The door handles were ornate and the overall appearance of the apartment left the impression that it had received a great deal of care and attention — a stark contrast to the apartment that Lena and Yevgeny were leaving behind them. Although the apartment was on the fifth floor, one floor higher than they had stipulated to be the maximum acceptable, the impregnable metal door with door handles — inspired by ancient Armenian designs — apparently overruled that inconvenience. "We'll take it!" the Slukhovs were all but saying, as they nodded their heads.

That evening, we received a call from the Slukhovs — Inge repeated what they were saying: " So, you … think … that … the apartment has enough greenery... around it and... you will... *take*... the apartment on Maskavas iela. *GREAT!*" So, the official "sign-out of" process was started on June 10. We arrived at the house and asked for their *dokumenty*.

"We need your birth certificate, Yevgeny."

"I dunno... there was some problem with it during the war —"

"Which war?"

"Ya know... the *World* war."

"Listen, Yevgeniy, you knew that we needed it — Inge told you."

"Sure, I *thought* I had it." "Well, maybe you can go get it. Where were you born?"

"In Latgale..."

"Great, they should have records at the registry," I blurted out naively. It turned out to be a simple task — requiring two weeks.

Our next stop was the House of Administration. When we arrived with Inge, the people were courteous, even jubilant. The Director, who had to approve all exchanges, said, "So, you're moving out, Mr. Slukhov? Fine... very good... and maybe you can take your Vukina neighbor with you — if there's a crankier old hag in Riga, we have yet to meet her!"

When we arrived back at the Slukhovs' apartment, we were invited in for more drinking and tale-swapping. We accepted — our curiosity about our future fellow tenants was growing exponentially with each visit. Lena and Yevgeny were amused by the story about our "eviction" from the apartment on Šertrūdes street. Then Inge asked about the neighbors that we were about to inherit.

"Well, there's the *Zality* 'Flooded' family." "That's a strange name. Why are they called the 'Flooded's?'"

"Don't know, but probably because their whistles are always wet... well, at least *his* is."

"He???!"

"Yeah, the son."

"Son of whom? ..."

"Of Anton Vladimirovich."

"So, he drinks all the time... useless guy. Good hands, though — if you need the radio fixed, Vasya'll do it for you... 'n better than anyone else," Lena added, trying to sound warmly reassuring.

Now that the second meal (and first bottle) had been consumed, with compliments given, Yevgeny was really opening up: "Now, *Zmei* Gorinitch's wife is darling, and so's the kid."

"Who's '*Zmei* Gorinitch'?"

"The son."

"She has another one?"

"No, it's the same — it's just that sometimes they call *Vasya* the 'Snake,' because he's good-looking or something."

"Un-hunh —"

"Now the mother, she's nice . . . so's the daughter . . . but Raisa doesn't let them work in the garden."

"No, really? Why not? It seems that there's room enough for all three families here."

"Yeah, well, she unearths other people's plants."

"Why?"

"I dunno, she just does . . . she's making moves to take over most of the garden. oh and watch out for the drinking buddies — they're no good."

"You mean Raisa Igorovna's drinking buddies?"

"No, no — Pavel's drinking buddies . . . one asked me for a bottle opener once. The next day, when I came back to work, our cassette/radio was stolen . . . we're gonna get him back for that."

"O.K. — but now, about Raisa Vukina —"

"Yeah, she's . . . well . . . just you watch out for her."

"O.K."

"And I forgot to mention . . . her son drinks."

"You already said that her son drinks."

"NO, that was the 'Flooded's son."

"The old crab's son drinks . . . and daughter-in-law too . . . but you'll be O.K. — just don't lend *him* any money . . . you'll never see it again. And as to Raisa — don't get her too mad, or she'll turn the water off on you — she did that once, and we had to replace our kitchen water boiler."

After recounting more evidence of brotherly love and mutual respect reigning between the three families, the couple began repeating themselves. By then, Inge and I both felt that we had obtained a good lay of the land; at the very least the precise locations of all the social land mines. We decided to leave, before the couple moved to the next phase of post-Soviet apartment swapping — the de facto *adoption* of the younger couple by the older one. We had also succeeded in drinking our quota of vodka so the road home would be a winding one.

The next steps in the process involved getting passports to the Houses of Administration of the new districts for signing. The procedure that we established involved Inge arranging for something or somebody to be dropped off with the right people in whatever agency necessary, and I would be the courier of documents or chauffeur of people. Although the various bureaucrats were a blur to me, a few made their marks. The most memorable was the police department in our second [transitional] apartment, on Maskavas Street. The first time that I drove to the police station, the section taking passports was closed a full twenty minutes earlier than was posted on their "hours open to the public." The sounds of a Name's day celebration emanated from the room. This celebrating in and of itself was nothing overwhelming, but that the precinct was open for passport stamping but three hours per day, two days of the week, made it frustrating.

The second time that I appeared in line, the precinct captain told us not to enter. Through the closed door, I heard that they were enthusiastically debating the plusses and minuses of gun ownership with the lady administrator. Upon having reached some provisional agreement on this issue, some ten minutes later, he proceeded to let in the next petitioner. When it came my turn, he took a look at the birth certificate and said that it was not acceptable …one of the letters of the town of birth was smudged. "But good sir, this birth certificate was accepted by both of the houses of administration." The police department chief threw me a look that said, "Yes sir, you just keep on talkin' there, yep. 'N when ya run outta steam, yer gonna do exactly as I say." Sure enough, Yevgeny had to order a new birth certificate — from the other side of the country — this request resulted in another seven-day lapse.

In the meantime, the trio that were leaving for St. Petersburg called us during this waiting period and the man said, "We've finished the process of signing out and my job in *St. Peter* is waiting for me. Would you mind paying us, so we could go?" Inge approved; I drove over to their apartment, confirmed that their passports had a "signed-out" stamp in them, and paid them the outstanding $2000. I was relieved to see several boxes of personal belongings stacked neatly in the living room. The dog also sensed that some big change was in the air — I didn't manage to finish *any* biscuits this time.

Eight days later, we received a call from the Slukhovs. Yevgeny was once again ready to be driven once to the police precinct of the new location. This would be the last step before we could sign into our new apartment. All told, the process had taken two months, three weeks and one day. That Inge signed herself and the children out of and into three different living spaces in the span of less than three months was testimony to the incredible opportunities that now existed for free movement, which in the past had been limited to KGB officers, gypsies and psychotics. Compared to other such transactions in the ex-Soviet Union, ours had been a lightning-quick, trouble-free one.

One key element that had made it so was my complete (official) absence from the process. For, although I was married to a Latvian, the right of residency, or for that matter cohabitation, was not conferred automatically with the marriage certificate. To paraphrase Orwell, this would have been a *squattersexcrime*. It appears that as a foreigner, I was expected to continue living in a hotel, until such time as the laws changed, to grant non-resident non-diplomats the official right to be signed into a location.[5] Ironically, resident non-Latvian citizens had a right to a space. However, non-resident Latvian citizens apparently underwent the same problems that I did. So there was even a period when, for example, a Latvian-American could return to Latvia and claim back his/her property . . . but could not live in it. Furthermore, any agreement gave the sub-lessee the same tenuous hold on an apartment that a New Yorker gives to a de facto sublessee on a rent-controlled space which does not allow de jure subletting without loss of rent-control rights (for anyone not from New York, suffice it to say that this situation is as complex as it sounds).

But even two months, three weeks and one day later, the ordeal was not *completely* over. On the same day that we received the permission to move into the new space, Lena called Inge, "Hi, sorry to bother you, but . . . we need a stove." Inge was flustered and asked three times what she had meant by that, as we had left her a perfectly good stove. I heard a series of "Whats?!" and a final "O.K., we'll come take a look at it . . ."

When we showed up, we were speechless. It looked like a band of thieving ex-cons had ransacked the apartment. The cabinets had been ripped off the kitchen walls, with most of the underlying tiles chipped off in the process. All the doorknobs, except for the one on the front door, had been removed. The wall-to-wall cabinets in the living room had simply been torn away, leaving large cracks in the wall in their wake. Lamp fixtures had been removed, as well as most electrical switches, in spite of the fact that when these people had moved *into* the apartment, all of these had been there, gratis. The wallpaper had been peeled away, as if the people leaving had decided, "We put this work into it — you certainly won't be getting it as part of the deal." In fact, besides the layout, the only element linking this space to the apartment that we had seen fourteen days earlier . . . was the blue delft–like tile in the bathroom, which for some inexplicable reason, they had left intact. Indeed, on the spot where the clean, functioning stove had been standing, there was another stove, with three popped, convex burners and two of four knobs removed. Inge looked at this scene, turned to me and said, "In my euphoric state, I completely forgot — one should never, ever pay the entire sum until the apartment has been inspected."

"That's alright, I think. There was more stuff that the Slukhovs had in Me aparks than can fit into this apartment . . . and I still think, that even with the tiles chipped, and the lamps gone, and the knobs taken off the doors . . . that this place looks better than what they've left us," I whispered.

And I believed that statement . . . except for the stove, that was — one would have had a hard time balancing anything larger than a Barbie's Playhouse wok on the burners that we were now scrutinizing.

Inge's father had been saving an oven for installation in his summer dacha. Inge called him from the apartment, explained the situation, and the next day he brought it over to the Slukhovs. The alternative would have been to stonewall them, which would have put the whole transaction at risk, insofar as they had the legal right to dispute the swap for a sixty-day period after it had been officially completed. One would have thought that those lamps had been Tiffany originals, and the door handles by Bulgari. In fact, I later saw those Armenian-style door handles in a hardware store for about $2.00 apiece.

Inge and I left the flat-cum-hovel and started talking about the repair work that would be necessary to complete ours, at the very least to bring it to western standards of the late 1960s. Anything more modern or expensive would have been impractical, insofar as it was possible that within a two-year period, an "owner" could show up to claim the property. In that case, we could be evicted . . . possibly with less warning or aplomb than had been rationed us two months earlier.

It was now mid-June of 1993; Inge had departed the previous week for a six-week training program to the U.S. I was following through on the courier work that Inge had assigned to me to shepherd the apartment-swapping along. It was then that I understood that this was a really boring town for kids and that entertaining Markus and Eliza would have to be my second job. The problem was just that there were no such things in Riga as gaming saloons, pinball machines, bowling alleys, miniature golf courses or a myriad of other entertainment venues that I had grown up with. The only thing that there seemed to be no shortage of were pirate videos, shot in movie theaters in the U.S. and dubbed-over in Russian by one fast-talking male with a high, whiny voice. It required a good deal of imagination to buy into the film when one would *see* Kim Basinger but hear a Jakov Smirnov sound-alike. The video rental stores almost all resembled the offices of Brooklyn bail bond services. They were filthy, small walk-ins, with creaky, splintered floors, and videos with hand-written labels, in tattered boxes, stacked high behind scratched Plexiglas barriers. *Blockbuster Video* stores these were not.

But I didn't let the lack of what I considered standard entertainment for kids get in the way. After we had watched all the hard-dying Willisovitch movies that we could, I decided that the occasionally sunny weather was too good to waste by being indoors. Markus was now ten years old, so I thought that it would be a good thing to teach him to play tennis. After all, I had been taught by my own father at a much earlier age to wield a wooden racquet and strike a white ball. So about every other Tuesday and Thursday, I packed Markus and Eliza into the car and took them to the courts. There were a total of nine open-air courts, in reasonably good shape, on the edge of the new district. We would start with some calisthenics, and then some hand-eye exercises. They would then hit the ball against the wall. Eliza liked to hit the ball about three times, and then pummel it with all the strength she could muster. After a while, she would forget some cardinal rule and the ball would be sent on a 45-degree trajectory a good distance over the board, onto the vacant property behind it, now overgrown with knee-high grass. Eliza would laugh, and with a mischievous look on her dimpled face, proceed to retrieve the ball. On the way, she would pick some flowers that were nestled in the tall weeds. If she caught sight of other balls, she would return victoriously with those as well. The process took no less than ten minutes, which I used productively to drill with Markus. Markus had the athleticism necessary to be a really good player, but after missing three times, he would take the racket and throw it somewhere, or hit a ball towards Tallinn. When Eliza returned, he would inevitably pick a fight with her. A year on, he still thought of her as fair game for any insult, shove, arm punch, or any number of aggressions that didn't cross some ill-defined pain threshold. "Listen, stupid, don't hit the balls to me, keep 'em on your side." "You can't even hit normally, you cow!" were two expressions that I heard with disturbing frequency. Finally, I would ask Eliza if she would mind being left alone to practice for fifteen minutes, to which she would invariably answer, "Well, *not* if you take Markus." Then I would take Markus to the Central Stage court and there I would give him my undivided attention, and soft volleys. Then he tried hard -- in one session, we rallied 63 times. Afterwards, I would take them to the café in the grandstand, and we would have some Pepsi or any number of carbonated beverages with funny names ("Spars" and "Tarhūns" were two of my favorites) that were still being manufactured in the CIS, before the advent of Coca-Cola.

Footnotes

[1] Home.

[2] White Stork Brandy was imported from Moldavia, which is a renowned wine-producing CIS Republic.

[3] There were strict limitations on the number of people allowed to move into major cities in the Soviet Union, including Riga. The actual reason for this limitation was the potential for massive migrations into cities, which not only boasted a fuller cultural life, but also fewer product shortages than in the countryside. In 1993, these laws were still in effect.

[4] I later heard of a nine-"sign-out," eight-"sign-into" case in St. Petersburg, which required a total of fifty-one separate trips to institutions. One might have thought that this was to acquire the lease rights to a wing of the Hermitage, but no, this was for the lease rights to a simple two-bedroom apartment.

[5] In the Soviet era, there were neither non-residents, nor aliens, nor even, with rare exceptions — such as Kim Philby and foreign wives of Soviet men — long-term visitors. Short-term visitors had to be registered with the local police and interior department agencies by the inviting organization. Furthermore, the KGB kept track of such visitors. Between 1991 and 1993 no new laws were yet in place in Latvia to codify the new "free-movement" situation.

23

A SONG AND A PRAYER

THE SONG FESTIVAL WAS TO take place in the first week of July. The Merry Baker's preparation for the festival began in earnest in the second week of June. Valdis went to the booth to assess the electric power capacity and distribution. He was good at those things. I was not. Mine were visions of huge lines of customers buying our products by the bag-full from smiling, cheerful salesclerks — not the visions of a wooden house going up like a tinderbox pile because one of the vendors had plugged in and turned on a microwave oven, grill oven, croque-monsieur maker, three drip-coffee machines and her blow dryer (for her nails, you know) into one really shoddy socket, by way of a gargantuan adapter. Valdis, perhaps on account of seeing so much go amuck in the world of airline ladders, de-icing platforms and luggage trolleys, had a very good eye for these eventualities. So Valdis was the first to do site inspections and modify the selling space to our needs. At the same time, Zigrīda contacted a seamstress to begin sewing new aprons, as well as planning the layout of the selling counter, centimeter by centimeter. I must admit that my head had never ached, until now, with thoughts of how to stack hundreds of wooden trays outside a booth once they had been emptied. Even Roberts the plumber got involved, taking it upon himself to make it possible for a group of salesgirls to circulate around the periphery, selling from rectangular baskets.

By the day of the first rehearsal concert, our booth — which was closer to the front seats than all the rest — was a veritable retailing "machine." Three salesgirls were positioned inside the booth, two were outside on the left of the booth, and two were on the right. The ones on the left were being drilled Prussian-style on the operation of the microwave oven over which they had charge. They also had an assistant, who would be running inside to get more product, bring a full thermos of coffee, or execute a number of replenishment tasks when the need arose. The salesgirls on the right side were standing ready behind a table that was piled high with cookies and pīrāgi. The counters inside the booth were groaning under the weight of pizzas, quiches and ham sandwiches on one side and Danish pastries, cinnamon swirls and honey buns on the other. Dried pretzels, each about eight inches wide, were hanging from colored ribbons, suspended from the rafters inside the booth. A few of these pretzels were hung on the eaves extending outside the booth. Not even the most myopic moron could miss the fact that some *serious* baked goods were on sale here. Altogether there were seven salesgirls, two assistants, Zigrīda, Ronalds, a driver and coordinator responsible for the transport of items as well as any emergencies that he would help with. Without a doubt, this was the most streamlined operation of any on the Song Festival grounds, including Dan Keen's short-skirted sales ladies.

We began our operations on Wednesday. We prepared ourselves for an onslaught. The amphitheater, however, turned out to be three-quarters empty. This was not even a "dress rehearsal"; the singers were still dressed in jeans and sweatshirts. As a result, we had a huge surplus of everything that we baked. We ended up returning a carload to the store, which was subsequently overwhelmed with product. We carefully downsized the orders for the following day. However, we had not scrutinized the weather report for weather on Thursday. Consequently, our downsizing of the order was insufficient to compensate for the fact that even fewer spectators attended the second rehearsal than had shown up for the first one. We returned the same amount of product as we had the previous day, but this time it was 10 percent heavier — the two salesgirls on the left had not been drilled on how to cover the pizzas during heavy rain showers.

For Friday, we listened for the weather report. The weather prognosis for the following day was good, and since this was to be the first real performance, we stocked up on items. Furthermore, we launched our mobile team of salesgirls. Each of them carried a wicker tray in front of her, laden with sandwiches and soft drinks. The trays were fastened with rubber, which our buyer had "obtained" from somewhere "special" — to me it seemed that several doctors would be wondering where the rubber tubes had disappeared from their stethoscopes. However, all's fair in love and baking, and we were battling the elements for our survival. During the set-up in the afternoon, gray clouds appeared on the horizon. By the early evening, the clouds did not clear up. The spectators that arrived early were soon drenched with partly sunny. Many people left halfway through the performance. Our personnel were getting bored. The girls on the inside were complaining their feet were aching from standing on the concrete; the girls on the left were complaining about having to move the mini-pizzas in and out of the booth "ten times a day." Ronalds and the accountant, on the other hand, were taking this opportunity to get to know each other intimately. Once again, we took a big hit on returned goods. The store managers, in turn, expressed frustration at not knowing what goods would be dumped on their shelves that evening, and consequently, what they should order for the following day.

Ultimately, this situation was demoralizing the bakers, who repeatedly saw their work returned, unappreciated. In some cases it was so waterlogged that the sole use of the prize-winning Danish would be to feed pigs or fling in a food fight, as one of the sticky-wet projectiles of the arsenal. This disappointment manifested itself through the goods that we received on the next day. The pizzas were lopsided; the ham, peppers, and other items were unevenly distributed on top; the golden sweet pretzels were flat and uninspiring. I had the misfortune of tasting a quiche slice. Apparently, one of the bakers couldn't have been bothered to look for the salt, so he substituted it with bacon fat. Besides being tasteless, the mass coated the whole inside of my mouth with something that I couldn't initially define. Then I cringed as I realized that if someone would thrust a two-foot wick down my throat, I could have illuminated the booth for at least three hours. As my stomach began refuting the mass, I could feel the heartburn coming up. "Goodness gracious," I thought to myself, "we shouldn't even bother sending them back to the stores." When Zigrīda arrived, I instructed her not to let the quiche slices be sold; "On Monday, when we clean up, we'll give them to the farmers for their pigs."

Sales on Saturday were just as dismal as on Friday. I had been told that this was supposed to be the gala performance. If so, it was a terrible disappointment for everyone involved. I had invited Markus and Eliza to come on this day, so that we could watch the performers together, walk around, enjoy some *shashliki* and play some of the carnival games that were set up on the periphery. Markus and Eliza came to the festival. They were doused with rain, yelled at by cross audience members and stepped on with muddy boots — after forty-five minutes, they asked to go home. I explained how valuable this ancient music was to world culture; they rolled their eyes. Inge's sister happened to have come to the event that day, and although she was with friends, she was visibly pleased to have an excuse to leave, and what better one than to having to take the sniffling niece and nephew home. Once, again, by the middle of the performance, the stands were almost half-empty.

On Saturday evening we had listened despondently to the weather forecast. Sunday's weather was to be a repeat of Saturday's, if not worse. Rainy, gray, and temperature not higher than fifty-eight degrees Fahrenheit. Zigrīda and I agreed at that moment to stay with the most conservative sales forecast possible, to minimize potential losses. Already, preliminary calculations from accounting revealed that we would be absorbing a big loss on this venture. Sure enough, as we were preparing the booth for the grand finale, the drizzle set in. Spectators were late in arriving, and went straight to their places, clutching their umbrellas, ponchos and family-sized plastic sheets. But an hour later, just as the diplomatic corps were seated in front, and the well-to-do Latvian expats filed in just behind them, the sun broke through the clouds. Almost instantly, the temperature rose by ten degrees. It was as if one-hundred-foot-high floodlights had been switched on; previously concealed booths threw off their camouflage. People started approaching our booth in unprecedented numbers. Parties of five and six were buying our *Kliņģeri*; others were asking to be photographed next to the salesgirls. The pizzas and Danish started flying off the countertops. One man said that he didn't want to be going back and forth, and that he was there with relatives, so if he could simply have ten of each item, that would be grand.

I was at the back of the amphitheater at this time, listening — in an effort to block out the pain that I felt with regards to this event — to the moving *Dievs Svētī Latviju*. The roughly twenty thousand performers on the stage rows looked dazzling. Upon hearing so many people singing "God Bless Latvia," my skin erupted in goose bumps. This song had been banned from all previous Song Festivals, on account of it being bourgeois nationalistic rubbish. The choral groups were now singing it with relish. It was not for no reason that the Baltic separation from the rest of the Soviet Union was called the "Singing Revolution."[1] All present joined in the chorus — over seventy thousand people were singing this song at one time. I listened to two more songs, the first of which was a Gregorian chant. Then I decided that it was time to go back. As I ambled slowly in the direction of the booth, I paid attention to the performers in full national costume, in the sunlight. The *tautastērpi* 'folk dresses' glowed. There were some dresses that boasted the traditional colors of the region, clasps, and medallions, shining brightly. Others were bedecked in ancient amber jewelry, preserved throughout several generations. Still other girls wore aquamarine-colored full-length satin dresses, topped by a robe that resembled a sari. They wore gold and brass jewelry and ornaments, including a brass headband that looked thoroughly Middle Eastern. I asked what region of the country they were from — it was the *Cēsu* district of the country, and the costumes were replicas of those that had been worn over one thousand years earlier. When I asked if they were descendants of the Assyrians, one of the girls cocked her head and said, "No, from the Zariņi."[2]

I came over the hill and saw the booth at this point, some twenty minutes after the sun had appeared. As the choruses started singing — or chanting — other songs and choral works, people's attention spans shortened. To me, looking from the top of a small rise, above the booth, it appeared that one out of every three of the sixty thousand spectators was making a beeline for the Merry Baker booth. The crowds of people stampeding our booth elated me. Fifteen minutes later, worry replaced my elation, as the crowds did not seem to be thinning out. Just before the halfway point of the almost four-hour-long concert, I asked Zigrīda how our stocks were holding out.

"Terribly," she replied, shaking her head, "the pizzas are all gone, our pastries will last for twenty more minutes, the last of the *kliņģeri*. Large sweet pretzels was sold, for three times its normal selling price in an auction — the expats from Chicago competed against the orchestra from Ohio. That was also almost a half-hour ago."

"Well, are the bakers still there at the bakery?"

"Nope, they've gone home an hour ago. The next shift won't be there in full for another hour. What we've got is all we've got."

At that point, I counted no less than twenty people converging on our booth from all sides. One customer pointed to our decorative pretzels. The salesclerk took it down and started saying something about it, apparently explaining to this customer he was requesting an item that had been hanging for five days in the booth, collecting dust. We were standing about thirty yards away. Before I had time to run to the the booth and say, "Those pretzels are rock hard, you can't sell them to people …," Zigrīda was in the booth, flashing her super salesman's smile. I realized that it was too late and could now hope only that the pretzel would not — ultimately — be given to a senior citizen without dentures of steel.

As I approached the booth, my mind feverishly assessed options. I suddenly realized that some items could be brought from the store. But when I tried to find Ronalds, the sole person who could organize such a delivery, I couldn't. He was gone … so was the accountant. They emerged from the forest, fifteen minutes later, holding hands, looking a lot like Christopher Atkins and Brooke Shields coming ashore from the Blue Lagoon. But by this time, it had become obvious to Zigrīda and me that not even the cost of *gasoline* would be covered by the sales of the handful of items that could be brought from the store on Sunday —- a handful was the amount usually left at the end of the weekend. So we just dropped back and watched, as two by two, the pastries were bought and the selling surfaces cleared. We prayed now that the onslaught of people would stop, so that at the very least, The Merry Baker wouldn't — to accompany the economic catastrophe that this event was turning out to be — also broadcast an image of incompetence. The hanging decorative pretzels were now being sold for a princely sum of two dollars apiece; the two crates of Friday's tasteless grease quiche — destined at the start of the day for the pig troughs — were brought out and sold for a 10-percent premium. It was all too reminiscent of the good old Soviet days, when items of questionable palatability would be sold for good money at public events. Perhaps most reminiscent of all, however, was that with a third of the program yet to go, we no longer even had the rock-hard pretzels and grease quiche to sell. Waves of customers came to the booth, only to be broken by the words, "Sorry, we've sold everything."

The next day, I got a call from Guntis, of the 7G club. After inviting me to the next meeting, he said, "So Boriss, I saw that you guys were at the Song Festival. Looks like you couldn't pull it off. When I went to your booth there was nothing left. Big projects like that ... guess you guys need a bigger bakery."

"No, Guntis. It wasn't the bakery's fault, it wasn't the managers' fault. It was *Pērkons'*[3] fault."

Footnotes

1 A. Lieven The Baltic Revolution, p. 110.

2 A common surname.

3 Perkons — God of thunder and rain. Probably derived from Viking belief
system of the ninth century.

24

LET THEM EAT CAKE

LATVIANS LOVED TO THINK BIG, in spite of their country's place in the world. No doubt, the years of real and imagined restraints had stifled their minds and souls. Now was the time to compensate, by thinking up plans that were larger than life ... and financing them completely with other people's money. In our case, none do I recall more vividly than the "Big Cake."

At the end of June, I was sitting in my office, wondering if the Hotel Metropole would add the custard/almond to its current array of raspberry marzipan and cinnamon rolls. The custard/almond Danish I had just finished sampling had a creamy-rich custard filling, highlighted around the edge of its roughly hexagonal form with a white almond-flavored frosting. The pastry had a hint of butter — enough to stimulate the taste buds, but not enough to drown the digestive tract. "Perfect," I thought to myself. But the thoughts were quickly interrupted by the appearance of Mr. Vincent Gailītis, (Vincent 'Little Rooster' in direct translation).

"Yes, Mr. What can I do for you?"

He smiled a wide smile, which brought a twinkle to his feverish eyes, and took my attention off his unshaven face, before he replied, "Well, my name is Mr. Gailītis and I just have the opportunity of the decade for you . . . if you agree to this partnership."

"Yes? Carry on."

"I'm the editor of a journal called *Nakts* 'Night,' which is an artistic-entertainment-political journal (a combination which was possible only in a country where 12 percent of the parliament members were artists by profession) . . . and as an advertising gesture, we would like to co-sponsor an event that we think you'd be interested in."

"Possibly, and what might that be?"

"The largest cake in the Baltics."

"Oh!? Tell me more."

"Yes, we at *Nakts* thought that you might be interested in making this cake three meters high."

"Well, that's an idea . . . we will certainly be famous after *that* now, won't we."

"Oh *yes*! Certainly after we put you on the front cover of the paper."

"Well, great . . . there's just one question . . . how big does the cake have to be?"

"Well, we've made all the measurements. The largest cake to-date has been the Lithuanian one which measured four meters by five meters . . . but that was a flat one —"

"And you want a cake that goes up vertically?"

"*Yeah*! Exactly."

In fact, he wanted that the cake was to be a pyramid, to a height of at least fifteen feet. It was to be twenty feet by twenty feet at the base. The word *Nakts* was to be boldly laid out in Marzipan on one side. The two sponsors' logos (once the sponsors were found) would be positioned on another two sides. The bakery could — he allowed — place its own logo on the fourth side. The cake was to be made in the middle of the square of the square, dominating it for a day. It would be a testimony to the greatness of Latvia. The Lithuanians would be cowed by this jest . . . This September 1st first-day-of-school ceremony would remain in the minds of participants forevermore . . .

"I'd like that too," I replied, once he paused for a moment from his dream-like reverie. "But there's a problem with the physics of it. When we talk about those sizes, the levels can't support one another — at least not in any meaningful way."

"Oh . . . I didn't think about that."

"Well, it's possible that the Soviet cakes could do that . . . if you were to use a week-old-sponge . . . but there's the problem of it being inedible . . . if you consider that a problem. I actually do — we prefer to see ourselves as the 'edible ingredients bakery.'"

"Well, yes, actually we do . . . yes, it should be edible."

"O.K. The only way around that is to build a supporting structure."

"Sure, sure. We can do that!"

"O.K. Now that that is solved, what kind of cake should it be?"

"Something good ... you know, maybe with whipped cream."

"Fine, I'll give it some thought . . . although I'll let you in on a secret. Whipped cream doesn't keep for very long in temperatures of twenty-two degrees [seventy-four Fahrenheit]."

"Oh, well then something else."

"Evidently. Now as concerns payment ..."

As it turned out, the paper had no funds for the venture, but promised us eight weeks of free advertising, as well as a full-cover photo. I stated that at least half of the cost of ingredients must be covered by a sponsor, but that I would, for the moment, take his word for the popularity of the journal, and could, in principle, accept the rest in advertising space. We agreed that he would contact me once he had found a sponsor.

I received a call from him two days later — he had found a sponsor in the form of the *Deutsch-Lettisch Bank,* so the project was on. I investigated later that day and found out that indeed, the nouveau riche of the city — along with the artist-parliamentarians — were buying that journal, so I agreed. In the interim I had also met with my co-directors and we agreed that although our reputation for pastries and *Klin̄ģeri* 'sweet pretzels' was well-established, we could use an advertising boost for our cakes.

I called our production director, "Ligita, do I have a proposal for you! We have a once-in-a-lifetime-opportunity to put this company's name on *everyone's* mind."

"Yes? How?!"

"Simple ... with about one ton of cake." There was silence on the phone. "Come on over when you get a chance, and we'll talk about it."

Ligita arrived a few minutes later, and we discussed platform proposals, angles, the dynamics of jam and butter cream and what we could expect canned peach slices to do when slanted at a forty-five-degree angle. We were talking the fourth great pyramid of the world. On that day, Dome square was to be jampacked with crowds, as thousands of schoolchildren made their traditional first-day-of-school pilgrimage to the Dome Cathedral ...

Two days before the event, a three-level wooden structure, rising fourteen feet in the air, stood in front of the radio building. Vincent had not received permission to place it in the middle of the square, as he had hoped, but next to the historic radio building. From the balcony of this edifice, Kārlis Ulmanis once gave speeches, meant to stir the crowds to a nationalistic frenzy. On the day before the event, a stage was set up in front of the Stock Exchange building, approximately seventy yards from the torte platform. I had been briefed, by phone, on the order of events. As a part of the ceremony, I was to say a few words following the Mayor's talk. That evening, I carefully rewrote the thirty words that I was to pronounce in Latvian. Anticipating that there would be a total of four (possibly lengthy) speeches before mine, I decided that it should be short.

The bakers arrived at six thirty in the morning onto the square, with buckets of cocoa butter cream. The sponge was carried in slabs on top of three-foot-by-five-foot plywood sheets. The first pieces of sponge were laid and trimmed into a uniform layer, that was seven feet long along the bottom edge, and five feet high. The sponge trimmings were taken away on the plywood sheet or in buckets. Three samurai decorators applied the first layer of frosting with blinding speed. The spatulas flashed in the sun as the yellow sponge soon turned brown. The temperature on the square was a pleasant sixty-eight degrees. The second layer of sponge was put down and covered with the cocoa butter cream frosting. By twelve, the cake was ready for its decorations. Assistants brought peach slices in two-gallon plastic buckets. They dropped off sugar decorations in the forms of green leaves, and daisies were dropped off in large cardboard boxes. Our tiger team of decorators went to work. By twelve thirty these master bakers were perspiring sufficiently to fill the same two-gallon buckets with sweat. The temperatures had by now risen to the mid-seventies. Those that had finished covering the first three layers I had invited to have a beer at our restaurant, which was around the corner.

The cake was cordoned off. The crowds began appearing at 1:00, two hours before the speeches and two hours, forty-five minutes before the cake was to be sliced and distributed. The *konditors* were scheduled to finish the decorating by one forty-five, as the speeches were to begin at two. Alongside the ribbons of chocolate relief, the cake masters left a swathe of elevated relief, resembling peonies; green leaves were laid, with great care, underneath gently curled peach slices. Next to them, they laid pineapples, cut to look like fuchsias. On one side of the cake, lay the *Nakts* logo, with its stylized moon and letters shaped like Chinese characters. On the other side, lay the three-foot-high *dlb* initials of the *deutsche-lettische* bank, on a round quarter-inch-thick base of marzipan. At one fifty-five, the bakers longingly viewed their *piece de resistance,* crowned with three whole pineapples. Ligita photographed the cake.

At two fifteen, about twenty minutes later than planned, the first speeches began. The square was packed with people; later accounts stated that there were almost five thousand present. The Minister of Education commenced,

Pryamid Cake. Domes Square, 1993.
(Photo Courtesy of Uldis Pāže.)

"Ladies and Gentlemen, it is a pleasure for us to celebrate the return to school for the youth of today . . ." I didn't recall the details of the speech, as I was doggedly preparing for my own twenty-five-word outburst. "Remember . . . accent on the first syllable, no matter what," I kept repeating to myself. As the second speech drew on, the crowds appeared restless. Everyone that I saw, on the stage and in the square below me, emanated beads of sweat. At about two thirty, the cordon around the cake started swinging wildly and became taut. The two people (I had been assured that two would be sufficient — others would be provided by *Nakts*) from my company, assigned to pass out plates and forks to all who wanted a piece of the torte, were visibly nervous. Seeing the over-sized high school boys grouping next to the cordon, I thought to myself, "Well, I suppose not everyone has had a chance to lunch today — that's fine, the torte is nothing if not filling . . ." During the third speech, which was droning on for fifteen minutes, one youth tried to climb onto the platform.

He was rebuffed by a plainclothes security guard. It was now 3:20, twenty minutes after the cake should have been distributed.

As I approached the microphone, and removed my glasses, I began, with a quiver in my voice, "Today is ... a big day. It is a pleasure for The Merry Baker to create a torte, almost five meters high, marking the first day of school for our *youth*, the *future* of this country ..." Or at least, that is what I thought that I had said. Apparently, what came out must have sounded more like "Well, *powderpuffs*, What are you *WAITING FOR*?! Never mind the pansies that are going to give you little plastic forks and nice clean paper plates as if this was some-kind-of *dejeuner sur l'herbes* ... Ya want it? *GRAB IT*!" because twenty seconds after I had started the minute-long speech, five strapping youths stormed the torte and started ripping chunks of it off. All but two policemen were far from the torte, restrained by the crowd and subsequently powerless to stop them. My two bakers with plates and forks resembled waiters trying to serve truffles to passengers fleeing the dining room of the sinking *Titanic*. As I ended with "... future," I looked up and saw one teenager, positioned on the side across from the Dome Church, taking fistfuls of frosting and jamming them into his open mouth and nostrils. Another, more considerate, guy with a large hand threw whole ten-inch-square chunks ten meters into the crowd. I saw someone crowned with a dark chunk of something, which must have been the lower limb of the "K" from "Nakts." The person receiving the crowning piece looked surprised; whether it was from wearing a dessert — or else by the fact that he was the fifth person to taste such a delicious butter cream, while standing a whole ten yards and fifty people away from the cake — I couldn't guess. One youth scrambled to the top as if he had just climbed Everest and began waving his arms about. Another one slipped, burying his face into the cake; when he arose he had half a pineapple slice attached to his left cheek, briefly resembling the mask of some Polynesian god. I saw one chunk careening in the air, and knocking off a schoolmarm's glasses. One of the organizers, standing to my right, kept repeating, "*Vai viņam nav kaunas? Vai viņam nav kaunas?* 'Have they no shame? have they no shame?'"

I was stunned, but since I had just addressed a crowd of fifteen thousand Latvians with at least thirty words in their own tongue, I was feeling far too proud to be angry. The deputy mayor turned around to me and said what I understood to be, "I'm sorry that you're watching this ... our people just aren't civilized enough to accept such an offer." I nodded as the cake-flinging progressed to a mad frenzy — I was sure to witness the first decapitation-by-decorations in my life.

The following day, I went to the bakery. The bakers were crushed. I could only apologize to them for the outcome of this event, which I simply hadn't foreseen. Ligita said that we should never have accepted to do something that was so demoralizing, and the bonuses that will be paid could not compensate for the anger that the bakers felt. I concurred that it was a terrible affront to the company and its employees that the mastery of the bakers could be treated with such disrespect, but it wasn't our fault; I added that if we stopped promoting our company, out of fear that the promotion will be turned into a mockery, then we would simply stop growing as a company. This calmed some nerves, but Ligita was still visibly upset throughout the day.

The following day, now two days after the event, I was sitting in the office, when the secretary ran in. She said the police were here. I invited the officers into my office. The commanding officer started asking me to detail what arrangements we had made to protect order around the cake. I replied that we had made none, unless he considered the passing out of plates and plastic spoons "protection." I added that *Nakts* had promised to make all those arrangements. The officer then began asking questions about whose idea this project was, and other seemingly irrelevant things. Finally, I asked him what he was getting at.

"We're investigating you, to see if we should press charges."

"On what count?"

"Willfully instigating a riot."

25

COSA NORTE

KARL MARX WROTE, IN *Das Kapital*, that the first stages of capitalism were marked by "wild capitalism," where the initial capital is raised by whatever means are possible. Even if this analysis were a little crude, it was, unfortunately, the one by which the Mafiya chiefs, themselves no doubt polished and educated people, seemed to swear by. Hence, nary a day went past without some armed robbery, extortion scheme, swindle, or other crime begin uncovered and published in the newspaper. I had heard of a few cases where West European investors had "hooked up" with a local "entrepreneur," and they gave him a small amount of money. He returned it with a 100-percent yield within a few months. The Western European investor then sent five, ten or twenty times more, and the "entrepreneur" was never heard from again. In short, this was a big "three-card Monty" set-up. But I could never have imagined, before my experiences here, to what extremes the "wild capitalists" would go to shake down the current economy. Well, I should have been warned through the first incident that took place ...

From the beginning of the year, tales of the Mafiya had been spreading wide and tall, throughout the city. Some of these allegations were even supported by waves of very specific crimes. From the disappearance of antiques and art from private apartments, to the crude expropriation of colored metals from public sites, railroad tracks and our apartment building, to a bomb exploding in a newly refurbished establishment, not a week went by without some Mafiya-linked crime being reported in the newspaper.

Most people with whom one discussed this situation simply shrugged their shoulders, as if one was lamenting over a bad season for the Dodgers. The common man said that the Mafiya was an extension of the government, and no government could be trusted, but at least this government was Latvian. Intellectuals hearkened to Karl Marx's momentous *Das Kapital*, and said that this phenomenon was a predictable, and indeed unavoidable, phase in the establishment of a capitalist society — the accumulation of capital by any means possible. German diplomats said that this was just "another" country of Ost Europa.

However, with the exception of the cold shower incident at the beginning of the year, neither I nor the company had had any direct contact with this catalyst of social change. Of course, I did set some parameters for minimizing exposure — the accountants avoided contacts with Mafiya-owned banks, while all import transactions were to be executed with full payment of customs duties and tariffs. Furthermore, cash registers were actually used to register sales, not just to adorn shop counters — while store clerks carry on the serious calculating work on large wooden abacuses (still the major trend in 1993). The Mafiya had a nose for cash transactions that weren't officially accounted for. That they had their own people at every customs point in the country was clear, as they targeted their most destructive activities against those companies that were later revealed to have been dealing in contraband goods.

Nonetheless, the unavoidable happened on one fine August day. As I pulled into the parking lot, I noticed that Valdis was outside, gesticulating excitedly to one of the workers. As I approached him, Valdis said, "I've got some bad news to tell you." Although this phrase was not an unusual one, it was not often that Valdis initiated the conversation with me, which meant I was going to be in for a particularly grave piece of news. I had expected something to the effect that, in spite of its use being banned except for the production of gingerbread at Christmas time, the propeller mixer had been used and caught the arm, or at least fingers, of a sleepy baker.

However, nothing had prepared me for the sight of the full office of people, wearing dejected expressions, as if they had been screaming at each other at the top of their lungs for the past hour, without result. Even the accountants, who were usually sequestered in their office-across-the-courtyard, were present. "So, what happened, did the department of health just announce that our pastries are spreading the plague in Riga?" I joked. Grim silence followed.

Zigrīda finally replied, "I wish it were just that. Boriss... we got a visit from the racket."

"What...?"

"They told us that we have to pay."

I then said that we should go into the back room and discuss this. I got a blow-by-blow account of this *nayezd* 'descent' by the racket. They had arrived without warning. Five of them entered the office. They asked who the *Nachal'nik* 'boss' was. The secretary referred them to Zigrīda, who was sitting in the back. After doing so, the secretary tried to go outside, but one of them blocked the door. He asked her, "*Kuda ti devushka – sidi spokoyno* 'Where you going, girl? Sit down quietly.'"[1] The five entered the back office, where two people could sit comfortably. Three of them sat down in front of Zigrīda. According to Juris, they had been taken from the same mold — with one-fourth-inch-high crewcuts and thick necks, with the only distinguishing features being scars or physical deformations in their visages. From the description, I could glean that they were anthropomorphic. They were dressed in jogging suits. At this point, the training suits were the utilitarian Soviet product, a blue gray with cherry red highlights in all the wrong places, garish and without *any* labels. With time, such uniforms were to boast brand-name labels such as Nike, Reebok, and Fila. All descriptions that Zigrīda gave me supported the notion that they were the proletarian-level Mafiya. The "spokesman," however, was of medium build. Zigrīda said that he had a particularly long scar on his cheek, and another on his neck. The others rocked nervously in their chairs, which were brought to the room by the secretary. Their eye movements belied an anticipation of physical action, in the form of combat, and a complete incoherence of subtleties of the "proposal" delivered by their spokesman.

"So, he said that we have to pay them for their protection. I said that we don't have money to do so — we're a small company producing bread... and in any event, our director would have to decide on this —," continued Zigrīda, with a tone of voice that reminded me of my grandfather's, when he used to launch into his "mowing down rows of Red Army cavalry as they charged our squad of six machine guns by the hundreds" account of his final hours in Russia.

"The 'talker' replied, 'fine, and when could we expect the director to be in?' I answered that the next day, in the afternoon, he would be here. He said that they would be there as well; then they left."

Before I had arrived that day, the biggest problem on my mind was trying to find out why the raspberries were not being picked the same time as last year. Now, the very functioning of the bakery was under threat, and not from late summer raspberries. I decided that I was going to do exactly what I would do in the U.S. of A. But before calling the police, I called Jay at the American embassy to tell him what happened and outline my plans. He warned me to be careful, but offered to provide me the contacts of the police department, which he would get through the Ministry of Interior. I told Jay that I appreciated what he was doing, and would be obliged for any pressure that he could put on the police department. "Sure, uh, Boriss, I think that we can certainly put a little pressure on the police, just by showing some interest in the case to our counterparts in the Ministry of Foreign Affairs. Of course, we can't contact the police department directly." I replied that I understood that he couldn't do that, and thanked him in advance for whatever he could do.

At the office the next morning, the rumor mill was turning at a pace that, if harnessed, would have generated electricity to suffice the bakery for a fortnight. Rumors ranged from the *vozmozhnost* 'possibility' that the gang was just a local one, to the *naverno* 'probability' that it was the *Pārdaugava* group of mobsters, who were renowned for drive-up shootings — someone recounted to me that they were once seen driving along the riverbank, shooting at a fleeing target out of machine pistols with silencers for fifty yards before hitting him. I wasn't sure whether I should have been awed by their tenacity or relieved that they were such lousy shots. Valdis took me aside, "Boriss, the Mafiya is using psychologists to convince people not to resist … Yeah, you might be standing in a café, and two people will appear at the next table and start talking to each other about how hopeless it is to resist the racket, because they 'control' the police, and have their own people planted in every government institution possible … the courts, Ministries …" He continued for five more minutes; I sensed surrender in his voice. Other workers contended that two of the ones who had paid their visit to us had served prison time for murder. Most variations were circulated as "facts gotten from the *inside*, and indisputable." I was beginning to get concerned — the Mafiya tales was one thing, the morale of my people was another, and it was hitting bottom-ditch.

Later that morning, I called the police department, special section working on racketeering, and arranged to file a report. As I drove to the police station that afternoon, I reflected on the risks of filing it. I had heard stories of police working in collaboration with the Mafiya. The Russian couple with the Bedlington terrier had recounted — when I had been sharing biscuits with the dog — "Santo's weekly routines." Santo owned the first floor of the high-rise in their apartment building. He made his rounds of each floor, offering to do "favors," godfather style, for the apartment building dwellers whom he liked. He seemed to have no occupation, but held long meetings in his apartment, several times a week. The couple told me that his bands were roaming through Rumbula, the used-car flea market center[22], skimming at least 10 percent off every car deal made, every car part traded, and every *shashlyk* 'shish-kebab' sold by the vendors. The Russian engineer said that he had frequently seen Santo carrying huge amounts of money out in large, transparent plastic bags, while walking his dog. This assertion had seemed highly suspect to me at the time, on account of the fact that Soviet plastic bags could not hold huge amounts of anything — I regularly watched our cleaning ladies take half-full bags of eggshells, apple peels and other organic refuse generated by the bakery to the garbage truck, only to have the bag burst wide open as they tried to heave them into the back. "And . . . ," I recalled the words of the engineer, "when he held council in his apartment, the first people in, and the last people out were the police officers from this precinct." The precinct headquarters were located not one hundred yards from his apartments. "So the police-Mafiya collaboration. But would it work on this scale? Are they collaborating at the ministerial level? Are they willing to risk an international incident if their 'pigeon' talks?" were some of many thoughts racing through my mind as I screeched the car into a parking spot.

When I walked through the main doors into the station, two people passed me who looked like the gangsters that Zigrīda had described — gray-blue and gray-red jogging suits, thick necks, short crewcuts. "If collusion it is, then they certainly can't be accused of hypocrisy," I thought. Sitting behind a large wooden booth with a thin glass window was a receptionist, dressed in a uniform. I mentioned who I was here to see and the officer made a call. Three minutes later, a man in his late twenties, dressed in jeans, wrinkled shirt, and a windbreaker, came down the stairs. He had a gun at his side. He didn't have an image that commanded authority, but at the same time, he didn't have the thick neck and short crewcut that the people from the other side boasted. The man led me up the stairs. In the stairwell, the paint was chipping off the walls. Telephone and other wires were running along the walls, fully exposed. In some cases, the plastic clamps that had been holding the wires in place had broken, and the wires dropped in arcs along the walls. The floor was covered with a brown linoleum, cracked in places. The ceilings were fourteen feet high. Suspended from them were some bent lamps. Invariably, one of a few lightbulbs would be missing. I was told to wait outside while the officer entered. A few minutes later, he reappeared and led me into the office of the chief. In fact, there were three desks in this well-lit room. The Captain's desk was on the right. Captain Eelisov stood up and reached his right hand out to shake my hand. His middle finger was missing. He was in his mid-thirties and had a complexion paler than Queen Victoria's. "So, what seems to be the problem?" he asked jovially, as if we were about to play cards. I described the situation, as briefly as possible. He posed some questions, and then concluded, "Hmm. Well, it's good that you came here. Sure, they might try to scare you, but don't give in, it's all a bluff. They'll say that they have 'plants' here, everywhere... but that's not true. They're afraid of us. We're the police. Who *wants* to go to jail?" He said this confidently, as matter-of-factly as any "godfather" would do, when he described his role in the greater scheme of things. In the meantime, I overheard, in the background, one of the officers telling another one, "Yeah, that Gerassimov job didn't end up very well. Three people in the hospital with gunshot wounds. One isn't going to make it. Gerassimov got away too. Hiding out."

"But what we need to have from you...," Eelisov continued, "is the total commitment to *follow through*. Of course it's not going to be easy, but it's the only way to put an end to the *banditi*."

"As I see it... I've got nothing to lose."

"Good. Now, from what you've told me, we don't have enough to go on. But don't worry, they'll be back. They spend a lot of time 'softening up' their targets... sometimes a month or more, if they need to. When you have a more concrete threat, come back to me."

Once at the office I recounted to Zigrīda and Valdis what he told me. I also instructed them that they should tell the racketeers, should the *banditi* show up in my absence, that Zigrīda and Valdis have full power to make financial decisions, so that the demands could be known earlier, and we could terminate this situation as quickly as possible. When word got out, a few hours later, that I had approached the police, the gossip hit a furious pitch. As I went down the corridor to the restroom, I overheard the following dialogue: "... and I heard that one man went to the police for protection, and not only did the police not help him, but they actually told about him to the Mafiya. Boy, did he get it... they found the body in the Daugava."

"Oh yeah, the police are working just hand in hand with the mob. *I* heard about this one store owner who went to the police, and the next day he got a phone call from the mob — told him that he had ten seconds to get out of his store. He ran into the basement just in time. Three seconds later, they blew the whole store front away. Oh you just gotta forget *that* approach..." By two o'clock, I had to leave — for sanity's sake.

That afternoon, they arrived again, unannounced, moments after I had left. Zigrīda later recounted that this time, they gave us a concrete proposal:

"When I started saying — once again — that we are a small, poor start-up company, the 'boss' said, 'Sure, sure, we've heard all of that before; that's irrelevant, we can accept two hundred lats at the beginning of the 'relationship,' and more with time, as the company grows.' I said that even this amount is too much. He then said that we don't need to pay in the way of an outside payment — his goal was not to 'cause any unnecessary burdens' to the accounting department nor to attract unnecessary attention — it could be conveniently arranged that the company would take into its workforce, as a baker, one of the boys. '. . . just take him on board — hire him.' He then pointed to the smallest, youngest man sitting behind him, and the latter nodded. I then asked, 'Will he have to work?' 'No,' the boss replied, 'He would just come in to pick up his paycheck.' 'Well,' I replied, 'it would depend on what the President says — we can't make such a decision without him.' 'Fine, consult with him, we'll be back tomorrow.' And then they left. What should we do, Boriss?"

"Well, not *that*, Zigrīda — once they're in officially, they'll destroy the whole business. They did that all the time in Moscow. Let me go to the police again. This time I can convince them that it is a pressing issue."

I had told both Eelisov and Jay that I would be fully prepared to involve myself personally in any undercover operations designed to catch the "banditi," that would be necessary. However, Jay called me the following morning and asked me not to do so. When I asked why not, Jay replied that the Ambassador had insisted that I not do this myself, as it could "bring some unforeseen complications to relations between us and the young government."

In any event, I went to Captain Eelisov and recounted what happened. He left the room for some twenty minutes. Inadvertently, I scrutinized his office; the walls were bare, and painted with a high-gloss beige color, which revealed all the imperfect contours of the plasterwork and previous paint coats. On the desk was some penholder from a Scandinavian police organization. On the shelves behind the desk were more plaques, pens and other paraphernalia that were the standard booty of exchange visits by foreign organizations. When he returned, he proffered to conduct a "sting operation" to catch the *banditi*. He started by saying that the next time they come, they were to be told that we had decided to pay them up front. He then proceeded to explain to me the details of what had to be done.

I reflected on the situation, and whether or not I should do this myself, in spite of what Jay had requested. I pondered the worst-case scenario, and besides admitting the impossibility of looking stylish in concrete shoes, I realized that no American businessmen had as yet been killed by the Mafiya in the Baltics or even Russia, at that point. Several in Moscow had been threatened, and a handful had seen their local business partners meet a dubious fate, but none had been killed.[3] I didn't know what the repercussions would be, but I could imagine that the disappearance and subsequent recovery of a bullet-ridden body of the owner of The Merry Baker — which produced nothing more profitable or addictive than chocolate eclairs with a unique custard-based filling — would subsequently force the Latvian Government to perform quite a song-and-dance in its effort to assure potential investors in the oil, transport, and communications industries that the investment environment was still A-O.K. for foreign direct investors. "Well," I concluded, "it's not like this is the most wonderful opportunity of my life."

As it turned out, the company plumber had been voicing his desire to "let him at 'em," thinking that it would be *budet zdorovo* 'jolly good show' to confront them. I met with Valdis; he confirmed that Roberts had never been as eager to do anything as much as he wanted to do this. "Weird" I thought to myself, but so be it. When the racketeers arrived later that day, they were told that they could collect on the following day. On the following day, the specialists from the police department arrived in the early afternoon, and wired the plumber up with a tape recorder and a microphone. He was massive enough that these items, in spite of their Soviet-style compactness[4], were not noticeable on his body. Had he stood less than 6 feet 2 inches tall and weighed much less than the 240 pounds that he did, then someone could have observed that he was carrying the aforementioned items on his body. As it was, with the help of his loose overalls, he could have concealed a small telephone booth.

The numbers from the banknotes to be used were written down on a piece of paper. The sheet was going to serve as the proof that money was extorted. Plainclothes policemen from the "section" were going to be milling around in the vicinity. The plumber was instructed to tell the *banditi* that he has the money, and to place an emphasis on the word "money" to elicit some confirmatory reaction from them. The latter would be recorded and used as evidence of extortion. This statement would serve as additional evidence. "They must say 'money,' or 'banknotes,' for this to be successful," the detectives repeated to Roberts. When the last of the band had left, Roberts was to say "they've left." I was proud of my co-directors who, though nervous, implemented the instructions flawlessly.

That afternoon, the racketeers arrived earlier than they had said they would. They entered the office and (according to Roberts) stormed down the hall. Then Roberts hollered that he had what they were looking for. He switched the tape recorder on. They returned to the front room, approached the desk where Roberts was sitting and asked where Zigrīda was. He stated that she was busy and couldn't be here, but that *he* had the money. The motor worked initially, but for some reason, the microphone stopped working. Or so Eelisov later told us. In any event, Roberts told the collectors that the President had asked him to give them the "*money*," as had been agreed, and if they wanted the "*banknotes*" then please to say so. "Are you trying to be funny, you #&$*#^/! Fat man? Van'ka, take the money," they replied. They took the money, left, and Roberts repeated three times, "they've left." Later, in his account of the encounter, Roberts said that the criminals were surprised by the relative ease with which they had received the money, even telling one another, "What, this guy doesn't value money?" and "Never got it this *&%*$# easy before."

In any event, the "milling-around, all-over-the-place" plainclothes policemen didn't apprehend the racketeers as they exited the building. The policemen didn't even try to catch them there. According to the account given me by Eelisov later, they didn't do so until forty-five minutes later, in Jūrmala, thirty-five kilometers away. The agents couldn't apprehend the criminals — who were no doubt laughing themselves silly at having taken twenty-five thousand Latvian rubles from a poor little start-up company without so much as a fist-fight — at once, because they "couldn't make a positive identification at the time." However, they told me later that they could do so thirty-five kilometers later, when the *cars* (not the scarred criminals inside) "looked suspect." Eelisov added that since this was apparently the first such sting, the *banditi* suspected nothing. He did not clarify, nor did I ask, whether the "first time" in his phrase referred to the *banditi* or his department.

Eelisov then called Zigrīda and Valdis into the headquarters to provide a positive identification, which the two co-directors gave. I went with them, to provide moral support. I looked at the "banditi" — I saw five of them. Three were boys in their late teens, pumped up like college football linebackers. They kept their heads down most of the time, and when they looked up, they did so briefly, nervously. One was slowly rubbing the one-fourth-inch-long blond hairs on his scalp. Another looked us over once out of the corner of his eye. The third one avoided eye contact with us. They gave me the impression that they were wondering how they got here — like they had sat on the wrong bus by accident. I could imagine that they had gotten the standard "*Van'ka, ne volnuysia, vsye bud'et normal'no. Nichevo firma nam nye zdelayet.* 'Little Ivan, don't worry, everything will be O.K. The pigeons won't do anything against us.'" — assurances before their "descent" onto The Merry Baker.

The two others, with more scars and deflated bodies, were older men. They were holding their heads up. The "boss" that Zigrīda pointed to had a deep scar running down four inches of his cheek. He had another one, a more horizontal one, which lay conspicuously above his right eye. His face reminded me of Tom Berenger's, in any of the films where Berenger had played the anti-hero-with-scar. The "boss" was gazing straight into a wall. But he wasn't nervous or despairing — he looked like someone waiting for a bus. Juris and Zigrīda signed the documents, identifying these as the men that had come to the office three days prior. We were told that the criminal accusations would be drawn up, along with the report, and be ready in two days.

That evening, I told the story to Inge, and she smiled. "Well, that was brave of your people... is the plumber's heart in order?"

"Sure — we gave him a bonus, five tortes of his choosing, and the week off — he'll need at least that much to make the rounds with his relatives telling them how it happened... the *stand-off*." We laughed. "Actually, Inge, I admire him — I'm not sure that I wouldn't have needed a stiff drink beforehand and a bathtub under my chair to catch all that I would have sweat."

Inge put her arms around me, "It would have been terrible if something had happened to you, you know the kids are getting used to you." At that point, the tinny, oddly-timed notes of the "African Fire Song" filled the room.

The next day, sometime around four in the afternoon, Zigrīda called me from the bread bakery. Her voice was quiet and morose. I told her to walk up to the office. She replied that she wouldn't walk up, but would have Valdis drive her the two-hundred-fifty yards up the street. This statement sounded odd to me, as she had frequently repeated she was grateful we had moved the bread production from the other plant, on account of the fact that she could exercise by taking the walk between plants in the fine summer weather. When she arrived and sat in front of my desk, I was shocked — I had never seen her looking so pale. I asked her what happened, and she began recounting the following story.

She was sitting in her office, which was in the back of the store, with the door facing the courtyard entry and parking lot. Since it was particularly warm that day, both the entry door to the plant, and the door to her office were open. Consequently, she had an unobstructed view of the driveway. As she was reviewing some employee records, a car came screeching to a halt outside, in front of the entry door to the bakery. The back door of the car swung open, and a man rolled out of the back seat, onto the ground, screamed and then lay still. "He was bent in strange directions, like he was dead. But it wasn't just a man, he had something on his face. It looked like a 'guerilla' [ski] mask. Another masked person in the front passenger seat of the car then turned to me and yelled, 'And this can happen to you, too. Don't press charges. Withdraw your statements.' The man in the ski-mask got up, jumped into the car and it sped off."

I tried as best I could to calm Zigrīda down, and say that these are ploys that they use against those that wish to press charges, because they are scared themselves. I then repeated the words of Captain Eelisov. Zigrīda replied only that it was easy for *me* to say that.

Then, late on the following morning, Zigrīda called me again. Her voice was trembling. I drove to her office right away. Once again, Zigrīda was besides herself, or as "besides herself" as a steely-nerved Director of Personnel of a Soviet food enterprise — used to dealing with the dregs of civilized society — could be. She then recounted that an elderly lady had come to the store and asked for "the director of personnel." Given what happened the day before, Zigrīda asked the sales clerk who it was. "The store clerk told me that it was just a late-middle-aged lady, so I walked out into the store. The lady threw herself at me. She was crazed. "*Ya Sashina Mama* 'I'm the mother of *Little Sasha*'. *Pozhalusta, ya* **umolyayu**, *nye nado pisat' zayavlyeniye!* 'Please, I *implore you*, don't press charges!' *On* **khoroshiy** *mal'chik. Yevo plokhiye lyudi zastavili eto delat.'* *Pozhaluysta, ya proshu, mat,' materyu, NYE PISHY.* 'He's a *good* boy. These bad people forced him to do it. I ask you, as one Mother to another. Please don't press charges!'"

Zigrīda recounted the other things that the hysterical woman said. The difficulty of raising him alone, without a father, the misunderstandings… "But he simply could not be mixed up with such bad elements as the police say he was… So please, I ask you, understand me — is it fair to condemn him, to put him in prison, with criminals who will destroy him? He'll die … please don't do it, don't press charges."

Again, I did my best to calm Zigrīda down and assure her that this visit was just a harmless mind-game the Mafiya were playing. However, I concluded by saying that I would never force her to do anything that would be dangerous to her health and "let your conscience dictate what you should do." Within a few hours, I was led to assume that the same was going on with Valdis, because by the afternoon, a few minutes before we were scheduled to go to the police station and sign the charges, both Zigrīda and Valdis came to me and said that they would quit rather than press charges. I ended by saying, "*Khorosho,* do what you think is right … just remember, that if nothing happens to them, then they could very well be right back, and from what I understand, all the money and sweat that we had put into this business will be lost."

"We understand, Boriss, but you see, we are not in the same situation as you are. They … they would never touch *you*, you're a *foreigner*."

When we went to the police, I waited outside, viewing the myriads of jogging suited, and jeans-wearing plainclothes policemen circulate in the halls. After some twenty minutes, Zigrīda and Valdis stepped out of the police captain's office, and I was motioned in. Eelisov asked me to review the statements of my directors. They had written only that which literally happened and what the racketeers actually said. Omitted were the myriad of insinuations, hints and gestures that were the guts of all the communications from such persons. My co-directors had written that no one had ever asked for money outright, and that they were never threatened. Eelisov told me that this was *slabo* 'weak,' and that I was going back on our agreement. I made some lame excuse and shrugged my shoulders. "I understand," he replied, smiling. We shook hands and parted. Subsequently, all charges against the racketeers were dropped. Although this outcome was a blow to justice, I was also aware that my colleagues had, under the circumstances, acted with notable bravery; I had no right to expect more of them. It would have been pushing the limits of human decency on my part to have demanded more of my partners, when it wasn't me who was sitting across a small wooden desk from people who snubbed out people's lives as easily as they did Marlboros. And as much a legend as I might have been in my own mind, I wasn't about to be a "Lethal Weapon" to the Mafiya — my current mission in life was to titillate thousands of ex-Soviet tastebuds with Danish, marzipan Napoleon Hats, and sinfully rich "Opera cakes." In gratitude to Eelisov and his men, we baked a twenty-pound cake for his department, for their annual ball. We fashioned a revolver out of marzipan.

With time I also realized that in its own way, this was probably the first such blow to the racketeers. I spoke with many Latvian businessmen afterwards, as well as my colleagues of the 7G club, and discovered that the "word in the street" was that over 90 percent of retail businesses were paying protection monies. This particular group must have seen that they were dealing with [crazy] people who weren't afraid to take their problems to the police, so why bother. Some four young men were, in fact, one statement short of having to spend the next five years behind bars. Whether they understood this, or whether their bosses had shrugged it off and went on to line up other retail targets that were waiting — like ripe plums — to fall into their outstretched hands, I don't know. But they never came back.

Footnotes

[1] Rumbula was a 100-acre complex which boasted over five hundred vehicles for sale at any one time, and had a spare-part section that included one hundred "car booths." Specifically, the vendors would take the wares that they were selling, and display them on the hoods and roofs of the cars that they had driven in with. In the 1980s, this complex had been a "market" alternative to the State-owned Lada Stores, which were forever short of key spare parts.

[2] Dyevushka — All women under the age of sixty . . . and some over, were referred to as "girls."

[3] This was to change in 1995, with the death of Paul Tatum, the co-owner and director of the Radisson Business Center in Moscow. He was assassinated by members of the Chechen Mafiya, who subsequently installed an "associate" of theirs in the director's position. Western businessmen were threatened regularly from that point on.

[4] A common joke was: "The Soviet Union makes the best watches in the world — they're the fastest." A similar joke concerned transistors — "the largest in the world!"

26

JUST DESSERTS

BY OCTOBER OF 1993, FIFTEEN months after opening, *Jautrais Maiznieks* was firmly imprinted in the minds of many who had been at the Song Festival, sampled our pastries, or trampled our torte. I figured that the business should grow slowly but surely, and I'd get back to searching for selling space further at the next stage, when issues of store leases were resolved and peoples' incomes had increased. I avoided "great advertising opportunities," and once again focused on learning about the culture.

I had the even-number-of-flowers routine down pat, but that was just a start. It was on the 22nd of October, 1993 that I recall being awakened by Inge. Normally, if I wasn't surveying the bakery's output of product in the morning, I would sleep until the bright hour of six forty-five in the morning. Now for some people, the so-called "morning people," including endorphin-crazed body-builders and five-mile joggers, this is well into the morning already. However, I am by nature a "night owl." Given an opportunity to set my own schedule, my window of sleep inevitably creeps towards a 1:00 A.M.–8:30 A.M. axis. My creative juices start flowing at about 9:30 P.M., when these joggers and "early birds" are contemplating bedtime. My concentration peaks at about midnight, two hours or more after the former category have been slumbering deeply. The morning, on the other hand, represents mental death and destruction. It's when fears and doubts coalesce together with fatigue, to create phantoms. In a word, Goya's *Sleep of Reason Produces Monsters*.

So when Inge woke me up at six thirty, I was despondent. "What's wrong?"

"Nothing, we have to get up."

"Grm, harumph, errr ... What the HELL HAPPENED NOW! God___ n it, can't a man sleep here?!"

"Boriss, darling, we have to wish Eliza a happy birthday."

"Hunhh?"

"Come on, GET UP."

"O.K., O.K., but it better be good." Sporting a yawn that would make a hippo nervous, I put on my bathrobe, and followed behind Inge. She picked up a bouquet of flowers which she had stashed on the balcony, and then took a wrapped present from under the bed. "Here, you take this!"

We proceeded to Eliza's room, which was still pitch black. Inge switched on the main light, sat on the bed, and started nudging her eight-year-old daughter. Eliza was in the deep caresses of rapid eye movement sleep; this nudging would no doubt come across as an earthquake or bus plunge in her dream. She opened her eyes about as wide as a dime is thick, and said, "The walls, the WALLS ... Mother? Oh, oh."

"Happy BIRTHDAY, *Dūdiṇa* 'Little Cupcake'!"

Eliza was still groggy, but managed a half-smile. She was young, but with time, she would learn to emulate joy and surprise, while her eyes would still be glazed over. "Give her the present, Boriss." I gave it to her, but added, "Inge, don't you think that we can let her go back to sleep now, that we've 'surprised' her?"

"No, no, she'll love the present ... go ahead, open it up." Eliza brushed her tussled hair back, quietly took the package, and unwrapped it. It was a Barbie doll, with a wedding outfit. Eliza managed a smile. Inge and I hugged her. Then Inge asked, "So how do you like it?"

"*Mṭṣ* 'It's nice,'" she grumbled, half-smiling, looked up with her eyes that had now widened to a quarter's edge width and then plopped her head back down on the pillow.

"O.K., Inge can we go now? I think that more than anything now, she would like to sleep some more."

"No, too late, we've already woken her up ... *Dūdiṇa*, tell me, do you *really* like the doll? You know, we were thinking of getting the one with the swimsuit," she continued, while gently shaking her daughter. This was enough to keep Eliza from falling asleep. She limply put her hand on the doll, drew herself up, and hugged the Barbie.

Inge continued the interrogation until Eliza mustered a whole smile, and squeaked, "It's exactly what I wanted. *Paldies* 'Thank you.'"

"Great, that's what we thought," Inge replied. She then jumped up and went to put the finishing touches on a large breakfast she had been preparing since what was probably four thirty in the morning. I turned to Eliza, "Is it always like this?" She nodded, with eyes closed, and put her head on her legs.

I learned — the hard way — that this ceremony was not limited to birthdays; the "Birthday Police" also did their work on Name days. Six times a year, I was dragged out of bed to subsequently inflict the same brutal "surprise" on other members of the family, followed by the same "so-do-you-like-your-*gift*?" interrogation. Loathed be the person who appeared ambivalent (although this is a pretty natural reaction to having bright lights flashed in one's eyes in the fifteen minutes prior to one's customary wake-up time; shaken to a "woken" state and forced to open two to four carefully wrapped presents that one could barely focus on). The interrogation would take a turn for the worse: "So, you don't like the gift?! Und vy NOT?!" in the case of projected ambivalence. Of course the said person wanted to say "I'm really happy about the gifts, but if it doesn't appear to you that I'm not ecstatic, which I am, it's just because you've woken me up in the middle of my REM sleep, and I'm having trouble adjusting," but on account of the fact that said person could easily confuse his own name with the Pope's at this time in the morning, he would normally say something like, "Mmgph, garggh, ubbaha, bus FALLING." Inge would then repeat, "*Nuu, nuu, nuu*" and firmly shake the child until a full explanation was forthcoming. The child would be given a few minutes to wake up, more lights were turned on, and then the truth would be ascertained.

I learned, within three or four episodes, that I should rise up quickly, open up the presents as if my life depended on doing so quicker than the Ferrari pit stop crew changed Michael Schumacher's front tires, smile idiotically — like a mental patient given a tubful of his favorite ice cream on a hot summer day — and exclaim how the purple apron, weird book or eelskin toothpick holder was *exactly* perfect for me. With the last word, my eyelids would come crashing down as quickly as they had been pried open, and I would collapse for another fourteen minutes of precious sleep.

On the other hand, absolutely nothing, save a bouquet of flowers, adorned the table in the evening. Sometimes Inge's parents and sister would come over, but usually, this was postponed until the following weekend. Birthday evenings were strictly a family event on the day they occurred, with an occasional friend of the child. Since I did not share the same sense of mission in playing with people's sleep patterns as did Inge, I tried to change the tradition, moving to an evening axis, as I had recalled it being for the past thirty-three years of my life. As it was, during the next two birthdays of Inge's, I tried to shift the crescendo towards the evening. I bought flowers during the day, came home early to prepare dinner, lit candles and tried to make it a festive event. Absolutely none of this succeeded in dampening Inge's crushing disappointment that she had not been brutally awoken in the morning. She would call during the day (usually several times) and utter something along the lines of "You know, I can't believe that you had *completely* forgotten my birthday." The birthday dinner resembled a funeral pyre. Within a year, I gritted my teeth, and acquiesced to the morning birthday ritual.

But what I didn't let up on was my belief that the kids should have great, unforgettable birthday parties with as many friends as they wanted. So, when I noticed the quiet, solemn party, where two invited friends were given some sweets, a cake and then left to their own devices, I swore that things would have to change.

In November, I was looking at the bakery's results of the previous three months, and saw that the cost-of-goods was rising rapidly. I discussed with Ligita and Zigrīda, suggesting possible reasons — spoilage, defective machinery, power surge and poor-quality raw materials. The replies were all negative. A week later, I received a call.

"Boriss, I think that we have found what is wrong." "Yes?"

"Yeah, I had asked Jurijs to check out some complaints about the oven, and he did so in the early morning of yesterday. He discovered a whole lot more *braķis* 'defective production' than the bakers had ever admitted to making in one night."

"Yes?"

"And the bakers were ashamed of that, so … they were hiding it."

"Hiding it?"

"Yeah … apparently, only the first of the three decks are being used. The other ones are not."

"I thought that they slow-baked the meringue in that oven."

"Yeah, but only in the top deck. They're taking the ruined production that comes out in the middle of the night, and pile it into decks two and three. Then they divide the stuff between bakers and take it home. The rest they sneak into a special bag and the cleaning lady hides it until the garbage truck comes."

"Ingenious … they'd make millions as bank robbers. But seriously Zigrīda, where's Ligita in all this? For Chrissake, she's the production director!"

"I know, I know. I asked her ... she refuses to get involved."

"What? She's a partner in this operation, *and* she's responsible for all production."

"She refuses to be a *stukatch*.[1]"

"WHAT?! But she's a *partner* — the bakers are stealing from *her* as well, doesn't she realize it?" This was met with a stony silence on the other end of the phone. I asked Zigrīda to talk with her again, insofar as she had been a friend of Zigrīda's. The next day I called.

"Nothing doing," said Zigrīda. "She said that you couldn't pay her enough to do that."

The next day I called. Sure enough she just kept repeating the word "stukatch, stukatch" until I stopped asking. I called Zigrīda again and suggested that we handle it differently and asked if she had any ideas.

"Sure, we can do what I did occasionally when we suspected someone of stealing — stand watch and catch them red-handed as they came out."

"Fine."

We then planned our stakeout. The following day, we walked casually out to the unpaved parking lot between the office and the bakery, at exactly 10:15, when the konditors working on the cakes would be departing. Our target was Gita. I didn't know her very well, except that I had associated her with a group of three "with heavy karma's"; three individuals who felt that although their profession was cake making, their vocation consisted of griping. Whenever I would pose the question, "Are there any other issues that you would like to discuss?" one of the three would inevitably say something along the lines of "This space is too small, when are we going to move out?" Another would chime in, "Why do we have to work in a half-basement?" while the third would round it out with a "Why do we have to make such complicated cakes?" I didn't pay much mind to this, as Zigrīda had warned me that they came from the "whining caste" of Latvia's inhabitants. She recommended that I just repeat, "Is it really all that bad?!" and they'll begin to think about the other bakeries that they can work at, where pay is half of what it was here, and where some owners even beat the bakers, and they will quiet down.

In any event, we were standing in the parking lot, when I asked Zigrīda which ones we would be checking.

"Which *ones*?! Boriss, we'll be lucky to snag one."

"Just one?!"

"Yeah, because what they'll do, is the first one'll get caught and then he'll run back to the window and tell the others that we're here."

"Why couldn't Juris stand there?"

"Oh no, that would destroy everything -- they'll suspect something. Even if Juris stops them from communicating through the window, they'll use hand signals, or the second one will have 'forgotten' something in the back which she'll have to run back and get—"

"I see, I see," I said sheepishly, ashamed for having assumed to have some 'tips' for a veteran of this business.

It was Zigrīda's idea to target one of the workers of the cake section — Gita.[2] As we were pretending to discuss the finer points of changing oil of the cars that we were standing next to, Gita rounded the corner. We calmly stepped in her path, and greeted her. Zigrīda asked her to show the contents of her plastic bag to me. She smiled nervously and did so. I found nothing but shoes, working clothes and the allotted amount of rolls — all was in order. Her smile turned into a smirk. I was feeling like the lowest of curs -- here I had not only tormented the girl with a cake plant located in a half-basement, but I was actually forcing her to show me the contents of her bag. I wanted to crawl into the smallest corner of our most dormant freezer. Then Zigrīda said, "Excuse me, but could I look in your handbag?" The smirk froze on the girl's face. "Yes, Gita, just for a second. *I'll* look, not Mr. Zemtzovs," added Zigrīda. Gita handed over the purse, as if it were an infant that she was afraid to let others hold. Zigrīda opened it, shook her head, smiled, and pulled out a peeled orange. "Hmm," I growled. Then she pulled out another. I was surprised. When she pulled out a third, my shame had turned to anger. "*Nu, nu. Viens apelsīns dlya ukrasheniye, odin dlya degustatsii, i odin yesche dlya vsyakoe sluchiye* 'So . . . one orange for decoration, one for tasting, and one more in case of emergency'?" Gita was silent.

Zigrīda took out a piece of paper and wrote up what had just occurred. She asked Gita to sign it, and me as well. After Gita left, Zigrīda turned to me, "You see, Boriss, they're treated too well here." I didn't know how to answer that one. I pondered replying: "Yes, you're absolutely right — as of tomorrow we will resume the public beatings of those bakers who stay longer than thirty seconds in the restroom! Salivating Dobermans at the doors in full battle regalia!" Instead, I answered that she, Zigrīda, should feel free to establish the level of order and discipline that she felt appropriate. Then, for what must have been the twentieth time in a year, I repeated the mantra that no one knew both these people and the relevant Latvian laws governing personnel issues better than *she,* and that I implicitly trusted her judgment. My only question to her was why did *we* have to carry out this inspection? She shrugged her shoulders and said, "*Citādi nekad nebūs kārtības* 'Otherwise, there will never be any order'."

I never saw Gita again. When we informed Ligita of this nab, her only reply was, allegedly, "Good, one thief less." I subsequently addressed the bakers on the "sin" of theft, and how ultimately, it affects them just as much as everyone else. For a short while afterwards, the cost-of-goods decreased. However, this attempt to steal items that were — in my mind — not even worth stealing, forced me to ponder whether or not Inge's earlier statements were not closer to the truth than I had given them credit for being.

Fortunately for the bakery, few establishments ended up reverting to such ploys to cover their own cash flow problems. Other establishments, particularly hotels, were increasing their orders rapidly. Our orders to the Metropole hotel now included close to a hundred Danish pastries and almost as many rolls.

Footnotes

[1]"Stukatch" was an individual who, in high Stalinist times, was the co-worker
   whose primary job function consisted of being a "snitch," reporting on
   the work and thoughts of fellow workers to the managing directors of
   the enterprise.The latter was done in full secrecy, sometimes masked as
   "chewing out by the boss" session, to keep the other employees guessing
   as to who the "stukatch" was.

[2] Not her real name

27

WINTER TRADITIONS

Although I had ordered some rum-soaked red and green cherries, chocolate angels and marzipan press molds in the forms of Santa Claus and Frosty the Snowman back in September, preparations for Christmas began in earnest after the first week of December. We agreed on work schedules, new Christmas cakes, how many hundreds of kilos of *Piparkūkas* 'Gingerbread' would be pressed out, and what advertising would be done. Zigrīda had considered it essential that there be additions to the standard shifts beginning on the morning of the 22nd. *Piparkūkas* are a tradition that was taken from the Swedes, who are the undisputed masters of the thin, crispy gingerbread cookie, intensified by inclusion of pepper. Nonetheless, the Latvian cookies were also not bad. We decided that our bakery should come as close as possible, without using treacle[1], to making *Piparkūkas* based on the pre-war recipe. Not being a connoisseur of gingerbread cookies — in fact, I have a congenital avoidance instinct to them that is even stronger than the one I have to English Christmas Cake — I was surprised to find that after trying the first one, I had trouble stopping myself from eating twenty small ones at a time. Along with the choice of natural ingredients, their slow mixture in the "propeller" mixer and the "aging" of the dough for two days, a key factor in assuring addiction to these cookies was to make them no thicker than two stacked quarters. Normally, using the pastry bread machine, achieving this thinness would have been child's play for the bakers. However, the bakers found that the *Piparkūkas* dough, laden with sugar, butter and molasses, would stick to the canvas sheets rather than going through the press from one side of the rolling press to the other. The machine would subsequently tear the dark brown flattened dough and deposit sections of it on the table, the floor, on the protective hand guards, on the bakers' noses and many other places besides the other side of the press. Consequently, over 1300 two-foot-by-three-foot sheets of dough had to be flattened by hand. I was concerned that the overtime pay would be quite substantial, but was told by my co-directors that the reputation of the bakery would be made or broken by the quality of the *Piparkūkas*. All doubts on the issue were dispelled about five minutes after I brought some home. The kids inhaled them. Inge told me that the two that she managed to save from their clutches were something otherworldly and "if I could place an advance order as the wife of the main co-founder for ten pounds of dough I would be much obliged, thank you."

My spirits were high, as I listened to the number of orders called in for the three days prior to Christmas Day — for the *Piparkūkas*, for all kinds of cakes, *Pīrādziņi ar speķi*[2], and other products. On the morning of the 22nd, the store shelves and baskets were full of product. However, the forecasted number of people failed to show up. Hundreds of kilos of rolls, pastries, and Kliņgeri were sent back. Zigrīda assured me that I shouldn't worry, for the next two days would make up for this miscalculation. Once again, for the 23rd, the bakers had worked around the clock, to ensure that the store shelves were groaning with product. And once again, no more customers passed through the store than would have been usual for a weekday. "Well," posited Zigrīda, "that means that perhaps we won't have the predicted number of people on the twenty-fourth?" I told her that she had spent more Christmases in Riga than I had, and that if she wasn't sure, she would do well to consult others besides myself.

On the 24th, after taking care of last-minute gift buying (as if there were any other kind for entrepreneurs), I went to the store. I was greeted by the sight of a long line of people, and one highly suspect *Kliņģeris* on the counter. The cake cabinet was completely empty. "What happened?! Where are the cakes?" I asked angrily. The store manager, flustered by my voice, replied, "The cake bakery can't keep up."

"Well, how long have you been without cakes?"

"Oh, for … a while … but they've called and said that a car is going to be here any minute …"

"How long is 'a while,' Zenta?"

"'About two little hours."

"*TWO HOURS*?!" I leaped to the phone, and called to the bakery. "Ligita can't come to the phone now, she's in the cake bakery."

"Fine, just tell her I called, and that . . . and that . . . this is ridiculous. Never mind."

We had met and we had agreed that the sponges would be made before hand. I was besides myself — it was the single best day for sales in the year, and because of poor planning, we were losing money [and customers] at an astounding rate. "Is Zigrīda there?" ". . . Yes, she is."

"Zigrīda, what is the problem?"

"Boriss, they just can't keep up. Someone is making the decorations by hand, and it's just going so slow — the cakes are ready, but Ligita says that they can't go out without at least pine branches on them."

"*Pine branches*?! You mean those light green ones with the little pinecones that look like . . . like *cat poop*?!" It was actually embarrassing to bring people into the cake plant when they were being made. I am sure that at no time before in culinary history had cat droppings been so accurately emulated, one could almost feel the bowel movement of the feline.

"The cakes can't go out because of THAT?! Where is that Ligita, I'll strangle her . . . Zigrīda, wait, can't they just put on the Christmas tree instead? Please, PLEASE try to convince Ligita that the Christmas tree is just fine for the holidays . . . if they do the pine branches, then leave the cones off . . . why can't they just use the marzipan press with the Santa Claus and the Snowman?"

"Ligita said that the presses don't work, and that neither of those two figures are *Latvian* Christmas symbols anyway — Boriss, they've finished another three, they're coming up the lift to get loaded in the car."

At that moment, I heard the deafening roar of the Soviet lift. It always sounded like it was groaning under the weight of a one-ton anvil. When it stopped, I resumed.

"Zigrīda, you mean they're sending a car with just three cakes?! Do you realize, there are fifteen people lined up here, and we have one . . . one 'Quasimodo Klingeris' to offer them?!"

"Yes, Boriss, I understand, but what do you want me to do? I can't very well go in there and start helping them. And the tensions are running pretty high down there anyway."

"O.K, O.K. I'm sorry, I know it's not your fault. It's just . . . a shame."

And I didn't dare enter the bakery myself. The last time that I entered the plant during a rush delivery preparation, my presence alone had been enough to erase the height of one step — the third one of the stairway between the cake bakery and the rest of the plant — from Edvins' subconscious memory;

he tripped and ended up wearing two pounds of an eight-pound German Chocolate Cake. And the frosting didn't even match his earring.

That evening, after a snow flurry in the afternoon, the ground was as white as my mood was black. The Merry Baker would be running a loss again this year, and the best sales day of the year had just been grossly mismanaged. It had been like the Song Festival all over again ... with the addition of marzipan cat droppings. Furthermore, the apartment renovation was falling disastrously behind schedule. Not even a brigade of the most steely-nerved, tee-totaling, amphetamine-popping construction people could "storm" it back on track. A March move-in would be out of the question.

"Looks like this'll be another cold, hard winter," I thought to myself. This would be the one, two ... third winter in a row, of this kind. The short days, and long nights — I hated them. It was as if God had gathered up all the gray clouds from every country in the southern hemisphere and stored them above Latvia for five months. The Swedes at least had learned to redress this circumstance by painting their houses gay tones of yellow, green, red, and blue, and lighting up the city of Stockholm with no regard to expense. The Soviet government, on the other hand, had banned the production of any color more vivid than dog crap ochre, and even *that* was relegated to interiors. Outside, one would find nothing more uplifting than beige, interspersed between a fleet of battleship-gray structures. It is not without reason, that even five years later, Werner Herzog chose the Latvian town of Kuldīga — as it stood in 1999, without almost any props or location modifications — to portray a Jewish Ghetto of Warsaw in the late nineteenth century.

"This'll be the third Christmas in a row to be spent with Inge's folks ... what had I done in my previous life to deserve that?" I was thinking as we drove along the poorly lit highway to Ogre. I still felt uncomfortable in their presence. Perhaps more accurately, I felt that they were uncomfortable in mine. Inge had told me on several occasions, "You're the American, from far away — they don't know how to treat you," and left the resolution of this issue to me. I repeated that I thought they didn't like the way I treated Markus. "Well ... that too."

I was still aghast at the liberties they allowed their only grandson. That they had an "only" granddaughter seemed to be of no relevance — they regularly recruited her to work in the kitchen, clean plates, help prepare the food and execute a number of chores. At the same time, the grandparents invited Markus to lounge on the couch, watch the T.V. station of his choice, eat as many snacks as he could stand. He greedily accepted this hospitality and took it one step further, by turning the volume of the T.V. high enough to disrupt others' conversations or play a pirated version of Nintendo until everyone was vomiting from the sound of the computer-synthesized "Super Mario" game's theme song. I had trouble digesting this double standard, and it took me a long time to get the truth from Inge; in Soviet times, the phrase "Every married couple should plant a tree, raise a son, and kill a snake" had been embedded in the mind of every young newlywed. I replied to her that this phrase could well explain the thick forests and the dearth of snakes in Latvia — I hadn't seen any over a five-year period — but it "doesn't explain why Markus should get away with everything at your parents' house, and your daughter with *nothing*."

"Oh, but that's because she has a 'character.'"

But this time, fuelled by my frustrations of the previous day, I continued the repartee:

"Yes, character . . . of a victim, I see. I won't get into that though, it'll ruin dinner. By the way, that's a very Central Asian-type saying, being that daughters don't count, and snakes are dangerous there."

"Could be."

"Now Inge, don't get me wrong, I love Markus too, I just don't think that coddling him, like your grandparents do, is going to help him in the long term."

"Sure, sure, let's talk about it when we get back home . . . in the meantime, could you help bring out these dishes . . . the best lessons are usually taught by example . . ."

"Ha, ha, ha," I guffawed as I took the Salad *Olivier* and dill pickles to the table.

Although my spirits were lower than they had been during the past two Christmases, I had also been deprived of normal conversation — one which did not focus on assessing fir branches, Santa Clauses, aesthetics of pine cones, or the "Latvian-ness" of snowmen for several weeks, so I wanted to talk. My Latvian was also to a point that I could use it without confusing birds and flowers, so I could converse somewhat normally. After sitting down at the table, I turned to Aija, Inge's mother, "Aija, you have made a very interesting-looking dish of fish, what is it?"

"It's a stuffed carp, Jewish-style."

"Jewish-style?"

"Yes, it means that some cod is added, along with onions, and put through a food grinder. Then some eggs are added, along with pepper and salt. It's then boiled and formed in the shape of a fish's body. The head is added later . . . it's actually more complicated than that, but that's the gist of it. Then we decorate with carrot slices and mayonnaise . . ."

"So I see, nice decoration. It's a shame to eat that. By the way, where did you learn that?"

"Oh, from my mother. She had been a nanny for a Jewish family that had left Riga to go to Finland during the first world war."

"Hmm. So, besides being saved from the hardships of war, I suppose, she learned to make all kinds of delicious foods."

"Yes," she nodded, pleased that someone had noticed her artistry. Along its two sides, the fish was highlighted by thin lines of mayonnaise, two of which continued past the gills to the head and ended with two large circles around the eyes. These circles were, in turn, topped by two eyebrows slanting upwards towards the front. The latter detail gave one the impression that the creature had "dolled itself up" for the event, but was currently suffering from stage fright.

After some shots of vodka, and Victor favorite home-made cranberry vodka/liqueur, Victor and I started feeling cheerier. After some very intensive but fruitless pleading, the kids resigned themselves to the fact that the parents and grandparents were going to indulge themselves in another half hour of useless conversations before the gifts were to be opened, so they went to another room and started playing a game.

"So, Victor, I guess that it has not always been this simple to celebrate Christmas."

"Oh, about that you're right. I remember, in the olden days, in nineteen fifty-seven, nineteen fifty-eight, we couldn't even celebrate it openly. If someone would have seen this tree, or heard us singing Christmas Carols, we would have been reported, and, and who knows what?"

"Like what *really* could have happened — Siberia?"

"Well, no," interjected Aija, "by then Stalin had been denounced and nobody was being sent to Siberia just like that."

"Wait a minute, now!... There *were* cases of people being sent to Siberia then... remember Ronalds?"

"Yes, but that was quite different. He was doing something with short-wave radios."

"Well anyway... but for singing Christmas Carols, no. People weren't being sent to Siberia, at least not by the time Inge was growing up. But I could've lost my job."

"Really?"

"Oh yes, if some informant were to have seen that we had a Christmas tree, and were singing Christmas carols, or if I didn't go to work on the twenty-fifth, then I would certainly have lost my job."

"But that, Boriss, is only because he was a foreman, a manager. A worker wouldn't have suffered anything," added Aija.

I asked if Victor ever celebrated Christmas together with his brothers, and recounted how we got together at my uncle's place on the 25th of December. Then two extended families — with other relatives dropping by all the time — would eat for six hours straight, while the parents consumed liters of Slivovitz.

"Slivovitz? You drank that too? I had some in Czechoslovakia when I was there, in … nineteen seventy-eight. No, we didn't get together for Christmas, no, that was too risky. *Especially* for Edgars, because of the war."

"I don't understand what that has to do with Christmas?"

"Oh, well, you saw that Edgars has only one arm … well, he lost the other one at the *Kurzemes katls*."[3] Then Victor went into great detail about how his brother had been considered a marginal member of society when he came back. How instead of being treated like a hero, he was treated like an enemy behind the lines afterwards, and he was prevented from attending university. "In fact, he had passed the exams to get in and been allowed to study for a year. Then one day, this 'commission' called him in. They asked him a few questions about what he had done during the war. Then they took out a file, where it stated how he had been wounded. He was told that he couldn't study further at the university, even though he had excellent marks."

"So … what did he do?" I asked.

"Well, he went into the Wholesale Food Trust. There, he became a big man in the warehousing of various foods . . . Yeah, he helped us out a lot afterwards."

Inge interjected, "Remember, Dad, when I was pregnant with Eliza, and the doctor told me that I needed to have a constant supply of that protein?"

"Yes …," added Aija, "so he was getting us this black caviar, a half-kilo tin after half-kilo tin. You were eating as much caviar everyday as the Ogre Regional Committee put together…"

"But anyway, Boriss, to answer your question…," continued Victor, "Edgars was being monitored closely for a long time after the war, and after Stalin's death, so if he had been caught celebrating Christmas… well, we don't know what would've happened. People who had fought in the war against the Reds were still being sent to Siberia in the seventies."

By this time, the kids made sure that we were ready for the opening of the gifts. The *'Opītis'* Gramps replied, "Markus, do you have some good poems lined up?"[4]

"Sure."

"And *you*, Eliza."

"Un-hunh."

"Go ahead then, you start …"

"Someone on Christmas day has just arrived on a sleigh, Come, barefoot children, Look at the sight!"

Markus was next, and started with singing *"Eglīte"* [Tannenbaum/O Christmas Tree]. Grandma followed, with a short piece on the jolly snowman. Everybody was amused when I started with an energetic version of "Sleighride." Out of courtesy to others, however, Inge allowed me to limit it to one couplet, later telling me — when I asked — that enthusiasm in a singer is good, but that is often better when accompanied with elements of melody and rhythm.

We returned in seven days to celebrate New Year's. I found that the menu and champagne did not depart from standards elsewhere, but my curiosity was piqued by the lead animals that were found on each of the plates around the table. This was another ancient Latvia tradition — the "fortune lead." Every December, a number of animal-shaped lead pieces would appear in the market and certain stores. They were molded in the shape of the creatures of the Chinese New Year. Like the fortune cookie, they contained a saying, typed on a small piece of paper. However, with this the similarity ended.

Firstly, one had to somehow pry the saying from the hollow of a very thick-walled lead piece. Furthermore, the makers of these pieces decided that the piece of paper would have to be drawn out of the animal's rear end. They then proceeded to make that opening to a realistic anatomic proportion. Later that evening, and fortunately *after* the main meal was consumed, I watched as five of my new relatives struggled to pull the rolled piece of paper out of a hole the diameter of a paper clip wire. They were sticking into it pins, needles, scissors blade tips, and any other sharp metal objects that they could get a hold of. It was not a pretty sight to see various utensils protruding from the rear ends of cute little dragons, pigs, and rats. Neither was it any prettier when *Opītis* started the plastic surgery — taking out a pen-knife and giving the creature a lunar-lake-sized anus. Once he opened his so that it looked like it had taken a howitzer shell in its bottom, he moved on, like a proctologist in wartime, to the other creatures.

I'm sure that I failed to hide my disappointment when the "wise saying" turned out to be some drivel such as "Getting up early is good," or "You must live life to please oneself." However, the true function of the animal was not as a mere receptacle for some pithy saying that anyone with a larger-than-paramecium-sized brain would forget within seconds. The true function took place through its *reincarnation*, which took place in the following manner: The creature was placed on a spoon; the spoon was held over a gas flame until the creature melted; the molten mass would then be tossed quickly into a pot of cold water; the metal would cool and then the reincarnated creature would be taken out. The abstract sculpture that resulted . . . was the premonition of how that year would be.

When *my* reincarnated creature came up out of the water, Inge exclaimed that my heretofore big-assed rat had *clearly* taken the form of an elf dancing on a hill, under a tree. Inge and my mother-in-law "oohed" and "aahed" at the amount of wealth that was found in the hill. "Excuse me for asking, I interjected, but how do you find that? I personally can't tell if it's an elf on a hill, or . . . or a dolphin thrown out of a whirlpool by the nuclear explosion. See the mushroom cloud?"

"What?! You really can't see the elf there, look..." I pretended to scrutinize, and nodded my head. "And, and these little lumps... that look like little pieces of gold... see ... that means *money!*"

"It's *that* easy, hunh. So we'll be rolling in dough this year, right?"

"Absolutely."

"But what if that was actually a whirlpool ... will that suck all the money down?"

"Oh stop, Borisss!"

"Sorry, sorry. Don't get me wròng. After all, you're right — it's about time that the business started bringing us bags of money!"

Footnotes

[1] A derivative of the sugar-making process, whose chemical formulation successfully combines the properties of molasses and nitroglycerin — warnings on labels still read that cans can become explosive a short time after opening.

[2] Crescent-shaped buns, filled with fried onions and some very, very un-lean bacon. One provided the fourteen times the U.S. daily recommended intake for saturated fat.

[3] The Courland firepot. Fall, 1943. This was the last series of battles that the Germans and their legions waged against the Russians. They did so to buy time for an orderly evacuation from the port of Liepaja. As their rearguard they placed Latvian legionnaires — while they beat a hasty retreat. "All" deserters caught, but particularly Latvian legionnaires, were shot.

[4] The Christmas tradition in Latvia involves, as in most other countries, the exchange of gifts. However, in Latvia, before any person, a child or a grown-up, can actually open any gifts, they must sing a song, recite a poem, or do a dance. There is no deviation from this rule, although Latvian poetry is replete with haiku equivalents — powerful and succinct.

28

TERROR DECOR

THE FINANCIAL RESULTS OF THE Merry Baker's operations in 1993 left much to be desired — a new business, for one. Nonetheless, on account of having eliminated a series of minor problems that year, I was optimistic that 1994 would be bullish. After all, the problems we had confronted could have happened in any bakery in the world — employees drinking on the job, thieving store clerks, and malfunctioning ovens that turned bread, effectively, into door stoppers. On the other hand we had expanded our wholesale business four-fold over the span of one year; we now supplied four major hotels, fifteen of the biggest cafes in Old Riga, ten restaurants, and we had just concluded an agreement with the airline catering operations. I decided to wait until the situation with real estate clears up, so that rental agreements could be signed.

In the meantime, we moved into a new office, closer to the bread plant/ bakery, and the accounting department once again joined us. As unhappy as I was with certain glitches in the operations, I also had to admit that although Christmas sales were a debacle, Ligita, Dace (the director of the savory production plant) and Zigrīda had worked admirably the previous year. They had been assigned the task of upholding certain quality and procedural standards, which they did consistently. As a result, the store and the wholesale operation had never before offered such an impressive array of baked and decorated goods as in the winter of 1994. There were now Linzertortes (using the aromatic and protein-rich raspberry jam), Black Forest Cakes and Ricotta Cheesecakes with a delicate natural orange-vanilla flavor. These had been my contribution.

However, the Latvian partner had also produced copiously. For the first years of her life, Ligita had apparently been beaten senseless with a Soviet basting brush whenever she approached chocolate; she decided to compensate for this deprivation now. Our chocolate tortes were available in all shades of brown and intensities of chocolate, ranging from euphoria-inducing dark chocolate, to a mulatto-light chocolate mocha torte. We had our own variation of the Opera torte[1], of a double Fudge cake and of a "chocolate-lover's, death-by-calories" mud pie. Our chocolate cakes redefined the genre. Furthermore, Ligita's feelings on the subject coincided with those of Riga's populace at large, so our cake sales were excellent that winter.

Our tortes, chocolate and otherwise, were still dry enough to justify the accompaniment of a full cup of coffee. My travels around Europe had convinced me that the moisture content of the locally made cakes was inversely proportional to the standard volume of the coffee or tea in a serving. In France and Italy, for example, where a proper post-dinner coffee involves no more than three thimbles of water, the cakes and desserts are so moist, that one is not "eating" anything so much as imbibing liqueur or sugar water sprayed between pieces of cotton candy. As a result, the cakes are no more than a few inches high — they would collapse on their own weight if they were higher. In France, even the wedding "cake" is a conical structure composed of between fifty and two hundred shortened eclairs, welded together with a caramel-colored sugar glaze. Italians have solved this physics problem by hiding plastic pedestals within the cake, to support sculptures of everything ranging from the relief of the wedding couple, to the Colloseum of Rome to Mickey Mouse in leather.

At the other extreme is England, where one can regularly find cakes that are five, six inches high and more. The sponges are thick, and the frosting relatively sparse. However, they complement a tea perfectly. In Middle Europe, including Latvia, the coffee beans are allotted more water than they are in France. Consequently the cakes are an inch or two higher than the Mediterranean ones, and one feels the sponge. However, the cake sponge is still moistened with liqueur or some sugar water. Furthermore, flavored butter cream, whipped cream, and marzipan are used generously throughout. Weight Watchers followers would find their daily diet consisting of orange juice, breakfast and a slice of a Merry Baker cake. Fortunately for the business, however, Weight Watchers had not yet arrived.

By the beginning of February, the renovation of the interior of our apartment was proceeding at a good pace. There was even cause to believe that it would be ready by summertime. At the end of the month, Chief Crooked Floor's crew had completed more than 80 percent of the work. I was told that the only work left was the finish. However, in late February, when I had last seen his crew — the remainder of it that hadn't succumbed to preservation-through-pickling — I began to harbor doubts about the contractor's ability to maintain high standards. Since I had been busy with the trip to Denmark, I hadn't reviewed the work completed since the 2nd of March. After receiving his phone call, now four weeks later, I said that I would contact him, but for now his men should not commence work on other parts of the house. In the beginning of April, I freed up time — in the evening — to view the work done on our new nest. Most of the work had been completed to an acceptable standard, but as I looked in the corner, behind some pressed and rumpled cardboard sheets (that had no doubt served as a bed), I saw mounds of broken tile. I started fuming, for I had had to purchase replacement tiles for the toilet three times. Each of those trips had been preceded by a sheepish "Well ... we have a little *nyepriyatnost* 'unpleasantness' message from the contractor. By the third time, the store had run out of the necessary quantity of the tiles with the light gray marbled pattern with beveled edges that Inge had picked out. There would be no more shipments of this pattern, we were led to understand, until the next millennium. I shouldn't have been surprised — we had purchased enough to tile half of the public toilets of Riga — let alone our ten-square-foot space. When I had relayed this information to the contractor, he had replied that he would locate something through his "contacts." I had been relieved to hear, a few days later, that he had found some real marble that was "identical" to what we had on the wall. He had also assured me that it could be placed in one strip, low and behind the toilet. I now raced to the "toilet-room." Behind the toilet, at exactly waste level to a male of average height, was a strip of gray marble. The marble was not only a different shade of gray, but when compared to the tile already in place, it appeared yellowish. In fact, the coloring of this strip of tile behind the toilet reminded me of the part of the wall into which the African rhino regularly piddled — with a straight-yellow power-stream — at the Washington Zoo. I groaned, in anticipation of Inge's reaction. Furthermore, the beautiful tiles on the top row, imprinted with a stylized cubist town, had been glued upside down. I had never thought to tell them how the tiles should have been hung. However, the abstract tower in the town's center was now poised downwards like a swinging phallus, on thirteen tiles running along the wall ... at eye level. At this point, I grasped — fully and without question — the Buster Keaton corollary of Murphy's Law:

"When Buster dies, he will be reincarnated over and over again as the general contractor working on one of Boriss' projects in Latvia."

As I walked around more, I was to uncover another specific of construction work in Latvia. Workers love antiques. It's ironic that these men, who can go into a project fit and clean-shaven, come wobbling out three weeks later looking like Grizzly Adams stand-ins, are irresistibly drawn to antique *objets d'art*. In fact this attraction does not stop at the admiration-from-a-respectable-distance. No, they like to incorporate the antiques into their working environment — give the stuff a "test run." In this case, our circa-1935 handpainted art deco coffee cups, from the Kuznetsov[2] porcelain factory of Riga, served as eye-catching receptacles for dozens of cigarette butts, some drill bits in water, and tea bags festering in three-week-old tea. The turn-of-the-century vase served to hold the wooden rulers and a large scratched metal level. Out of curiosity, I went upstairs to the attic. Next to the box in which these coffee cups had been carefully packed, the regular glasses, mugs and plates for everyday use — in full view to all passersby — were lying untouched. My first impulse was to take these downstairs and ask the workers why they hadn't used these instead. But sense got the better of me and I dropped the issue. Nonetheless, for the next two years, I made sure to remove all antiques from the construction area. However, I forgot to execute this procedure a few years later, when we were having some insulated windows installed. For the worker, I had left a stool and a stepladder in the corner of the room where I assumed the first window would be replaced, but I had — absent-mindedly — left the two 100-year-old art nouveau chairs with original *gobelēns* hand-loomed material in the opposite corner. When I returned in the afternoon, he was screwing in the window hinges while dancing a rumba on one of the antique chairs — with his mountain boots. I abruptly asked him to get off, but it was too late; by then, what had been an ornately loomed orchid-pattern looked like an impromptu rendition of Muesli that our cat might have clawed out over a few weeks under the influence of catnip.

In any event, and unrelated to the coffee cups, I called Chief Crooked Floor the next day to tell him that his services would no longer be needed, and that he could come back and collect his materials. I told him that, for financial reasons, the finish work would be completed at a later time. The finish work involved the restoration of the parquet floors, the laying of tiles in the kitchen between the counter and the cabinetry, as well as the wallpapering and painting of all rooms.

We decided to rely on a different source of labor for these tasks. In fact, Inge's father had a list of workers that he had called on for the finish of high-quality interior jobs in the past, or so he claimed. The first *meistars* that he had recommended was his younger brother. He said simply that "Janis can do floors." Inge approved the choice, while I held my breath. Within one week, "Janis" took to repairing the parquet floor, which he did with great success. Seemingly indelible stains disappeared, with a combination of burning and chemical treatments, meticulously applied by this jovial man with a wide smile. He explained then that waxing would not make the floor impervious to water and recommended a lacquer. After he had varnished it, the floor was as smooth and free of blemishes as any that I had seen in the West. I couldn't help asking him where he had received his apprenticeship. "A few places — the Benjamin mansion in Jūrmala, Rundāle... a few museums in Riga... you know, wherever the ladies needed a handsome man." The floor still sagged in the middle of the living room, but that wasn't due to Uncle Janis' workmanship; it was the result of an uneven settling of the house over the past sixty years, exaggerated by the tanks that had rolled by our street in the 1940s and to the lumber trucks that thundered past *Meža Prospekts* these days. *Meža Prospekts* was the main North-South thoroughfare of the neighborhood, and it wasn't a full forty meters from the house.

I was now convinced that Inge's father could find the right people for the job. When he arrived with the *Molliari* or painter/wallpaper/tiling specialist, we started him right off with the task of tiling the kitchen. Two days later, he finished it. Given the warped condition of the locally manufactured tiles, he had done an excellent job of it — like making a perfectly straight wall from scallop shells. We subsequently gave him the task of wallpapering the smallest bedroom in the house. A few days later, we returned. Inge and I would have executed perfect cartwheels from the joy of seeing how the work was done, if not that I would have broken the glass door and we would have been extracting shards of glass from my thighs for the next three days. To Inge's critical eye, it was a neat job. To mine, it was nothing short of divine inspiration; the seams between the sheets of wallpaper were invisible; the patterns matched perfectly at the edges of each sheet of wallpaper.

"Well Uldis, you certainly did a good job here. I think that we can entrust the finish of the entire interior to you." Uldis smiled.

"Yeah? Glad you like it... mind if I have a smoke?" "No, go ahead."

After looking around and seeing a few cans of opened and emptied tins of Baltic sprats, I asked if we couldn't bring some dry foodstuffs for him. He answered negatively, saying that the store was just down the street, and he could easily go there whenever he needed something.

"O.K., then I'll be back at the end of the week. Keep up the good work, and call if you need anything."

I arrived back in four days, as agreed. The second room was done just as neatly as the first. However, the third room had a few mismatching patterns. Not enough to cause the work to be redone, but enough to cast a shadow of doubt on his capacity to complete future work as well as he had in the first two rooms. Although I did not detect any alcohol on his breath, I sensed that he was burned out.

"Your work has progressed well, but I'm concerned that you might be getting tired, and lonely. Why don't you take a week off?"

Uldis scratched his head, and replied, "I usually like to stay at a place until the job is done … but I'll think about it."

"Good. I mean, sure, we'd like this place to be finished as soon as possible, but … we're not slave drivers." The comment prompted a hearty laugh from the *molliaris*, and he shook his head, "No, no, of course not. But don't worry, I'll be fine."

I repeated that he knew where the tramway was, and it would be quite acceptable to us if he were to ride it to the train station when he had had enough and come back later well-rested.

When I returned to the house a week later, I had expected the job to be done. Instead, the apartment had been trashed. Furniture had been upended or thrown about. There was a stench of alcohol, cigarettes and vomit. The opened and empty cans of Baltic sprats I had seen during the previous visit were still scattered everywhere, but they were now overflowing with cigarette butts. Those butts that hadn't fit onto the mound in the can were scattered in rings around the stools. The toilet seat was half off the toilet. "Uldis!" I yelled. There was no answer. I wandered into the living room. I looked at the walls and stopped in my tracks. The wallpaper displayed varying degrees of alignment as one progressed along the walls from the starting point. The first strips were straight up and down. The last ones were cocked at a ten-degree angle. Furthermore, the first strips were pristine, while swathes of some gray substance covered the last ones. It looked, at a glance, as if Uldis had invited some coal-mining friends to play a vertical rendition of *Twister* -– without using the mat, and before the wallpaper had set in place. I heard some rustling of cloth. I glanced down on the floor. Behind four empty bottles of *Kristāls degvīns* 'Crystal fire-wine' was a brown-green form of some sort. As I approached the blanket mass, it groaned. Uldis popped his head out. His hands, coated gray, were shaking.

"Uldis, what happened?"

"Unnhh. *Ya nye ... ochen sebya ...* 'I ... I'm not ... doing very well ...'"

"Can you get up?"

"Yeah ... just a minute."

I went to the kitchen to boil up some tea, but was put off from this assignment by the mounds of still-moist wallpaper glue on the floor. No water to be found anywhere, except some bottled sparkling mineral water of dubious origin. I poured it into a pot anyway, and placed it on the stove. I returned to the room. Uldis had risen, but was standing on one leg, balancing himself against the wall. He resembled nothing so much as a dog, whose leg had been crushed, and was now confused by its helplessness.

"Uldis, what happened to your foot?"

"Well ...," he drawled, "I ... twisted it a little ... when I was going down the steps."

I looked closer. Between his foot and his shin was a purple mango. "A little? You've got a bad sprain there, if not a break. Let me help you — I'm taking you home."

"No, don't need to ... absolutely not. Don't bother ... my, uh friends are coming for me."

"When?"

"In a couple a' days."

"Oh? Well, by then, you'll be able to smoke another two packs of cigarettes and if you jump around on your one good foot long enough, then you could lose another five kilos of weight while you make a royal mess of a couple more walls. Thanks, but no thanks. Let's go, I'll take you."

I walked him downstairs, he limped to the car, and I drove him home. As his wife stared at him, tears welled up in her eyes. She kept repeating, "Where did you disappear to ... why didn't you call me?"

I had never realized before what esoteric waves, what invisible force emanated from the walls of our house that turned normal men into drooling savages within three weeks. Could it have been the spirits of the previous owners, who had been trundled up and sent to an icy wasteland to die? Could it have been the ghosts of German soldiers who fled and were shot? The house was a four-minute stroll (I later timed it) from a tramway stop and a five-minute walk from the telephone booth. It might as well have been in the wilds of Alaska.

I returned and, once again, took in the crooked wallpaper. It dawned on me — as I followed the trail of black handprints from the bottom of one end of the south wall, to the top right — that I had overlooked the Keystone Cops' corollary to Murphy's law: "After the Keystone Cops die, they will be reincarnated as construction workers who will be working on Boriss' construction projects in Latvia ... whether Buster hires them or not."

From that point on, through the month of June, I oversaw all work ... closely — I could have been accused of voyeurism. I didn't care. By this point I had solemnly sworn that our house would no longer be the laughingstock of the interior decorator's world.

Footnotes

[1] A thin cake containing two layers of light chocolate and two layers of dark chocolate ganache. Developed in France at the beginning of the eighteenth century.

[2] Kuznetsov porcelain factory was the largest and best-known porcelain factory in pre-war Latvia. The first one was founded in Moscow in 1830. But experts agree that the founder had produced primarily tavernware in that factory. Sixty-five years later, he opened another factory in Riga to cater to a more upscale market.

29

LESSONS IN THE TRADE

PARTIALLY TO KEEP THE PACE of innovation and quality maintenance high and partially as a reward to the managers for work well done, I had organized a "training trip" to Denmark for late April. I went with five others — Ligita, two bakers, and Zigrīda, to Hillerod, Denmark.

We were given a tour of Hillerod, and had the bakery "lab" to ourselves for three days. In his plant, Preben demonstrated the fabrication of several more baked products. During this course, the bakers made more shapes from puff pastry dough than could be used in hundred years of baking. We added dozens more marzipan "pieces" to the list of what we could make; some five- and eight-grain breads were added to the list of exotic breads already made. Ligita, without prompting, decided to make pizzas that looked like the ones that we ate at one of the Turkish-run pizzerias in town.

Furthermore, Preben demonstrated the use of still other equipment. There was a freezer that served as a proving cabinet (into which formed pastries were placed to rise before baking). A timer permitted the temperature to rise (or fall) between 2 and 110 degrees Fahrenheit. More practically, the cabinet allowed the Danish baker to start work as late as six in the morning, insofar as the first products would be puffy and ready for the oven at exactly that moment. To achieve the same result, his predecessors had to arrive no later than three in the morning. But by far the most interesting piece of equipment was a small metallic tube on wheels, which created perfectly formed butter cookies. Preben turned a crank, as if he were adjusting the trajectory of the mortar. But instead of firing something forward, the device scooted along the table, defecating perfectly formed, one-inch round butter cookies.

Zigrīda and Ligita also sampled a McDonald's Big Mac for the first time; the former said that it was better than she had expected, and the latter was surprised that someone could call that a meal — the bun was *"zem kritikas* 'below criticism.'" When I told her that several new hamburger restaurants would be opening in Riga, and we could offer them our alternative, Ligita agreed immediately. Zigrīda was amazed at the "freewheeling, fill every nook-and-cranny with product" manner in which the windows were decorated. I myself had long before become accustomed to the way that Riga's retailers decorated their windows, which manifested a fine eye for the derelict, ultimately demonstrating that no self-respecting Soviet merchandiser could ever have been accused of enticing a customer. Some windows were replete with faded packages, spider webs and burned-out light bulbs. Other shop windows even boasted empty containers, a reminder of days foregone, when "there was everything."[1]

The trip was dampened only slightly by the fact that on the third day there, when I called Inge, she informed me that Eliza had been diagnosed with hepatitis. I was besides myself for the morning, but calmed down after realizing that I couldn't go back for two more days, I was both the organizer and translator here and wouldn't be of much help anyway. As it turned out, she was afflicted with hepatitis A, which broke out in different sections of Riga every year when the ice melted and the various rivers overflowed to taint the city's water supply.

April also marked the second parliamentary elections, and it was noteworthy that besides the five ex-barmen, twelve artists and eleven physicians, thirteen repatriated Latvians[2] were also elected into the Parliament.

Western business practices were also taking hold. This development was tied to the active participation of some Western direct investors, such as IBM, along with the pressures exerted by investment funds. The Norwegian division of Alcatel started one of the funds, in cooperation with the Norwegian and Latvian governments. It had allotted one million dollars to start up a "Norwegian-Latvian Fund" to invest in small businesses. An economist friend of Inge's, Dainis, was heading up the fund. During one of our get-togethers, he asked me if I didn't need a source of consistently high-quality flour. I replied that I did, and explained how the bakers were veritable alchemists, changing the recipes on a weekly basis to accommodate changes in the flour of unknown provenance. For example, out of one shipment of Ukrainian flour, we created puffy, light, golden pastries that were a pleasure to view and divine to taste. During the next shipment, however, the quality overseers had allowed the flour to include some old cream-of-wheat; the same pastries turned out flat, pale-colored and gritty — in short, expensive swine meal. So I told Dainis that if his flour was equivalent in quality to, or better than, the one we were receiving from the large Latvian mill in Dobele, then we would take his without question, particularly if it was cheaper. "But Dainis, remember, our business relies on consistency for its *survival*," I added.

A key parameter was the gluten content, which had to be no less than 25 percent, and preferably 26 percent. Gluten is the chewing gum-like substance that provides two key elements to white bread — its spongy consistency, and its protein content. Unfortunately, gluten is also not visible to the naked eye, and cannot be separated, through a visual screening, from the rest of the flour, even with a microscope. It can be practically measured in only one of two ways — through laboratory chemical testing, or through "washing." "Washing" consists of taking a certain quantity of flour, and kneading a measured amount of water into it. The dough ball is subsequently washed under a faucet, using the same motions that one would use to wash a sock, until all the elements besides the gluten wash off. The remaining ball, which looks identical to a large piece of already-chewed gum, can be weighed. The weight of the dried gluten ball, compared to the weight of the flour used, reveals the gluten content of the flour.

As one could imagine, the latter technique was impracticable, when one went through twenty sacks of flour per shift. Besides, we could not afford to have a stash of "reserved flour" that could be used in the event of having received "poor-quality" flour. At the same time, an apparatus for measuring the gluten cost upwards of $15,000. Such a device was standard equipment in mills — not in the retail bakeries buying from them. Preben said that if you order a certain quality of flour from the mill, that should suffice; "we only measure for gluten in the school–theory class."

In short, we were at the mercy of the mills. But *Dobeles Dzirnavnieks* had given us a run of six weeks without any bad flour so Ligita and Zigrīda were happy. Nonetheless, I decided to give Dainis a break. He investigated the gluten content of his "*Augstākā Labuma* 'Highest Quality'" flour and reported that it was 26.3 percent. This was a full point better than the one that we used, so the bread would be fluffier, chewier, and whiter still, than the best that we had. The woven PVC bags[3] with the new flour would be identified by the name *Baltā Dzirnava* 'the White Mill.' I passed on the information about its quality to the plant. Everyone was excited that we would have a flour that would result in an even finer product than the one we had now. Some ten days later, when I had forgotten completely about this issue, I received a call from Zigrīda.

It started with a solemn questioning about how my family was doing. I had learned that the more circumspect her greeting to me, the grimmer I could expect the subsequent news to be. When she asked how my family back in the States was doing, I knew that we had a major crisis on our hands.

"Zigrīda, *Shto sluchilas* 'What happened?'"

"Nobody's buying our products ... sales are down by one-third in the store."

"Why?"

"The production ... is completely flat."

"What?! Then obviously, the new flour hasn't arrived."

"The ones marked '*Baltā Dzirnava*'? It has ... that's what the bakers have been using."

I rushed to the store. On the way, I glanced in some of the state bread stores, and saw that the white bread looked about as it did all the time. This bode poorly for us. When all the bread in town was flat, and our situation was, subsequently, not worse than elsewhere, people would understand that it was a "bad flour day." "But if *we* were the only ones ..." I reflected, in horror, as I burst into the store. Along the back wall, towards the top, I looked at our prized "French sticks." They were some pathetic cross between a baguette and Lavash. Our famed Danish were inverted saucers ... without teacups, while our cinnamon loafs resembled nothing so much as giant Brazilian centipedes. I lunged and broke one of the loaves open. It was an unsavory grayish-white color. Zigrīda looked to the ground.

To the question, "What happened to the flour?" no one at the mill could respond. I called the Fund — Dainis was gone for a week, with a couple of company executives, for management training in Norway. We removed the bags for return to the *Baltā Dzirnava* mill. The answer I received a few weeks later, after promising that I wouldn't tell anyone. The owner of the mill had gone on a business/fishing trip. He had put his cousin in charge "being as he was family and all." This cousin proceeded to mix the *Trešā Sorte* Third Category of flour (used only in trace quantities in second-grade cookies, but primarily for feeding farm animals), generously into the *Augstākā Labuma* 'Highest Category' bags. He pocketed the difference in profit, which he promptly spent at the nearest bar. Dainis made no more business overtures to me for several years afterwards.

We moved into the house in early summer, as the weather was turning nice, so the first thing that we gloated over was the patio. There we discovered how close the house was to nature — namely the tropics, as the flamingos, one hundred yards away, wailed out their spring mating call. Some East Asian herons chimed in to make cacophony of it. But there was something perversely comforting to know that, unlike the other denizens of the city, we wouldn't be bothered by the squawking of common seagulls or pigeons — we would have the distinction of being tormented by flamingos.

After having been in two rooms totaling 430 square feet, the addition of almost 1000 was pleasant . . . if not a little overwhelming. Four of us could now enjoy eating a meal seated, together. A refrigerator could fit in the kitchen without displacing the stove. It was like having moved from New York's lower Eastside to Westchester County . . . at the expense of only a fifteen-minute commute.

In the new apartment, the first thing that we had to do was re-orient our buying patterns. Specifically, we went to a new market. It was much smaller, more charming, than the Central Market. The begging dogs were finer sorts — a golden setter and a labrador were among the lot.

The end of June meant two things — the beginning of the warm season, with the relentless attacks of bloodthirsty mobs of mosquitoes . . . and second anniversary of The Merry Baker. The results of the first two full years of The Merry Baker's operations were inconclusive. I reassessed the progress achieved to date. I reflected on the results that I had just read, and for the first time, experienced a sensation of futility. I looked again at the financial summaries; sales would increase during one month and then fall precipitously the next. There seemed to be a seasonal nature to the business . . . but the seasons changed every year.

We had to turn the situation around. I started by consulting some of my foreign contacts about the future direction that The Merry Baker could take. The Europeans with whom I spoke still seemed to be convinced that the baking of Western-European-style breads would be the key to success. My observations of two failed ventures, which had baked quite respectable *baguettes*, told me that in spite of what the French and Germans in Riga would like to have reported back to their compatriots, crusty bread was still not something that people "couldn't live without."

So, without having obtained a clear-cut solution, I decided that the answer might lie in reaching out to new clients, who might have more of a foreign-customer base. We signed a contract with the company that catered the airlines. Several informal, family-style restaurants had opened up in the previous six months and I convinced them that if they had foreign clientele, then our bread and *only* our bread "met their standard." Another one agreed to take the Danish, because the owner felt that his restaurant had to become the "breakfast spot" of Riga, and the American manager had succeeded in convincing him that without good Danish pastries, he could not claim to be a breakfast capital of Kzyl Orda[4], let alone Riga. The owner accepted the suggestion, ordered the pastries, and to both the manager's relief and my own — within one month — the Osiris restaurant became the best-known city center location for a continental breakfast amongst expatriates.

It appeared that in the fall, we would reach our target of $100,000 sales per month.

Footnotes

[1] A sentiment best summarized in the anecdote: "Before, Ivanov was written on the sign outside, and you'd find meat inside. Now, Meat is written on the sign outside, and you'll find Ivanov inside."

[2] Sometimes referred to as expatriates, depending on their fidelity.

[3] This was a radical departure from the current practice, which involved providing the flour either in recycled '*Dobeles Dzirnavnieks*' bags, or more often than not, in rough hemp bags. They could double as a monk's cassock if one were in need of penitence. Carrying them on one's back left great big red welts, and they had probably been banned in the U.S. in the beginning of the eighteenth century.

[4] The pre-Soviet capital of Kazakhstan. Overrun today by goats, mules and neo-communists.

30

MELTING PODA

As MUCH AS WE HAD HEARD about our infamous downstairs neighbor Raisa Vukina, the first encounter with her did not take place until almost four weeks after we had moved in. I was exiting our apartment, and she was strolling past. Upon seeing me, she turned to face me.

"*Privet* 'Greetings.' You know, there's that little apple tree there, next to our lawn. Do you plan to use it? If you were to give it to me, I would give you the plot next to the fence ... and fifty kilos of elephant manure."

Her face was deadpan, a little forlorn; the tone of voice was disarming, like that of a little old lady asking the Boy Scout to help her cross the street. My first impulse was to say, "Why of course we would! What need do we have for a stunted apple tree [we already have two other examples of this gnarly genus on the other plot] and the land under it, when we can have over one hundred pounds of elephant shit, out of which one can fashion *ultra chic* ashtrays and umbrella stands!" However I decided to err on the side of caution and call Inge. She descended, greeted Raisa, listened to the proposal, and promptly replied — "No. We do want that land which is ours, even if we haven't already started cultivating it." Raisa lowered her gaze, slowly turned around and walked away — we had just crushed her will to live.

Two days later, the water pressure in our apartment disappeared — completely. Inge was in the shower. By the time I realized what had happened,

Inge was already dialing downstairs. Considering her wild-eyed grimacing, Inge was restrained as she asked, "We have no water — what happened?"

"Nothing, the water pressure is low today. So, when Svyeta (Raisa's daughter-in-law) is preparing food, the pressure might disappear for you," and promptly hung up.

"*Oy zaraza* 'Oh what an infection!' that old lady! Boriss, could you go down and check the water pressure?"

"Sure can."

I descended to the garage, but did not remember where the entry point of water into the house was. As I stumbled to the middle of the enormous basement, Raisa came out from her quarter. "They've restored the pressure. You can go back now." By the time I went back upstairs, the water pressure was indeed restored.

But we *had* settled in, getting used to the idiosyncrasies of the house and the neighborhood. Regarding the house, the toilet room was rather compact; we warned the taller guests to watch their knees when closing the door. They had no choice — when the door was closed a tall person's knees just about came up to their eyeballs. When it rained, sheets of water would come rushing between the end of the roof and the rain-gutters. The gutters had not fulfilled any water-carrying function for a good fifteen years, but did admirably as high-rise compost ditches harboring flora and fauna that thrived directly under the branches of tall pines.

At first we were afraid that the shell of the house wouldn't outlast our next pair of shoes, so we harbored a complaint at the House of Administration about the trucks and the roof. The administrators in turn replied that they were powerless to act on the issue of the lumber trucks, but that a certain bridge across the lake was being repaired and that when this would be completed, the trucks would no longer drive this way. When we asked how long that would be before the bridge was in place, they replied, "Very soon — within three years."

"Great, well, if our house survives that long, we'll be very grateful. In the meantime, please tell us if there's anybody who has a need for fallen chunks of stucco — we have a plentiful supply in the garden."

"Well, it's not *our* fault. You know that the Soviets tried to destroy this section of town."

The lady then explained how the city authorities, on orders from Moscow, re-routed major trucks and military vehicles along *Ezermalas* street and *Me a Prospekts*, which ringed the neighborhood. Then they intentionally let the houses fall into disrepair, gradually condemning them and evacuating the inhabitants of the most dangerous ones to high-rises in the new sections of town. They figured that after twenty more years, the houses would collapse unto themselves. Then they could just bulldoze them down. We asked why the Soviet authorities had wanted to do that, since this was an architecturally unique collection of homes, the likes of which had long since disappeared in most of Western Europe. The answer was that they were considered "bourgeois" and a German enclave by the Soviet authorities. After the story, she must have taken pity on us and offered to send someone over to repair our roof... if we could foot a third of the bill. She tried to soften the request by adding, "Normally we don't have any money in the budget for anything less life-threatening than collapsing walls... but we'll make an exception in your case."

By now we had become used to our new neighborhood. We had become used to the drunks directly across the street, the Director of the Latvian Privatization Agency walking his dog next to us. Our next-door neighbor to the right was an ex-newscaster of Radio Free Europe, whose mother had received the property back through privatization. Next door to him was the community shelter for a gypsy *tabor*. Rumor had it that they had purchased it for $20,000 in 1991. A more likely story is that they just squatted it. If so, the group had a great respect for the neighborhood, as the house was seldom occupied. But when it was occupied, it was bursting at the rafters. On two occasions where the gypsies drove in with their two twenty-five-year-old buses — boasting originally red paint faded to salmon and tires balding in all possible places — then it could be stated with certainty that no house in the Baltics was as full as theirs. Children and elders were swarming around the dilapidated structure like ants on a disturbed hill. One summer, they augmented their own population with that of thirty-five Hare Krishna revelers, and their buses with the Rama *Ratha-Yatra* cart. Krishnas poured out of the gate and *Hare'd* into the street, bypassing the dark-skinned children — holding brightly colored books — in the yard. As the cult of begging goes, this convention must have rivaled the General Council of Constance of 1415 for the Catholic churches, when church tithe collection procedures were finally standardized. So if someone has been swindled out of money in an airport, in the late '90s, through a technique not involving roses or thick radiantly covered books, then that person can be sure it was the result of the Riga Krishna-Gypsy Convention of 1995.

On the other hand, the most finely renovated house, boasting the most nicely landscaped yard, belonged to the most ruthless Russian mafiosi of Latvia. Five business partners had met strange fates in the span of eighteen months — in cars, elevators, rivers and stairwells. Yet the house was staid and respectable. The only hint that this house belonged to someone of that ilk was the floodlight on the lawn. The lamp was activated when anyone passed by on the sidewalk, or a car drove by. The resulting light was bright enough to illuminate the entire twenty-five-foot expanse of street in front of the house, the trees fifty yards away and the owls perched on their branches ... as well as providing the lumens necessary to conduct three interrogations simultaneously in the ten-foot-long driveway to the house. Besides that, there were no guards visible, no dogs or any other security outside the mundane beige walls of the house.

Across the street from this residence and a little to the left stood the house once belonging to Ludvigs Bolšteins, Brigadier General of the Border Guards in June of 1940, when the Red Army invaded Latvia. He had been a vociferous opponent of the treaty that the President had signed, which would allow the Soviets to station their army at key strategic points of Latvia, in preparation for an allied invasion. Upon hearing that the Soviet troops entered Latvian territory at Zilupe on June 21, Bolšteins took the pistol out of his holster and blew his brains out.

In October, we moved the office to new premises, and the accounting department finally moved with us. The first day, they were quite at a loss as to where to put the teapot and the firewood. We reminded them that the wood would no longer be necessary — these desktop computers were not the fire-powered variety — and bought a drip coffeemaker to corroborate the modernization. Soon, the accountants converted to Merrild coffee for a morning lift and Microsoft Excel for the accounting spreadsheets. Our office, from a cursory glance, began to resemble one from the end and not the beginning of the twentieth century. Valdis later confided to me that this move was also timely; the alcoholic whose apartment we had leased for the accountants had indeed signed five other "exclusive" rental agreements with other parties, and those people had been going to court regularly to contest their claims.

The board had also agreed, following the trip to Denmark, to purchase new equipment. We had applied for and received monies — this had been the fruits of a World Bank initiative to develop small and medium-sized manufacturing industry. Upon receipt of the loan, we acquired the equipment necessary to expand our wholesale production capacity; we ordered a semi-automatic roll former, two rack ovens, two planetary mixers, refrigerators, stand-up freezers (including one with the electronic, pre-set deep-freeze-to-ready-for-oven cycle) and one of the cookie-dropping devices that Preben had shown us during our trip. We divided the equipment almost evenly between the two plants. We also acquired a Western-style refrigerated display cabinet, which featured four shelves upon which the cakes could be displayed. To understand the radical novelty of this last purchase, one had only to view the existing display cabinets, which in 1994 consisted of dented aluminum boxes with scratched plexiglas panes. Ours was the first three-level, clean-glass, illuminated cake cabinet in Riga.

In fact, at about this time, without especially intending to, I met a great deal of Latvian expatriates, who had returned, for one reason or another, to their "homeland." It should have been no surprise to me as well, for of the ethnic Latvian population worldwide, more than 20 percent resided outside the country. The most reliable non-KGB statistics, proffered by the historians of the "Occupation of Latvia Museum," showed that in 1960, while the native population of Latvia numbered approximately 1.3 million persons, some 300,000 émigré Latvians lived outside of Latvia.

Over one-third of these resided in Russia. Although a large part of these had been forbidden from returning to their native land after serving their terms in the forced-labor camps, many had simply stayed in Russia — and even in Siberia — out of inertia. Year by year, these 120,000-odd Latvians were being assimilated into the greater Russian population, just as Stalin had planned.

At the same time, in the 1960s, approximately 130,000 emigrant Latvians lived in the United States, Canada, Australia, Germany, Sweden, and various countries in South America. If one were to add the direct descendants of these émigrés, one could find over 200,000 people of Latvian descent in the U.S. alone. Some of these children of the *Trimda* Diaspora had even achieved fame and fortune in their new homelands. Among the most famous Latvian descendants of the diaspora, one could count Mr. Georgs Miķelsons, who was the CEO of *Transair* airlines in Indiana; the Zariņš brothers, who were teaching surgeons at the Harvard and Stanford Medical Schools; Mariss Jansons, conductor of the Pittsburgh Symphony Orchestra; Arvids Blūmentāls, the man upon which the Crocodile Dundee character was based; Ed Viesturs, the first man to climb twelve of the highest fourteen mountains without oxygen. Thousands of others made significant contributions to their new countries as farmers, lawyers, technical professionals, and even score-writers for television cartoons.[1]

However, in 1994 most of the Latvian expatriates that I met felt it their moral obligation to give armchair lectures to their poor-country cousins, as if the latter had made it a personal goal to live in squalor and poverty. These expatriates, many of them in their sixties and seventies and armed with memories of pre-war Latvia, railed on how "This country should be like

America, Australia [or a dozen other places that uncle Joe had made sure that Latvia would *not* be like for many, many generations] ... and people should have two cars per family, a large house with a dishwasher..." In spite of their intent, in so lecturing, these re-pats did little more than ignite bonfires of material envy in the souls of their relatives.

Fortunately for this country however, other Latvian re-pats viewed their time in the country as a Peace Corps equivalent. Many were working for measly salaries in government institutions, and in so doing, tried to establish a reduced-corruption, "use-your-noggin-for-the-greater-good" environment in these agencies. Some, such as the lawyer Vaira Paegle, became selfless and hard-working politicians themselves. Vaira Vīķe-Freiberga, a retired professor of linguistics at the University of Montreal, is currently the President of Latvia.

And yet another one actually bailed out The Merry Baker. The Grots family of Boston had re-acquired a property on Brīvības iela, the main thoroughfare of the city. Martins, the son of the owner and at the time the purchasing engineer for the Polarbek Company (which was going to build the first Radisson hotel in the Baltics), had mentioned that his father had inherited a residential property and a two-story building with storefront space on *Brīvības* Street in Riga. Martins had been given the power-of-attorney to develop and manage it. At one American Chamber of Commerce luncheon, I mentioned the problems of finding retail space; he offered to lease us one hundred square meters. The following week, I went to *Brīvības* Freedom Street to inspect the building. The location was superb — with doctors' and lawyers' offices in the adjacent buildings and a steady flow of pedestrian traffic. However, the outside of the building looked decrepit. Our potential space was occupied by a "sewing co-operative," which looked like some shop in the Bronx that wanting to avoid notoriety at all costs. Wooden boards covered the inside pairs of the double windows. A nondescript handpainted sign hung next to the door. When I entered, I was mildly shocked to see bare light bulbs illuminating the ten sewing stations spread out over the space. The floor, which consisted of partially painted wooden planks, had three different levels. I was warned not to step off the rug walkway — in several spots, the boards had rotted through, exposing holes. When the sweatshop dominatrix asked me what I wanted to do in the space, I said that I didn't know yet. To this, she replied: "Yeah, well, that's what happens — these buildings come back into the hands of their pre-war owners, and just like that, perfectly good businesses are thrown out *na volye sud'bi* 'to the winds of fate.'" The following week, I told Martins that I agreed to take the space, if he would agree to accord us a few months free rent, in exchange for executing the major improvements that this space called for. He agreed. We would, if all things went *normāli*, have a new store on Riga's main street in six months' time. If things went "*kā vienmēr*'as always,'" then the store would be ready in eight.

Another social group had coalesced, during the Soviet Union's "Stagnation" era, called the *Saules Brāļi* 'Sun Brothers.' They had acquired this nickname on account of their outdoor lifestyle and scant attention to hygiene, as a result of which they had complexions that reminded one of vacationers in the Bahamas. They were also remarkably innovative when it came to earning for a drink. One day in November, shortly after St. Martin's Day,[2] a man in the neighborhood complained of having eaten a goose with a "very fishy" taste. After this complaint reached the ears of the local authorities (apparently the family's holiday had been completely ruined by this event), they investigated the story and found that three enterprising *Saules Brāļi* had been responsible for the fishy goose. They had burrowed a hole under the fence to the pelican area of the zoo, dragged one of its denizens out, killed it, sawed the bill to the size of a goose's (approximated, but filed) and sold it as the perfect Martin's Day feast. A week later, the guard at the zoo was doubled. But the brotherhood was irrepressible; within three years, swans, ducks and even lowly pigeons were a rare sight in the city.

During the fall, in our house, we learned to decline the "It's a great deal — I have a radio cassette player/book/wooden doll/carriage frame-without-the-carriage that I'll give you in exchange for a twenty-lat loan" come-ons from Pavel and "Zmei Gorinitch" when they were drunk. The only exception was when Pavel came by with a voluminous brown bundle. He said, "Hey Boriss, if you lend me twenty lats, I'll let you keep this $&#@#*/!!! ancient-as-all-hell book. I was curious what book he could be plugging so energetically. I leafed through some pages and realized this was a Bible, at least 110 years old, whose cover and first few pages had been torn off. The text was in old Latvian, printed with a Gothic font. As I looked at Pavel's engorged red face, I though to myself that I'd better make an exception to the rule and take him up on the offer, before another thirty pages of this book find a second use as window insulation.

   I could state unequivocally, that my impression of the Latvian expatriates and repatriates at this point was more favorable than that formed by my neighbors.

The equipment that we had ordered arrived in December, along with a Danish technician to install them. He worked quickly and efficiently. He had brought all his tools in one metal box that was two feet long and one foot high. He worked for four days. Within this time, ten pieces of equipment were installed. Preben was on hand to show how each one worked. When the last one was connected, and Preben turned it on, Valdis rubbed his head. He turned to me and said, "Wow, now *that* I understand . . . where can I find a mechanic like that?"

The production was distinctly fluffier, higher and more evenly browned. The production was also distinctly freer of foreign materials, thanks to the mechanical dough sifter.

Once again, the year did *not* start with a large bag of money being brought from the bakery, although several bags of new pastries did make their way to our table, the most interesting of which was called the "wasp's surprise." There was nothing even vaguely associating the pastry and a wasp (although later on Ligita attempted to convince us that because of the spacing of the two sides that were receiving custard and jam, it looked like a wasp's head). Although we had implemented a system for the sampling, reviewing, naming, and introducing new cakes, Ligita had apparently thought that puff pastries did not need to undergo the same treatment. In general, she was still ill-disposed to any systems, which had as a side effect the limitation of her artistic liberties. My explanations about how "standardization is what the clients want," once they have tried something of ours that they like, were not well received. When I clarified that *repeat* customers would be the ones to help her and the bakers achieve higher salaries, she retorted, "What's wrong with new customers?"

One conversation that I hadn't properly girded for took place in February 1995. It started with a suggestion that something new be developed, now that the holiday crunch was over (and had been for nearly a month). Two weeks later there was nothing.

"Good morning, Ligita, how are you doing?"

"Just fine."

"So, Ligita, what about those new cakes? How are they coming along?"

"Not very well."

"Why not?"

"Uh, I'm not . . . inspired."

"Anything I can do to help?"

"Nope."

"Do you need some supplies — do you have all the marzipan you need?"

"Yes."

"You know, it would be grand if we could have something new for March. You know, on the fifteenth will be St. Patrick's Day."

"What's that name of the pastry?"

*Author (right), with Ligita Svirido, Director of Quality Control (left),
working on new product development*

"It's an Irish-American holiday, where everyone dresses in green, and eats green things ... like cakes, for example."

"That wouldn't go over here — there are no Irish-Latvians. Besides, I don't use food coloring in the foods — they're artificial."

"Oh, now I understand your concern. In Soviet times perhaps the food colors were derived purely from poisonous chemicals. Today, however, food colorings are all tested."

"On animals?"

"Well, yes, I suppose so. They were at least, twenty years ago, when they were developed ..."

"I think that Western food colors contain more chemicals than our [domestically produced] ones."

"Fine, then use ours."

"Are you telling me what to do? Maybe you want to do this yourself?"

"No, please, Ligita, understand, I'm just giving some ideas."

"If you think that you can do it better than me, then you should. After all, *I* was *only* selected to be one of the chefs working on the banquet for Saddam Hussein when he met with our leaders in nineteen eighty-four. *He* ate dishes that *I* prepared!"

"Damn, and you *also* blew the chance to poison him … even giving him elephant-size portions of Western-made food coloring would have helped … *anything*," I wanted to say, but restrained myself, instead quietly confirming, "Wow, that's impressive, I didn't know that."

"Ha, ha … I know my worth."

At this point, I could do no better than smile politely. I could never "win" with Ligita. Once, in fact, I had "won" some argument with her, and for three days afterwards, the cakes looked so awful, customers were asking who in the bakery had died. I couldn't afford to replace her because she had also developed, over the course of her ten years of food-service experience at the best restaurants of Riga, an unerring taste for what the Riga populace desired. She was able to take foreign recipes and alter them to meet this taste. Consequently, after these conversations, I would regularly slam the telephone down, storm out of the office, and curse up and down the street, then return and continue my work as if nothing had transpired.

Sure enough, three days later, we had a green rum butter cream cake — decorated with green leaves and green cherries, that was nothing short of a masterpiece. So, to keep the innovative process going at a healthy clip, Zigrīda and I accepted the "wasp's surprise" as the name of the pastry.

I also noticed the clientele changing. We had started to attract a new socio-ethnic-economic class. Over the course of two years, as the economy of Moscow blossomed — fueled by Western investments — the effects trickled down to the economy of Latvia. I didn't know this at the time, but the massive river of goods flowing to Russia's capital city of ten million people was fed, to no small extent, by tributaries that started in Latvia. Cottage industries were booming throughout this country, manufacturing everything from shampoo to canned meat. One Latvian coffee roaster sold more than forty tons of coffee monthly under a noted Russian brand. Furthermore, over one-third the items shipped to Moscow from Western Europe or America, were transiting through Riga or Ventspils. One Frenchman that I met in 1995 stated that of the twenty-seven containers of coffee and chocolates shipped to Moscow every two months, half of them were shipped through the Port of Riga.

And of the cash streaming back to Latvia, most of it gathered into a wide river back to Riga. One day, a man came into The Merry Baker on Brīvības street. He was dressed in a Hugo Boss suit. He had a quarter pound of gold chains on his neck, signifying that he was a *Jaunkrievs* 'New Russian.' He said, with a slightly Caucasian accent, "A wantcha ta make a cake for ma dad. It's gonna be his eightieth birthday."

"And how would you like the cake decorated?"

"Ah dunno, maybe with some animals."

"Animals from the zoo, from the hunt —"

"Don't botha me with details — *you* make cakes! Ah just want the cake to, to be a *SKAZKA* FAIRY TALE."

"All right, and how big a cake would you like?"

He gestured the size that would be about ten pounds. The clerk nodded, and asked what the price range should be.

The man waved his arms and said, "Don't botha me with the details, Ah toldja, it's ma pa's eightieth birthday!"

With such clients, we couldn't go wrong. And we didn't. At the end of February, the accountant showed the final results of the previous year. Although modest, it was the first profit that the company had shown since its inception, and most of it came during the last four months. After two years of work, the company had reached the black.

"Great work, Zigrīda, Jurijs, Ligita!"

"Yeah, but we still have to get our quality up," said Zigrīda. Ligita threw a Terminator glance at Zigrīda and said, "And we still need to get another store … which you have been promising for two years …"

"All right, all right, guys, but just for a moment … be good to yourselves, congratulate one another. *GREAT WORK* . . ." I brought out a bottle of champagne and uncorked it.

"So … I don't know about you guys, but I'm going to toast to our first good year … I hope that you'll join me, because I hate drinking alone."

They raised their glasses and lifted them.

"And maybe we can move to the office closer to the bread bakery — everyone'll fit there."

"Yep."

Footnotes

[1] The Emmy-winning score for the 2000 Batman cartoon was composed by a Latvian-American.

[2] A traditional feast day in Germanic countries.

31

FOOD MORGUE

NINETEEN NINETY-FIVE — THIS WAS GOING to be our year of *victory*. Both our bakery plants were glistening with new equipment. We would finally have our second store. The number of recipes that we had compiled was impressive, and the taste of the final products outstanding. Most importantly, men in thick leather jackets were coming in and ordering incredible tortes for their family members. Riga's first supermarket, entitled Maxi Market, opened its doors in the Purvciems district, and we had convinced them to install our "mini-bake-off shop" within their store. Both the supermarket, with proper wheeled carts and a bake-off shop, were novelties. It was amusing to watch mafiosi officers wheeling around carts, listening to their wives through brick-sized mobile phones, as the latter communicated them purchase orders. "What, what @A)*(%& brand of mayonnaise did you want?" Our bake-off shop was a respite for them, as they would munch through half of a freshly baked baguette before even getting to the check-out counter.

Thus, in early 1995, we were on our way of reaching 85,000 Ls per month, or $160,000 in turnover — almost $2,000,000 per year. The economy was going fine. Victory was at hand.

On a personal note, I also began to get accustomed to the proper social etiquette for birthdays and name-days, getting used to the fact that the birthday person is obliged to treat the others to hors d'oeuvres, to alcohol, and even to a cake — the burden of celebration lies on the shoulders of the birthday boy/girl. So, during my first two years, when I downplayed my birthday, thinking that I had been communicating, "Now, now, I don't want to be treated special because I'm the boss," I was instead broadcasting, "I am a real tightwad skinflint, lacking even a rudimentary respect for Latvian social etiquette." After seeing enough frowns, I had subsequently remembered to set a birthday and Name day table for others on those days.

Of course there *were* exceptions to this rule, as I discovered in March of 1995. The fact that the company had actually made a profit meant that the paperwork had to be filed in another section of the Internal Revenue Service office. Natalie, our chief accountant, stated that this was so because as a company with predominantly foreign capital, we had the right to offset the taxes due this year with tax credits from the previous two years. Our filing was about to be one day late, so she had to receive permission to file late. She went on Thursday in the morning. That afternoon I called, to ask for details of the trip.

"Well, I registered the filing today … but with difficulty."

"Just registered the filing? You were going to confirm the tax credits."

"Yes, yes, but … I couldn't."

"Why not?"

"Because the office was closed today at eleven thirty."

"Eleven thirty? Is today a holiday?"

"Well, not statewide, but in the IRS office it was."

"What do you mean?!"

"Boriss, it was the Director's Name day."

"Yes … and?"

"Nobody would see me."

"At eleven thirty in the morning?!"

"Boriss, you wouldn't believe it, I've never seen anything like it in my life. As I came to the door of the deputy assistant's office, two men from 'Dilo's' carried a crate past me — it was overflowing with sausages, hams, pate's, you name it. They could barely carry it up the stairs, and they were *big* guys. Then, as I sat down, some clerk ran by with two bottles of French Cognac. She yelled to somebody, 'Take the rest of that case and the two other ones to the Director's office.' The Deputy assistant was just furious with me for coming in *so late*. She wouldn't be able to do anything that day, except making sure that we weren't fined for a late filing. Boriss, I'm not sure if she was angry with me for coming when the excitement had already started, or, or because I had only brought a one-kilo cake. Everyone was in such a frenzied state. You know, I just had a glimpse through the door — the table was *full* of food. Of course, I called back to the store so that I could take a three-kilogram torte instead, so that we wouldn't appear like — like we were *disrespectful* or something. By the time I brought it to the door, I couldn't get back in. But I *finally* convinced the accountant to take it. I hope she did, but I'm not sure she could get back up the stairs without falling on top of the cake, she was in such a *state*."

I thanked Natalie and mentioned that it should be a date to mark in our calendars for the future. Then I realized how it was that "Dilo" got away with paying such relatively low social security taxes; half of his workers didn't officially work at his establishments.

On the advice of a Canadian manager with food-service experience, I enacted a new rule — all name days from the previous Monday through Thursday would be celebrated on Friday at three o'clock in the afternoon in the office, or after the last shift in the bakery. I reasoned that this was fair while not jeopardizing the business.

The new powerful, two-cart rotating oven that we had acquired for the bread bakery could bake almost five hundred French breads per hour. This production capacity was not only impressive — it was also a full two hundred more than could be sold on a good *day*, let alone an hour. On the other hand, our rolls were selling very well — thousands a day. I couldn't understand why rolls sold so much better than our sliced bread, until coming back from a visit to an apartment of some of Riga's more aggressive socio-economic climbers.

The acquisition of household appliances followed a strange sequence in Riga. In the West, appliances were acquired in the order that they are invented, produced, and marketed. For example, in America, the introduction of electric ovens followed the introduction of gas ones; electric toasters followed these electric stoves into the average American household in the late 1930s; household washing machines, with push-button controls and wringers housed in the same unit, appeared in the 1950s; dishwashers were popularized in the 1960s, and so on.

But most of these discoveries, developed over the course of sixty years and subsequently introduced at the rate of one or two new appliances per decade, had bypassed the Soviet proletarian; the leadership apparently didn't believe in the value of work-saving utensils, thinking instead that the work-starved populace would relish, for example, processing food with the help of an aluminum spoon and an axe hammer. Consequently, beginning in 1993, the 5 percent of the Riga population that had a relative abundance of disposable income, started purchasing these items in the order that it felt to be the most appropriate. For example, after acquiring a TV and VCR, many started with the replacement of their washing machines. They too didn't think that a bathroom was the most appropriate location for a jet turbine.

By 1995, the average post-Soviet Latvian consumer, who four years earlier had been living on an appliance offering of Lithuanian televisions, circa-1960 Byelorussian refrigerator/freezer units that maintained a "just-below-room-temperature" coolness in the summer, *Riga* washing machines and wing-blade coffee grinders[1] (ironically, an item that made its debut in America in the late 1980s) — was confronted with a mind-boggling choice. The first Bosch washing machines — equally silent but more energy-efficient than the Vyatka, hit town in 1994 — along with microwave ovens, dishwashers, food processors, blenders and toasters. So the question arose, "What does one buy first?" There was no standard answer. In 1995, it wouldn't be unusual to find a well-to-do household with a modern multi-system Sony video recorder and multi-system television set, large Samsung stereo center, a Bosch washing machine, an Electrolux dishwasher, and a Moulinex microwave. But, next to the state-of-the-art dishwasher would be a circa-1950s refrigerator, whose freezer door wouldn't quite close because it hadn't been defrosted the month before. And somehow, this made sense — since Latvians had experience only with poor-quality refrigerators, they never thought that 34–40 degrees was ever an important goal for a refrigerator. Furthermore, there was no frozen food, no tradition of iced beverages and all the ice cream ever made somehow came only in single-size servings. Consequently, if the freezer section frosted into a near solid white block within a week of cleaning, that was O.K., as long as one could stick a *Plombīrs* ice cream sausage inside. Judging by Inge's use of the refrigerator, few people understood the real purpose of the big white box. A few times upon returning home famished, I would open the refrigerator door, and pull out a bowl of marinated mushrooms or chicken or soup made "some time" before. However, as I was about to bite into the first mushroom or chicken wing, I would notice a patch of light pale green, or yellow fur on the chicken wing out of the corner of my eye. I would rear back and confirm that the leg in question is a health hazard. "Oh yuck," I would whisper as I lowered the fork or spoon. After experiencing half-a-dozen close encounters of the fur kind, I couldn't resist telling Inge that when I opened the big white door, I understood that I should not be expecting to find leftovers of the consumable variety anymore. When she appeared puzzled, I quickly added that I have just been examining items of her "food morgue," and "pray-tell-what-scientific-breakthrough-could-I-expect-you-to-announce-at-the-end-of-it-all." She was not amused.

This "appliance ignorance" spread to all sectors of society. In the bakery, I usually found the butter lying on some table, at room temperature -- on the verge of melting. At the same time, the refrigerators would be stuffed with oranges — or worse yet — strawberries. The bakers would put creams in the refrigerator, which was a good thing, but they would also put the cake sponge in them — uncovered. This was a bad thing, for cake sponge would go Death Valley-dry after even a few hours in our industrial refrigerators. When I saw this, now one year since Preben's last training session, I understood why people complained that our cakes were "dry." Preben had lectured the cake team on this problem a dozen times... even going through one of his "berserk" phases when demonstrating — about leaving unbagged sponge all over the bakery. We had subsequently purchased thick plastic bags for the bakers to put the sponges in. Within two weeks, however, the sponges were being swaddled in a clear plastic cling film... that didn't quite cling. In the meantime, one hundred and fifty dollars of thick PVC bags, custom made for storing cake sponges in the refrigerator or freezer, were being used to transport rolls to customers and dirty laundry to the cleaners.

But the ignorance had its positive points; for two years our bread roll business flourished on account of the phenomenon. Loaves of white (or dark) bread are purchased weekly by millions of Americans, who then take a few slices out of the plastic bag and throw the bag back into the refrigerator or freezer. When they take the bag out again, they take some slices and throw them into the toaster, etc. But if one could imagine that the bread didn't come in plastic bags, or sliced, then the natural response would probably be, "like, why bother?"; throwing a loaf of factory #36 white baton bread into the refrigerator would only mean "party time" for the green, furry genus of mold. And slicing bread to fit into a toaster would require the skill of a diamond cutter, not to mention having to sharpen the knife all the time.

As a consequence, the *rebyata or zēni* 'guys' would get together and watch the international hockey matches on a late-model wide-screen television set, would drink lukewarm beer or vodka (which was the way it had always been), and eat ham sandwiches — made with our fresh rolls. And *that* was good for our business — very good; at 5-6 santimes apiece, our rolls were up to three-quarters the price of the same in any of Europe's medium-sized cities. Our other products were from 60 percent to 80 percent cheaper than their Western European counterparts.

But as great as our roll business was between 1994 and 1996, "appliance ignorance" swept down once again to rob us of our advantage. In 1996, Rigans began worshipping the microwave. The microwave oven must have hit a purchase rate of 80 percent amongst the middle and upper classes, from what I could tell from conversations with Inge, my acquaintances, and the bakery crowd. I'm certain that along with any foodstuffs which the microwave was explicitly designed, no small quantity of eggs, whole cans of mackerel and wet woolen socks also received the 800 watt waves during this period. Unfortunately, this appliance had a different effect on our business than did the lack of toasters. In a conversation that I had on this subject with Zigrīda, it came out that people were complaining about the bread getting terribly tough after being heated up. I remembered, from my days as a buss-boy in a French restaurant, that when the bread, which had been sliced for lunch, was warmed up in the microwave for the evening tables, it had a useful half-life of twenty minutes. Afterwards, the crust turned hard, very hard; even moderately enthusiastic mandible contact could cause gums to bleed profusely — not a pleasant feeling when one expected to taste and feel only Grand Marnier-enhanced pate de Campagne on a silky-soft slice of French bread. Even in the case of fresh bread, the microwave turned the crust into a leather-like ring around the bread, giving one the distinct impression that the baker had dropped his chewing gum into the dough during mixing of that particular batch. So when Zigrīda said that "a few times they mentioned microwave ovens, you know how people are hurrying these days, and it's so convenient," it didn't take long for me to realize what was happening. I explained to Zigrīda, and added, that people would find out the culprit soon enough by themselves, but in the meantime, recommend that they just use the regular oven . . . and tell them not to dry their little pets in the microwave either — she would score big customer relationship management points with that.

Well before that time we had started making loaves of white bread, and cutting them by hand — intentionally too thick to be placed in a non-industrial toaster. However, when the managers of the large bakeries traveled to the West, they discovered the obvious. They then installed automated slicers, powered with Rolls-Royce motors. By late 1996, a competition had erupted between these factories on who could deliver the lowest-priced sliced bread. Since we could never pretend to be price leaders in manufacturing, this was a competition that I was glad to be avoiding. Besides, the appliance gurus of Riga had now focused elsewhere; even six months after the first "*Tostermaize*" hit the market, I noticed that the trend-setting Phillips shop still had no toasters displayed in their windows. On the other hand, the three tastefully lit non-citric juicers-with-self-contained-peel-and-detritus-catchers displayed prominently on different stands, signaled that this apparatus was to be the latest rage. When I later walked into a café that was perpetually "raging," and had a fresh-squeezed kiwi juice, it took me half an hour of water drinking afterwards to get the peel hairs out my throat.

But what I hadn't noticed is that the toasters *were* being purchased, slowly but surely, and not just by the upper-crust Rigans.

Footnotes

[1] Latvia's "Straume" plant had been the major producer of wing-blade coffee grinders for the entire Comecon region, since the late 1970s. The factory was based in Latvia because of the preponderance of coffee drinkers in the Baltic Republics (in most of the ex-USSR, tea is the hot beverage of choice). Burr grinders and two-spout espresso machines from Hungary were standard equipment in almost all Baltic cafes, restaurants and theater buffets in the Soviet period.

32

STICKY FINGERS

IN JUNE OF 1995, THE first economic crisis struck Latvia. This was a bank collapse, the cause of which was a bank president who believed he could foist a Russian-style pyramid scheme on investors and savers. As a back-up, it was rumored that he had planned to bribe the President of the Bank of Latvia to devalue the Lat, such that he could repay all interest at laughable dollar rates. His plans went awry, and he spent the next five years in prison; he hadn't counted on the fact that the President of the Bank of Latvia was paid a Western-level salary. Consequently, with a salary well over $100,000 per annum, the President of the Bank was impervious to the offers of half that amount to create an African-style spontaneous devaluation. The Prime Minister, on the other hand, with his annual compensation of $10,000, was of a different opinion. In any event, the fall of the Banka Baltija triggered a shock to the entire banking system, and subsequently to the economy. Our pensioner client base simply dropped away at that point. Wives of small business men also stayed away for several months.

But the underlying problem — a lack of enforced laws and marginal ethics — did not go away. Every week, one was confronted with situations that would be rare in most of the United States. For example, I was once in a hurry to get from one side of the Old Town to the other.

I pressed on the gas as I left the parking lot, but the ten seconds saved was not enough, particularly when I saw the two long lines of cars streaming over one hundred yards from the light. "Rats, this is absurd. I'm stuck. Damn. Oh, oh, I'll take the 'third lane.'" This was a lane that existed in the minds of all motorists who were hurrying, in the same manner, to get on the road to the center of town. It was the right hand lane, and in Denmark, or any comparable city in Western Europe whose road engineers had assumed that drivers are capable of maneuvering and staying in lanes of 3.5 meters width, it would simply have been the third lane. Here there was only a right lane about six meters wide, so that even inebriated bus drivers could be confident that they were "in the lane."

As the light turned green, I followed the one car in front of me, across the lanes going east, then across the tramway tracks, and finally... to be alerted to the existence of a bright green imp, waving its wand. When the hyper-excitement of avoiding the twenty-five cars ahead of me at the light subsided, I realized that the *Ceļu policija* 'Road Police' had finally caught up with me, after my having attained a record two-month-long respite from violations. It was at times like this that I wondered how come, in the States, I had driven for fourteen years and didn't get as much as one moving violation, while here — I got tickets more often than I got head colds. "Rats, I'm gonna get nailed now," I thought to myself. As I pulled over and behind the parked police car, I was wondering what I would say. When the policeman gestured for me to get out of the car, I realized that there was nothing I *could* say, being as my violation was so flagrant. Quietly, I opened the door of the police car and sat down in the passenger's seat, as was the custom on such occasions. The officer, a man in his late twenties, finished writing a ticket for the previous third-laner, then turned to me.

"So, what do you have to say for yourself?"

I frowned and replied, "Nothing. I was wrong."

"That's right, there is no lane there. O.K., so what do we do? The standard fine is fifteen to twenty lats ($28-$36) for such a violation..."

I shook my head, communicating that I didn't have that much on me.

"Oh but I see here that you are an American citizen. Interesting... with this Russian name." I nodded, still frowning.

"So, what would an American be doing so far from home, in Latvia?"

"I'm the director of a local company."

"Oh, which one — by the way, you seem to be doing very well with the Latvian, too, even though you have a pretty thick accent."

"The Merry Baker."

"*REALLY*?! Well, well, not bad — a friend of mine buys from nowhere else — a very good reputation it has indeed. Hmm..."

I nodded impatiently.

"So, how do you like it here?" he continued.

"Good so far, but it's cold," I replied quickly, to let him understand that I had no time for idle chit-chat.

"Well, that's for sure... tell you what, you've lucked out today. Normally, like I said, the fine is fifteen to twenty lats. But today, if you can do without a receipt, we're giving an 'entrepreneur's discount' — the ticket'll cost you only five lats."

"What a bargain...," I thought to myself as I chuckled and said, "Where I come from, they call it an offer '*you can't refuse*,'" as I handed over the crisp five-lat bill.

"Pleasant journey, and I hope that you enjoy your stay here," he said with a smile, placing the five-lat bill in a billfold bulging with the same. I left, of course without any documentation of my meeting.

Worse yet, could it be a societal illness? I dropped the thought until a few weeks later, when I walked into the bakery, in search of Zigrīda, and heard a great commotion.

"It was *him*. They said that *we* put that thing in the pastry. Who could have done it?"

I heard Zigrīda trying to calm everyone down: "Maybe it just *fell* into the dough. Could that be?"

I used the moment of silence to ask, "Is something wrong?" I asked her.

"Well yes, Boriss. We almost killed someone."

"*WHAT?!*"

"In fact, we almost killed *Yakubovitch.*"

"Who's he?" I asked naively, suspecting that she was recounting the name of another of the stars in her personal constellation, but whom no one else even knew.

"*Yakubovitch*? He's the master of ceremonies for a famous show in *Russia*."

"Which one?"

"*Pole Chudyess* 'Field of Dreams.'"[1]

"Oh, that's right! ... We're killing off famous TV personalities with our cakes now?"

"No... it wasn't one of our cakes. It was just one of our Danish pastries. The company that was sponsoring the event, 'BNL', says that there was a *thumbtack* in the pastry that he bit into. He could have died."

"Oh, come on, that's ridiculous," I retorted.

"Ridiculous, maybe. But here is the thumbtack that they gave us."

Zigrīda then picked up a thumbtack that was lying next to the half-eaten pastry. It was the Soviet model of thumbtack, which consisted of an uncoated steel metal button, through which a wedge-shaped hole had been punched. The sharp punched portion constituted the pin portion of the tack. The resulting hole on top of the thumbtack looked like a reverse slice of pie. This particular thumbtack was rusted in many places.

"That is just . . . unbelievable. You are saying that of all the hundreds of orders this week, during *one* of the orders, one of our bakers dropped a thumbtack into the dough . . . or the topping, and *that* particular pastry ended up going to the most famous MC of the most famous television show in Russia? I can't . . . no, I *won't* believe it," I said.

Zigrīda shrugged her shoulders.

I was thinking, "This just takes the cake. We'll be at the center of an international scandal now. And it had to be done with one of these rusty Soviet 'punched-through-head-becomes-needle' thumbtacks; and rusted too."

Zigrīda looked at me with a puzzled expression. When I finished ruminating, I turned to her.

"Seriously, Zigrīda, I don't know how to react to this, what do you think?"

"I think that . . . we should just let it blow over. If there is some content to this, then we *will* be contacted."

"Won't that be too late?"

"BNL is a club whose reputation isn't . . . spectacular. They probably just wanted to do this to get a refund or something."

I followed Zigrīda's judgment. We reimbursed the billiard club for two dozen pastries, and didn't hear a word more about the incident . . . from anybody.

More and more often, I brought up the issue of the high cost-of-goods. Once again, we staked out a spot and caught a thief. For a while the cost-of-goods decreased. I found out only later what superficial effects all our thief-catching activities actually had. Our "hot fingers" prize for creativity in lifting went to Katrina. Valdis and Zigrīda were taking their turn inspecting the bags of exiting bakers. As usual, they showed up unannounced. When they walked through the door, three bakers were leaving. Zigrīda asked one to show the contents of the bag — all was in order. At the same time, Katrina showed her handbag to Valdis. He pointed to the plastic bag. Katrina replied, "Well, there are . . . personal . . . you know, *feminine* things there." Valdis nodded and waved her on. But Zigrīda, apparently having seen this out of the corner of her eye said,

"Stop, Katrina, you say that you have things which you are embarrassed to show Valdis. I understand you, you can show them to *me*." Zigrīda proceeded to look in the bag. She pulled off the uniform, which was on top, and saw a stocking underneath which, she later said to me, looked suspect. She lifted it up. At the foot of the stocking were three dark forms. Zigrīda reached in and pulled out, one by one, three of our chocolate truffles, elegantly wrapped in our attractive paper doilies. With that feat, Katrina took her place at the top of our "hot fingers" list of those creative geniuses that had decided, at the wrong moment, to take their work home with them.

But, in retrospect, I had to admit that this activity was part of the epidemic of thievery afflicting the whole country. Managing directors were fabricating false receipts for everything from paper to flowers; it was accepted practice to claim to be employing only one-third of the workers that one actually *was* employing, to minimize the payment of taxes. In politics, the scene was derelict. Even the Green Party received long-term leases on old buildings and other capital goodies that were written off the balance sheets of the city government, which they astutely traded for others or passed off to their representatives. I once had the opportunity to sit down with a high-ranking city official in an informal setting; he confided to me that it was possible to steal, because it was easy to lie. He said, "It's hard not to lie, because the first thing that you had to deny — in order to become a communist party member — is that you believe in God. After that, all the other lies are little ones."

The penultimate "appropriator", however, was an ex–Vice-Minister of Agriculture. He quietly "persuaded" the privatization board of Latvia to sell his company the ownership rights to six of Latvia's largest food or beverage concerns. Andris Šķēle was so successful (both on the "privatization" front and in politics) that, in 1997, he was declared Europe's wealthiest Prime Minister; his net worth was valued at over $40 million. Mind you, this was Europe's third-smallest nation, out of twenty-three. If the nation's leading representative had amassed such a fortune treading on the very edge of legality, and not at all along the footpath of Western ethical norms, then what about the hoi polloi?

By early 1998, the company was once again in respectable shape with three stores, a long-term contract for bun production with the largest hot dog vendor in the Baltics and an internal control mechanism that was still, perhaps, full of holes, but smaller ones. We decided to consolidate our production by refurbishing and moving into a larger facility, which we did in February 1998.

Six months later, the rug was taken out from us; the Russian Financial

Crisis struck. The crisis in Russia spelled doom for the luxury end of the Latvian economy. Beginning in September, our autumn sales dropped by 30 percent, in comparison to the previous year. Although December sales were more or less stable, January and February figures gave the impression that Riga's inhabitants had gone on a two-day fast. Overnight, the *New Russians*, along with the Latvian artists, politicians and bankers, stopped coming to the stores.

One by one, my hypotheses about the soundness of our strategy proved to be unfounded. The widespread use of toasters — which had finally captured the imaginations of the Riga populace — and widespread availability of machine-sliced bread crippled our roll business. At the same time our wholesale business customers were seduced away from us, one-by-one. In some cases they opened in-house bakeries themselves, based on our example. In other cases they switched entirely to purchasing goods in cash – at an 18% discount — from small upstart 'left'(illegal) bakeries that avoided paying taxes.

At the same time, while I focused on maintaining demand, our internal control systems deteriorated to occasional snooping parries of the senior managers into the ranks of the bakers, who once again grew bold and sticky-fingered. I believe that, ultimately, it was a question of pride; my co-managers couldn't bear to admit openly that their fellow countrymen were kleptomaniacs. Instead, they took every opportunity to lessen the perceived fallout of theft, and played down the issue.

Finally, I consciously failed to observe at least two cardinal rules of any successful business — not to limit a majority of sales to just one very small customer segment, and not to expand into other sectors prematurely. In the case of our bakery, a disproportionate portion of profits were coming from one group — businessmen who were selling into Russia. At the same time, my unilateral decision to expand into the restaurant business a few years earlier, detracted from the core baking business, while contributing only pennies to the entire operation... but wow, was it fun. I could strongly suggest for anyone that suffers from a budding inferiority complex, to open up a three-star restaurant one hundred and fifty yards from the nearest Parliament, House of Commons or Congress ... but that's another story.

Ultimately, the Russian Financial Crisis that appeared in late 1998 probably just drove the final nails into the coffin, instead of being the primary reason for the company's bankruptcy; for my family life it was also a blessing in disguise. In May of 1999 I filed a request with the Latvian register of companies to declare the company insolvent.

Footnotes

[1] Polye Chudess is the Wheel of Fortune of Russia — enjoying the same
notoriety throughout Russia and the former Soviet republics as Wheel of
Fortune did in the U.S.

33

EPILOGUE

The making of bread is a brutal process, pitting a billion-year-old fungus against baby plants. The bakers merely mediate. The heterotrophic yeast fungi, technically called *Saccharomyces cerevisiae*, are hardy organisms, which survive off just about anything containing sugar. The baby wheat seeds contain some of these sugars. But they also contain a good amount of gluten. This gluten is tough enough to hold most of the carbon dioxide that the sugar-gobbling yeast cells flatulate out during the eating process. The baker — like a good referee — prevents either from getting the upper hand unfairly. At first, he lets the yeast go to work, while the flour gets bloated and inflated. He then "punches" the flour down, fundamentally breaking the gum now surrounding large pockets of carbon dioxide.

This forces the yeast to work more, but it can't work as hard as it did, while the gluten breaks into smaller pieces, and can't flex as much as it did. So the struggle slows, and gets even-handed –- the pores become smaller and evenly-sized. At this time, the bread-shaped dough is placed in the "proving" cabinet. The foes rise (again), in their final glorious battle. At precisely this moment, the skilled baker moves the dough from the humid, 38-degree proving cabinet to the oven. The four-hundred-degree oven quickly halts all dynamics between flour and yeast. The end product is the combined result of all the steps taken — from mixing to baking; if even one step in the process has not been performed well, then the end product emerges a failure.

I liken my business and its struggle between the market and the environment, to this struggle between the baker, the yeast and the flour; in my case, the final product didn't come out the way it should have. Like many a baker, I couldn't pinpoint exactly why.

However, the story of The Merry Baker, or its first parent company Vērdiņš, was neither the summary of my life, nor the story of Riga, which continued to grow as a world-class city.

I stayed happily married and Inge increased her qualifications, advancing within the World Bank to become the first country manager selected from the host country, as well as becoming a specialist on Pension systems. Markus is finishing the Stockholm School of Economics program for business (and has a practical example of how *not* to establish one). Besides studying philosophy, Eliza has become an editor of a counterculture e-journal of some renown in this country. She is also devoted to the replacement cat which, in turn, provides frequent amusement to family and friends with his preference for being vacuumed over being brushed.

Zigrīda, Ligita and Valdis all landed securely on their feet in the company that purchased the remnants of the 'Merry Baker's parent company.

When, in the course of brooding over the collapse, I wonder whether it was worth it, ex-customers never fail to cheer me up. Not that pastries are really a vital aspect of one's existence, or a cornerstone of an emerging economy, but I'm reminded that I did more than just support a few Latvian mills to unload second-grade flour and third-grade beet sugar; "You gave color and novelty to pastries—" claimed one regular customer. "Before you, in the best pastry shop in town, there were nine pastries, that had been there [forever]. When I first went to your store and saw different colors and different pastries, I was. . . shocked. . . and the the next time I walked in, there was something *new.*" Other, more macroeconomically-focussed persons said that my operations had helped keep out the flood of cheap(-but colorful) Danish jelly rolls that had inundated Poland and Lithuania(no doubt providing a formidable challenge to the maintenance of a positive balance-of-payments equation). But whatever – I *had* established a business in the Wild East and it made a small bit of their gray, monotonous lives, cheerier.

Finally, two years after the failure of the company, Latvia recovered from the Russian Financial Crisis of 1998. Riga's economy burgeoned, attracting an entire set of businesses that could and did complement the casinos, lingerie boutiques, and film-developing stores that had dominated the cityscape in

1994. This new retail movement included Reebok, Benetton, Mango and Nike stores, three chains of real supermarkets and appliance stores to fit any budget. Today, Riga is a stunning gem of a city. It has a smart international airport, a range of hotels (with listening devices removed) for all tastes, restaurants featuring cuisines ranging from Scandinavian smorgasbord to Armenian to Sushi bars. In fact, several western-style pizzerias have burgeoned into city-wide chains, without exceptional difficulties or even back-stabbing with rusty-knived blades.

The city boasts a few hundred millionaires; racketeering has been all but eliminated (the crux of the Mafiya having by now moved into highly lucrative businesses of oil trading, wood export, and contraband liquor manufacturing); the Opera House's productions are once again drawing attention from all of Europe — boasting the only production of *The Magic Flute* featuring a transparent washing machine as a prop; there are now more than a dozen nightclubs; no less than forty upscale bars have sprouted that rival any in New York or Chicago, and renovated downtown department stores now carry everything from the latest Italian women's fashions to Macanudo cigars. Alongside the Mercedeses, Audis, VWs, Fords, and Renaults that have replaced most of the Volgas and Zhigulis of 1992, one can get gasoline at Texaco or Statoil stations. The unwashed *baboushki* still ride in airless railway cars, but now you can occasionally see them thumbing through their bags and pulling out Nokia phones to take calls from their compote-carrying comrades. And this is just the beginning, for on the 20th of September of 2003, 69% of the voting population had voted to join the European Union. Romano Prodi's comment on this was 'welcome home.'

This result should have been no surprise to anyone who follows Eastern European affairs even casually — it was also the natural evolution for any country that had been ripped from the fold of a Greater Europe of 1939, in which it had been comfortably settled. But there are still moments when, in my heart of hearts, I long for Ivankin's gas truck. Ka-chunk.

Acknowledgment

Thanks to Paul Zemtzov, who assisted intensively with the final edit, and to countless others who helped with advice or encouraging words.